ADVERTISING AND HONG KONG SOCIETY

Advertising and Hong Kong Society

Edited by

Kara Chan

The Chinese University Press

Advertising and Hong Kong Society
   Edited by Kara Chan

© **The Chinese University of Hong Kong**, 2006

ISBN 962–996–264–0

THE CHINESE UNIVERSITY PRESS
The Chinese University of Hong Kong
SHA TIN, N.T., HONG KONG
Fax: +852 2603 6692
    +852 2603 7355
E-mail: cup@cuhk.edu.hk
Web-site: www.chineseupress.com

Printed in Hong Kong

Dedicated to

Pang Hon

Table of Contents

Preface

*T*his book is about the roles of advertising in the Hong Kong society. Hong Kong is one of the advertising centers of the world. Advertising and other marketing communication industries in Hong Kong are highly sophisticated, fast-paced, and money-driven. The intense competition is unrivaled anywhere in the region—or globally. Advertisers are demanding and competition among advertising agencies is extremely keen. Advertising is one of the most dynamic industries in Hong Kong. It reinforces the development of Hong Kong into a high-income economy and assists global advertisers to explore the mainland Chinese market for consumer products and other goods and services. It also fuels the advertising industries in the Asian and mainland Chinese regions by providing high caliber advertising management personnel and creative talents.

While other advertising books focus on how to maximize the persuasion process while minimizing its cost to the advertiser, this book considers the social, psychological, legal, and ethical impact that may result from a campaign or from advertising generally. It provides readers with an understanding of the role of advertising as a form of social communication. It enhances the sensitivity of prospective advertising practitioners to the social consequences of their work, and provides them with sufficient understanding of the regulatory environment to enable them to avoid unnecessary legal entanglement and, we hope, to develop their sense of professional ethics. This book aims at providing suggestions and solutions to make advertising better for society while also more effective for marketers.

In the first two chapters types of communication indicators, advertising indicators, and an overview of the Hong Kong advertising scene will be laid out. There are basically three types of advertising indicators: production indicators are about the creation of advertising messages; distribution indicators reflect how advertising messages are circulated in society; reception indicators refer to audiences' perception and evaluation of advertising. The advertising message itself provides scholars with rich contents for analysis. Analysis of advertising messages can be conducted in a quantitative way, such as analysis of its information content and cultural values, or in a qualitative way such as its symbolic meanings. Readers who are not familiar with Hong Kong society and its advertising scene will benefit from reading Chapter 2. It starts with analysis of the economic and social environments and continues with an analysis of the advertising industries. While Chapter 1 gives the framework or the bones of the advertising system, Chapter 2 gives the details or the flesh. Manpower statistics, billing by advertising agencies, advertising expenditure by product category, and media consumption figures are among the many statistics presented.

Public service announcements, a specific type of advertising by the Hong Kong SAR government, are the focus of study in Chapter 3. It investigates how political ideology is portrayed in Hong Kong. The chapter begins with a review of the production of public service announcements and continues with the thesis that political ideology in public service announcements reflects the political changes that Hong Kong society faced before 1997 and is facing after 1997.

Chapters 4 and 5 discuss how Hong Kong people perceive advertising. Major criticisms of advertising are summarized in Chapter 4. Chapter 4 also traces a series of opinion survey findings about public attitudes toward advertising. Chapter 5 specifically discusses what constitutes offensive advertising. The chapter attempts to answer these questions: What products and services do consumers find offensive in advertising? What appeals do they feel are offensive? What is the degree of tolerance to offensive advertisements in different media? What do people do when they feel that a particular advertisement is offensive?

Chapter 6 deals with the regulation of advertising in Hong Kong. The regulatory framework, the regulatory bodies, features of television advertising standards, and the ethical issues involved including truthful presentation, children as an advertising target, and sexual appeals are discussed.

Chapters 7 to 9 investigate advertising contents or advertising messages. Chapter 7 provides a framework for analyzing the symbolic meaning of advertising. It provides readers with a critical study viewpoint in order to "read in depth" an advertisement within its broader social, cultural, and political context. Examples of critical reading are given to illustrate the process. Chapter 8 is a quantitative analysis of print advertising in Hong Kong over a period of 50 years from 1949 to 1998. Altogether 4,080 advertisements are studied in three Chinese newspapers and one English newspaper to map the changes in cultural values manifested in advertising. Reflective hypothesis is adopted and readers can see how cultural values in advertising reflect the social and economic changes in Hong Kong society. Chapter 9 analyzes gender portrayal and the images of beauty promoted in advertising in Hong Kong. The author examines the cultural connection between advertising and the construct of beauty in Hong Kong, and specifically how the symbolic meanings of skin-whitening and body slimming concepts share, construe, and interrogate gender culture in Hong Kong.

The last two chapters, Chapters 10 and 11, discuss advertising and minors. Children and adolescents are the focus of a study of advertising and consumer socialization. Chapter 10 adopts a developmental approach and discusses various cognitive and social changes in children from an early age to young adults. It follows with a survey of Hong Kong children's understanding of television advertising, perceived truthfulness of television commercials, and their perception of parental influence in watching commercials. Chapter 11 discusses developmental changes during adolescence, adoption of materialistic value orientation, and advertising exposure among adolescents, as well as advertising and smoking, and advertising and self-perception of body image.

Various research techniques have been used in the studies in this book including semiotic analysis, content analysis, surveys, and secondary data analysis. This is the first book to examine advertising and Hong Kong society. We think that the book should be useful for scholars and the general public who are interested in the social impact of advertising.

Advertising professionals and practitioners will also benefit from the book by studying advertising in a broader social and economic context.

The editor would like to express our thanks to the Hong Kong Baptist University students who have taken the course "Social communication and Advertising" during the years 1993–2005. Many ideas in the book originate from their class discussion and the group projects that they have completed. The editor would like to thank the book chapter contributors for their support and efforts. The editor would also like to thank Miss Shelby Chan of The Chinese University Press for her patience and assistance. Last but not least, the editor would like to thank her colleagues in the Department of Communication Studies for their inspiration and generous sharing of research ideas.

Chapter 1

Social Communication and Advertising Indicators

Fanny Fong-yee Chan
Kara Chan
Joseph Man Chan

*T*his chapter is divided into two parts. The first part reviews the concept of communication indicators and discusses the theoretical as well as methodological issues involved in communication indicators research. The second part tries to apply the concept to construct and analyze the existing advertising indicators in Hong Kong.

Conceptualizing Communication Indicators

Communication indicators are indexes of the state of production, distribution, and reception of messages in a social system. Indicators of message production refer to the characteristics and encoding practices of media institutions and communication professionals. Indicators of the message distribution system pertain to the availability and capacity of communication channels. Reception indicators are the audience's consumption and evaluation of various forms of communication. Associated with production are the messages that constitute the symbolic system. It can be analyzed in volume and orientation as communication indicators too.

Media, communication, and culture are three interrelated concepts with one being the subset of the other as far as the scope is concerned.

Culture, in a broad sense, includes social actions, values, and beliefs (Rosengren 1986). Media are usually restricted to communication via mass-oriented channels. Communication includes mass-mediated communication, computer-mediated communication, and interpersonal communication. However, it is not as encompassing as culture. With communication so delimited, new media like satellite television and online broadcast, as well as small and traditional media such as storytelling and photocopying machine, should all be included in the study of communication indicators. In fact, the simultaneous monitoring of both the modern and traditional media is essential for a developing nation that attempts to harness all communication resources for the sake of development (Tehranian 1979).

At the industrial and organizational level, communication can be viewed from the perspective of ecological theory which relates environmental pressure to organizational structure and resource

Figure 1.1: The three interrelated concepts

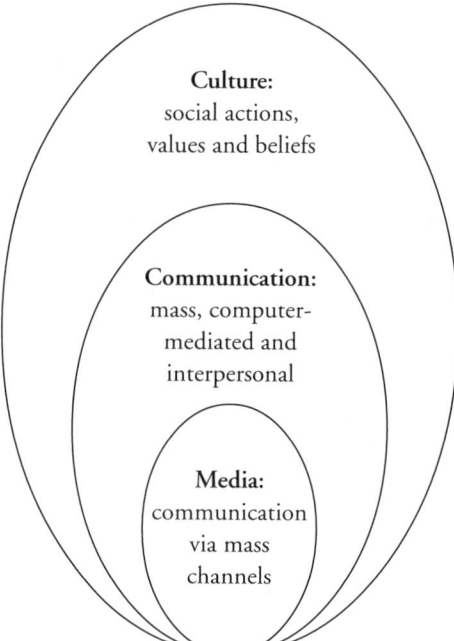

acquisition (Dimmick & Rothenbuhler 1984). It is the survival of species that is at the heart of ecological theory in biology. In our case, each species is a set of communication organizations composed of television stations or newspapers or advertising agencies. Communication, as a social subsystem, is interrelated with other social subsystems. The social context in general and the regulatory framework in particular sets the parametric constraints on communication. Any change in the environment will set pressure for communications to adapt. It follows that socioeconomic indicators such as per capita GNP (Gross National Product), education level, and occupational structure are relevant to the study of communication indicators as well. The global context can also affect communication within a nation. In this shrinking world, no society can afford to be a closed system, and international exchange of information is inevitable. The import and export figures of books, television programs, trans-border data, media goods (such as VCD, DVD, etc.) and the like are therefore legitimate indicators.

Like social indicators, communication indicators can also be distinguished as objective and subjective ones. Objective and subjective indicators have different emphases and they two together form a full picture of the communication environment. Objective indicators relate to facticity. The penetration of video-cassette recorders (VCR) and the average time people spend on television are illustrative examples. Subjective indicators relate to people's subjective evaluation of the objective media environment. In this case, what matters is people's perception. Perceived reality and actual reality should be equally stressed as they often interact in shaping social outcome.

Theoretical Issues

The basic function of communication indicators, and for that matter, social indicators, is to reflect the state of the situation, serving as a feedback to a communication system and as a basis for forecasting communication development and for planning social changes. Communication indicators can serve theoretical purposes too. To say the least, theoretical consideration is implied in conceptualizing and measuring these indicators. This theoretical value of communication indicators can be further enhanced if they are (1) measured longitudinally, (2) grounded theoretically, and (3) subjected to analytical and theoretical use.

Social change is at the core of the problematics in social science. Without longitudinal measures, it is difficult, if not impossible, to draw meaningful conclusions about the processes of change and development trends. In fact, merely as feedback indexes for policy-making, communication indicators are much more useful if they are measured over time. Longitudinal indicators provide a basis for testing hypotheses and theoretical assumptions too.

The analytical and theoretical values of an indicator may change as a result of the way it is conceptualized and measured. For instance, the box office of movies in a nation itself may be a relatively straightforward indicator of cinema attendance. However, the ratio of the box office of local productions to foreign films may serve as a criterion for testing if Western media necessarily dominate local productions in a third world country, as the theory of media imperialism expects. In the latter case, the ratio serves an analytical and theoretical purpose.

The value of a given indicator also depends on the way it is used. When used alone, the indicator is merely descriptive in nature. However, when used to correlate with another variable or when used to answer a research question, it can serve an analytical or explanatory purpose. The advertising expenditure, for instance, is a common index of the marketing communication environment. A longitudinal correlation between this advertising index and the GNP over the years, however, will test the relationship between advertising and economic growth. The increase of the advertising index can also be used to explain the rise of commercial centrist newspapers in Hong Kong in the 1970s (Chan and Lee 1991). While the theoretical use of communication indicators is desirable, we shall not limit ourselves to such use. Communication indicators *per se* have their own values. They are meant, first of all, to index the messages as well as the state of production, distribution, and reception of messages.

There are three orientations in the study of communication indicators. The first is the cultural indicators approach pioneered by George Gerbner and his colleagues (e.g. with Gross 1976; with Gross, Morgan and Signorielli 1986) since the early 1970s. The major concern of this approach is to test if television has cultivation effects on the audience. According to this theory, exposure to the symbolic reality portrayed on television will cultivate the audience's social perceptions. To test this theory, analysis of the symbolic content and survey of the audience's perceived reality are often compared to see if they correlate. Along similar lines and broader in conceptualization is the cultural indicator studies performed by Karl Rosengren (e.g. 1984; 1986) and his European colleagues. They are more interested in finding out the cultivation effects of mass communication on people's values and beliefs.

The second orientation is the "information society" approach initiated by researchers in the Research Institute of Telecommunications and Economics in Japan (e.g. Ito 1980). The chief concern of the Japanese researchers is to measure and compare the degree to which societies are informatized. To do this, they develop information-based indexes to measure people's information-related expenditure as well as their supply and consumption of information in society per year.

The third approach is the study of communication indicators as an extension of the social scientists' and social planners' concern for development. Within this orientation, development indicators are broadened in scope to include economic, social, and cultural (communication) indicators. Majid Tehranian (1979) has provided an illustrative study of this type. He has amassed the statistics for various media, ranging from the number of libraries to the length of telecommunications network, in his effort to relate communications development. Both the second and third approaches are concerned about development in a general sense. However, they differ in their choice of the criterion for social evaluation and level of methodological sophistication. All the above three approaches have informed us one way or the other when conceptualizing communication indicators.

Methodological Issues

In general, communication indicators can be observed at all levels of analysis—individual, group, institutional, and societal. While individuals may be the unit of observation, indicators are often analyzed at the group level or above. The specific level of analysis is determined chiefly by the nature of the communication components in which one is interested. For instance, media consumption, often observed on an individual basis, is presented as group statistics. Media imports and exports are aggregated data on institutional or societal basis.

The methods that are particularly useful for the study of communication indicators include survey, content analysis, and data aggregation. The survey method can be used for generating indicators about all aspects—except the content—of communication. Examples include media penetration, audience's evaluation of the communication environment, and communicator's encoding practices. Content analysis is applicable to indexing the symbolic system carried by the media or artifact in terms of volume, content orientation, and type. Data aggregation is useful for recording the monetary value of communications, the proliferation of information technology, the imports and exports of information goods and the like.

Despite that economics and sociology are more developed as social science disciplines, the indicators they often use have not won universal acceptance. For instance, people are still debating whether per capita GNP is a valid measure of the welfare of a nation. Communication being a younger discipline, indicator measurement possesses even greater problem. This is particularly true in measuring subjective indicators. The variations in question wording and measurement scale, for example, may change the results. Without equivalent indicators, it becomes very difficult to compare the state of communication across nations.

Another striking problem with communication indicator measurement relates to the nature of communication messages. While practical formulae can be devised to measure the supply and consumption of all messages (audio, visual, or print, etc.), in terms of a basic unit, it is much more difficult, if not impossible, to distinguish information from misinformation (Ito 1980). The quality of communication is very difficult to measure. The measurement of contents may also involve the interpretation of meanings which is vulnerable to subjective evaluation. Controversy often creeps in as a result. This implies that the development of universal indicators for message-decoding will be a long and painstaking process.

The measurements of communication indicators in a given society may have to change as new communication technology and new forms of media are introduced. For example, the VCR and DVD recorders that people use for time-shifting purpose provides a good illustration. VCR and DVD recorders have changed the way many people watch television. Besides, some television programs are put online for downloading nowadays. Thus to measure television consumption, we must sum up the time respondents spend with "direct" television watching as well as time spend with "pre-recorded" television programs and online television programs. In conclusion, whatever methods we used to measure communication, we have to bear in mind the two words—"validity" and "reliability"—and try to maximize the two. To obtain more meaningful and useful results, communication indicators should be measured comparably and longitudinally.

Advertising Indicators in Hong Kong

After introducing the concept of communication indictor and its possible measurement, we now apply the concept to map the state of advertising communication in Hong Kong. Heavy advertising expenditure has become the lifeblood of many communications of Hong Kong. As a result, the state of the advertising industry becomes reflective of the general media environment.

Production of Advertising Messages

Advertising expenditure is the most straightforward way to indicate the status of production of advertising messages. ACNielsen (2004), the world's leading provider of market research, acquired Survey Research Group (SRG) in 1994. SRG was the company that specialized in compiling figures of advertising expenditure by different product categories for the major mass media in Hong Kong (ACNielsen 2004). It calculates advertising spend based on published rate cards and offers advertising expenditure measurement and audience measurement. Reports on monthly and year-to-month advertising expenditures by product category and by brand are provided in a hard copy format on a monthly basis. As the advertising market becomes increasingly competitive, clients require more timely report on an interactive platform. They also request to combine information about advertising expenditure with the visual presentation of the advertisements in an integrated manner. As a result, admanGo has started its services.

admanGo (2004), founded in 1999, works with major advertisers, advertising agencies, and media in Hong Kong to develop an extensive advertising archive of all major mass media. At the end of 2004, its online advertising library carries over 100,000 advertisements from 15 television channels, 100 newspapers and magazines, radio, billboards, RoadShow (pre-recorded television program shown on bus), M-Channel, bus and tram panels and shelters, direct marketing and in-store promotions, etc. It provides competitive advertising monitoring service through an online platform. By clicking on the thumbnails of advertisements (see Figure 1.2), subscribed users can see the two-dimensional print advertisements, hear the radio spots as well as watch the television commercials. It also prepares detailed reports about advertising expenditure by different product categories, media, brands, and campaigns (see Figure 1.3).

Figure 1.2: A sample report on advertising monitoring service

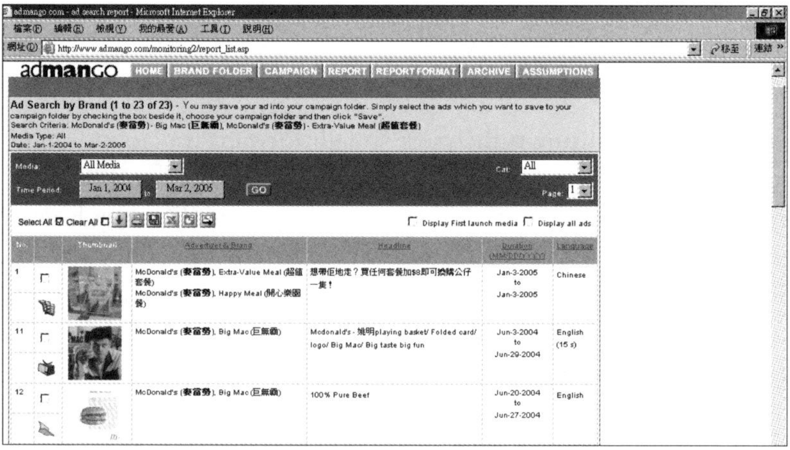

Source: admanGo (2004)

Figure 1.3: A sample report on advertising expenditure

Source: admanGo (2004)

Another indicator for advertising production is the Hong Kong advertising agency income report released by Association of Accredited Advertising Agents of Hong Kong (HK4As, refer to Chapter 2 for the figures). It provides online report of the top ten Hong Kong advertising agencies' billings with breakdown of source of income by geographical level (i.e., income from Hong Kong and income from Mainland China). However, they recently stop releasing reports about the advertising agency billings because some advertising agencies refused to provide the figures in consideration of commercial interests.

Apart from advertising expenditure and billings, advertising manpower also reflects the hardware of the production status of advertising. The Vocational Training Council conducts regular manpower surveys for major manufacturing as well as servicing industries in Hong Kong. The first round of manpower survey for the advertising and public relations industry was conducted in 1987 with the coverage of advertising agencies, public relations agencies, and advertising/PR departments of selected big companies and media agencies in Hong Kong. The number of technical manpower and their training requirement of the advertising and public relations industry were surveyed and reported every two years. However, the manpower statistics are reported by technical level (managerial, supervisory, technical support) rather than by functional departments (i.e., account servicing, creative, production and media, etc.). The number of advertising programs offered by local colleges or universities and the number of intakes every year also serve as indicators of the production of advertising messages. They somehow indicate the potential supply of manpower and the sophistication of formal advertising training that people receive before entering the industry.

Distribution of Advertising Messages

There are numerous available channels for the distribution of advertising messages in Hong Kong. The traditional one includes television, radio, newspapers, magazines, cinemas, Mass Transit Railway (MTR) and Kowloon Canton Railway (KCR) stations, trains, outdoor billboards, etc. Internet advertising is becoming more and more popular. New means for advertising have also appeared, for example, SMS through mobile phones, TVs in karaokes or even on bus (RoadShow and M-Channel broadcast on buses and mini buses). The availability of more and more advertising channels will certainly encourage intramedia and intermedia competition. This may cause the redistribution of the advertising pie.

Television

Television has become the major advertising medium in Hong Kong. It contributed 41.7% of the total media expenditure in 2002 and was regarded as the most important medium (admanGo 2004). It is also the main entertainment staple of the people in Hong Kong. Perhaps it is the most popular advertising medium in Hong Kong for an advertiser to build up the highest reach of population within the shortest time. At present, Hong Kong has two Chinese television channels: Television Broadcast Limited (TVB) and Asia Television Limited (ATV); and two English television channels: TVB Pearl and ATV World; all of which provide free television program services to the Hong Kong audience. Usually a one-hour television program will embed four commercial breaks and each commercial break has four to seven advertisements. Pay television program services are also available in Hong Kong, for example, Star TV, exTV, and Cable TV. There are different types of television advertising, for example, spot television commercials, advertising magazines, product sponsorship, title sponsorship, and product placement. There are altogether four types of product sponsorship, including prop sponsorship (i.e., the product is displayed inside a program), scene sponsorship (i.e., a particular scene of a program is specially written to expose the product), character sponsorship (i.e., a particular character in the program bears close association with the product), and theme sponsorship (i.e., the central theme of the program is tailor-made to tie in the product) (Television Broadcasts Limited 2003).

Radio

At present, Hong Kong has 13 radio channels—three operated by Hong Kong Commercial Broadcasting Company Limited (Commercial Radio), three by Metro Broadcast Corporation Limited (Metro Broadcast), and seven by Radio Television Hong Kong (RTHK). RTHK is funded by government but is editorially independent. It does not accept commercial advertisements.

Newspapers and Magazines

Hong Kong has been a hotbed of publications. It has two English newspapers: *South China Morning Post* and *Hong Kong Standard* and more than twelve Chinese daily newspapers. They include *Oriental Daily News, Apple Daily, The Sun, Ming Pao, Sing Pao, Hong Kong Economic Times, Ta Kung Pao, Wen Wei Po, Sing Tao Daily*, etc. Due to the keen competition in the market, some advertisers publicize whole-page ads and some even insert advertisements in headlines. There are more than 50 magazines in Hong Kong. They could be further divided into subcategories, including art, business, car, children's, computer, food and cooking, health and fitness, men's, news and politics, society and culture, teen's, trade, and women's. Thus advertisers could choose to place their advertisements in magazines with relevant topics. Some familiar one includes *Yazhou Zhoukan, Next Magazine, East Weekly, Yes, Yellow Bus*, etc. Some free distributed newspapers and magazines like *Metro, Recruit, Jiujik* also give rooms for advertising messages. Audience surveys were carried out to check readership of Hong Kong newspapers and magazines (see Chapter 2 for detailed figures).

RoadShow and M-Channel

Recently many transportation vehicles such as buses and mini-buses have become new platforms for advertising. This implies that advertising exists everywhere even on the way to work. RoadShow is owned by Kowloon Motor Bus which broadcast on over 5,000 buses and mini-buses. M-Channel is owned by StarEast Limited in 2001. It broadcasts on New World Bus and in some shopping malls.

Advertising revenue is a way to indicate the volume of advertising carried by different media and the distribution of advertising messages. admanGo (2004) compiles data about advertising revenue by different media every month. Regulation is another indicator for advertising distribution. As we know, the restrictions put on some product categories will surely have their effects on the distribution of advertising messages. For example, tobacco advertisements are not allowed on broadcast media in Hong Kong since 1991. Some products are allowed to advertise on broadcast media outside prime time hours, e.g., alcoholic drinks and condoms (see Chapter 6 for advertising regulations).

Reception of Advertising Messages

Reception refers to audiences' perception and evaluation of advertising messages. From time to time, there are studies to explore public opinion toward advertising in Hong Kong. Different aspects of advertising viewing and attitudes have been measured including exposure, general opinions, perceived credibility of advertising, opinions on unacceptable products and services, complaints about advertising, children's understanding of advertising, and advertisements praised by the audience.

Exposure and Attention to Advertising

Exposure to advertising is the first step to examine before further studying other aspects of advertising. In order for an advertisement to be effective, one needs to have essential exposure to it. Questions such as "What do you usually do when advertisements are on" (Chan 1995a) could be used to check audiences' exposure and attentiveness to advertising.

General Opinions

This is a relatively well-researched area among all the advertising indicators. Many studies were carried out to investigate public attitudes toward advertising (e.g. Chan 1995a; Martin et al. 1994; Sin and Cheng 1984). The details of questions asked and the major findings are summarized in Chapter 4.

Perceived Credibility of Advertising

Apart from attitudes, credibility is another widely studied area in advertising research. Advertising is always being accused for not telling the truth. That issue is even critical for children since they do not have the ability to differentiate between advertising claims and the reality. Therefore various studies were conducted to see whether people believe in what advertising said. Statements such as "Products don't perform as well as the ads claim" (Martin et al. 1994) and "In general, advertisements do not present a true picture of the product advertised" (Sin and Cheng 1984) were employed. MDR Technology Limited (1994) conducted a household survey to collect public opinions on advertising for the Broadcasting Authority. It asked respondents to indicate their extent of believing in the claims of television commercials on a 0–10 point scale.

Opinions on Unacceptable Products and Services

Offensive advertising became another hot issue in advertising. Consumers' views on offensive advertising were explored in order to identify what product/service advertisements consumers find offensive and the effect of it. Usually respondents were asked to indicate their level of personal offensiveness towards a list of products/services, e.g., chatline services, gambling, condoms, underwear, funeral services, etc. (Prendergast, Ho and Phau 2002). Reasons for finding advertisements offensive, level of tolerance of offensive advertisements and impact on purchase intentions could also be probed (see Chapter 5 for details). Questions such as "Have you ever watched any commercials in non-designated languages" and "Do you think it is necessary to prohibit the broadcast of commercials of female sanitary products during family viewing hours" were asked in the study conducted by MDR Technology Limited (1994).

Complaints about Advertising

Complaints about specific advertisement are an indicator of public dissatisfaction of advertising. When the public feels annoyed by an advertisement they come across on broadcasting media, they can lodge a complaint to the Hong Kong Broadcasting Authority. The Broadcasting Authority keeps an online complaints archive and issues press releases regularly about the number of complaints received, the reasons of complaints, and their decisions on complaint cases since 2001 (Hong Kong Broadcasting Authority 2004). There is no official body regulating advertising in other media such as print and outdoor advertisements in Hong Kong. People usually make complaints to the news media, the Consumer Council, or internet chat rooms.

Children's Understanding of Advertising

Educators and parents concern themselves with advertising which takes advantage of children's incompetence to understand. Chan (2000) used the three questions "When we are watching television, sometimes the program stops and there are other messages coming up, what these are", "What do commercials want you to do," and "Why do television stations carry such messages" to examine children's understanding of advertising. Children were also asked to recall their favorite television commercials and to explain what the commercials said by reading storyboards of different commercials (see Chapter 10 for details). The statement "Advertising has a bad influence on children" was presented to the respondents to see how they viewed the impact of advertising on children (Sin and Cheng 1984).

Advertisements Praised by Audience

In spite of the strong criticisms advertising received from the audiences, the Hong Kong audience does express their liking of some commercials.

Asia Television Limited (ATV) and the Hong Kong Advertisers Association organized every year "The Most Popular Television Commercials Award" since 1995. There is a theme for the event every year. For example, the theme for 2005 was "We grow up with ads." The selection process consists several stages. First, the ATV committee select 300 commercials from all the commercials shown in Hong Kong in the past year. A panel of judges from advertisers, advertising agencies, and related industries then select a pool of 38 short-listed commercials. Finally, the public was invited to vote for ten commercials they like the most. The ten commercials with the highest votes from the professional judges and the public will receive "The Most Popular TV Commercials Award." Those who participate in the voting are probably people who enjoy watching television commercials.

The advertising messages that constitute the symbolic system can also be analyzed in volume and orientation as communication indicators. Research studies have focused on four aspects of the advertising messages, including gender portrayal, information contents, cultural values, and symbolic meaning of visuals and texts employed.

Gender Portrayal

Advertising is sometimes accused of creating and further reinforcing gender stereotypes. Content analysis can be conducted to see whether gender stereotype exists in advertising. Items included in content analysis range from how frequently males or females act as central figures in advertisements, roles of the central figures to product price (Siu 1996). Yik (1999) and Moon and Chan (2002) have conducted similar studies but with the focus on television advertising to children.

Information Contents

Studies were conducted to examine the information contents of Hong Kong television advertisements. The first information content analysis of television commercials in Hong Kong was conducted in 1986 using Resnick and Stern's (1977) evaluation criteria. Commercials were analyzed to see if it contained one or more of the fourteen information cues including availability, performance, components, etc. The study also examines whether the presence of information cues depend on types of product advertised, duration of the commercials, and broadcast day, time and channel. Altogether 235 commercials were studied and 47% contained one or more information cues (Chan 1986). A replicate study of 341 Hong Kong commercials were conducted (Chan 1995b). There are also studies about the information contents of corporate advertising (Kwok 1994; Tse 2004).

Cultural Values

Advertising is said to reflect cultural values. Chan (1999) conducted a study to explore the cultural values embedded in Hong Kong's newspaper advertising for the period 1946 to 1996. Altogether 580 print advertisements were analyzed to see whether they contained any of the following 32 cultural values including adventure, beauty, quality, and safety, etc. The same coding frame was used to compare cultural values in Hong Kong and Mainland Chinese television commercials (Chan and Cheng 2003). An extensive study of 4,080 print advertisements in four newspapers for the period 1949 to 1998 is included in Chapter 8.

Symbolic Meaning of Advertising

Some scholars tried to read against the advertisements by doing textual analysis. This is what Katherine Frith (1997) called to "undress" advertisements. Frith (1997) argued that one have to deconstruct an ad in order to understand "what" and "how" it means. During this process, three levels of meaning should be addressed, namely surface meaning, the advertisers' intended meaning, and the cultural or ideological meaning (see Chapter 7).

One particular way of deconstructive reading and interpretation of a problem or text in an advertisement to reveal the hidden motivations behind the text is called "discourse analysis." This method has been used by scholars to deconstruct television commercials that target at children (Wong 1997), slimming advertisements (Chapter 9), banking

Table 1.1: A summary of different advertising indicators

Production	Distribution	Reception
Advertising expenditure	*Advertising expenditure by different media*	*Exposure and attention*
Advertising revenue		*Attitude*
Manpower in the advertising industry	*Advertising regulations*	*Credibility*
	Ratings and readership	*Offensive advertising*
Students enrolled in advertising programs		*Complaints*
		Understanding
Coding practices of advertising personnel		*Liking*
Message Content		
Gender portrayal, Information contents, Cultural values, Symbolic meaning		

commercials (Wong 2000) as well as public services announcements in Hong Kong (Cuklanz and Wong 1999; and Chapter 3).

Table 1.1 summarizes different advertising indicators described in this chapter.

Conclusion

Hong Kong people enjoy pluralistic and well-developed communication systems. Communications in Hong Kong appear to have benefited from its economic advancement by virtue of the advertising revenue and social consumption power. With the advanced technology and the transformation in lifestyle, we witness a number of changes in the media world. The ever-changing communication activities in Hong Kong require timely monitoring and updated research methodology.

As discussed above, we could employ indicators of message production, distribution, and reception to map the states of communication in a society. Communication indicators help us master information about media consumption and the shifts in the media market. Likewise, for any communication activities to be effective, one needs to have precise research of the three states (the production, distribution, and reception of messages). The states of production, distribution, and reception are three intertwined paths (see Figure 1.4).

Figure 1.4: The three interactive states: production, distribution, and reception

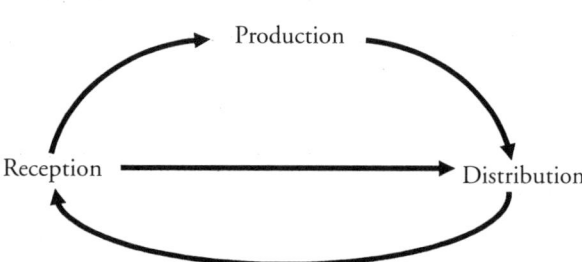

The way of production significantly affects the way of distribution and it further exerts effects on reception. On the contrary, the state of message reception provides feedback for message production and distribution. Take advertising as an example, the way of production (e.g., the production cost and the creative manpower) decides the way of distribution of advertisements (e.g., to be placed at what venue or channels). This again influences people's perception of the advertisements they watch or hear, which in turn provides hints for production and distribution of advertising messages. To succeed in today's fast-changing as well as complex markets, it is not enough to simply know what products and services people are consuming but we must know why. Therefore the reception indicators deal with not only "what" but also "why."

With advertising as an example, this chapter illustrates the theoretical as well as methodological aspects in studying communication indicators and, in particular, the advertising indicators. As reviewed above, advertising indicators in Hong Kong are widely developed and researched with lots of efforts directing to the reception of advertising messages. Among all the advertising indicators, public attitude toward advertising was the most elaborated area. Interestingly, there are relatively few studies about online advertising though this domain is getting more and more popular. One area that attracts little research attention is the code of practices of advertising practitioners. It is supposed to be one of the advertising production indicators, yet our review fails to find any published studies on this. Hong Kong does not publish any code of practices for advertising practitioners. Perhaps this is the reason why this indicator remains untapped. It is hoped that in the future we will see more studies in these two areas.

References

admanGo's website. Advertising expenditures by media. http://www.admango.com (accessed September 2, 2004).

ACNielsen's website. Advertising expenditures by industry. http://www.acnielsen. com.hk/search_result.asp (accessed September 2, 2004).

Chan, J. M., and C. C. Lee. 1991. *Mass media and political transition: The Hong Kong press in China's orbit.* NY: Guilford Press.

Chan, K. 1986. Lack of information in TV commercials. *Media & Marketing*, November 25:15–16.

———. 1995a. *Hong Kong television advertising: The good, the bad and the ugly.* Hong Kong: Department of Communication Studies, Hong Kong Baptist University.

———. 1995b. Information content of television advertising in Hong Kong and China. *Journal of Asian Pacific Communication* 6(4):231–44.

———. 1999. Cultural values in Hong Kong newspaper advertising, 1946–96. *International Journal of Advertising* 18(4):537–54.

———. 2000. Hong Kong children's understanding of television advertising. *Journal of Marketing Communications* 6(1):37–52.

———, and H. Cheng. 2003. One country, two systems: Cultural values reflected in Chinese and Hong Kong television commercials. *Gazette* 64(4):383–98.

Cuklanz, L., and W. S. Wong. 1999. Ideological themes in Hong Kong public service announcements: Implications for China's future. In Randy Kluver and John Powers, eds. *Civic Discourse, Civil Society and the Chinese Communities*, 93–107. Stamford, CT: Ablex.

Dimmick, J., and E. Rothenbuhler 1984. The theory of the Niche: Quantifying competition among media industries. *Journal of Communication* 34(1):103–19.

Frith, K. T. 1997. Undressing the ad: Reading culture in advertising. In K.T. Frith, ed. *Undressing the ad: Reading culture in advertising*, 17. NY: Peter Lang.

Gerbner, G., and L. Gross. 1976. Living with television: The violence profile. *Journal of Communication* 26(2):173–89.

———, L. Gross, M. Morgan and N. Signorielli 1986. Living with television: The dynamics of the cultivation process. In J. Bryant and D. Zillmann, eds. *Perspectives on Media Effects*, 17–40. Hillsdale, NJ: Erlbaum.

Hong Kong Broadcasting Authority's website. Complaint archives. http://www. hkba.org.hk/cn/complaints/archives.html (accessed September 3, 2004).

Ito, Y. 1980. The "Johoka Shakai" approach to the study of communication in Japan. *Keio Communication Rreview* (March):13–40.

Kwok, W. Y. 1994. *Corporate advertising in Hong Kong: An information analysis.* Unpublished M.Phil dissertation, The Chinese University of Hong Kong.

Martin, E. F., Y. M. Cheng, G. B. Wilson, and Y. W. Tsu 1994. Advertising images among Hong Kong Chinese: Use of individual modernity and Western orientation clusters in determining market segmentation. *Asian Journal of Communication* 4(1):12–32.

MDR Technology Limited. 1994. *Survey on television broadcasting 1993/94.* Hong Kong: MDR Technology Ltd.

Moon, Y. S., and K. Chan. 2002. Cross-cultural study of gender portrayal in children's television commercials: Korea and Hong Kong. *Asian Journal of Communication* 12(2):100–19.

Prendergast, G., H. Benny, and I. Phau. 2002. A Hong Kong view of offensive advertising. *Journal of Marketing Communications* 8(1):165–177.

Resnik, A., and B. L. Stern. 1977. An analysis of information content in television advertising. *Journal of Marketing* 41(1):50–53.

Rosengren, K. 1984. Cultural indicators for the comparative study of culture. In G. Melischek, K. Rosengren, and J. Stappers, eds. *Cultural indicators: An international symposium,* 11–33. Vienna: Akademie der Wissenschaften.

———. 1986. Media linkages between culture and other societal systems. In M. McLaughlin, ed. *Communication Yearbook*, vol. 9, 19–56. Beverly Hills, CA: Sage Publications.

Sin, Y. M., and W. L. Cheng. 1984. *Advertising in Hong Kong: The consumer view.* Hong Kong: Research Committee, Faculty of Business Administration, The Chinese University of Hong Kong.

Siu, W. S. 1996. Gender portrayal in Hong Kong and Singapore television advertisements. *Journal of Asian Business* 12(3):47–63.

Wong, W. S. 1997. Construction of ideal childhood: Reading and decoding TV advertisements directed at children in Hong Kong. *Hong Kong Cultural Studies Bulletin*, Spring: 75–84.

———. 2000. The rise of consumer culture in a Chinese society: A reading of banking television commercials in the 1970s of Hong Kong. *Mass Communication and Society* 3(4): 393–413.

Tehranian, M. 1979. Socio-economic and communication indicators in development planning: A case study of Iran. Paris: UNESCO.

Television Broadcasts Limited. 2003. *Product sponsorship brochure.* Hong Kong: Marketing and Sales Division, Television Broadcasts Limited.

Tse, W. M. 2004. An information content analysis of Hong Kong corporate advertising: A comparison between public utilities sector and private sector. Unpublished M.Phil. dissertation, Hong Kong Baptist University.

Yik, H. 1999. A content analysis of children's television advertising in Hong Kong. Unpublished M.Phil. dissertation, Hong Kong Baptist University.

Acknowledgements

Part of this chapter has been published in J. M. Chan and P.S.N. Lee (1992), "Communication Indicators in Hong Kong: Conceptual Issues, Findings and Implications." In S. Lau, P. Wan, M. Lee and S. Wong, eds. *The Development of Social Indicators Research in Chinese Societies* (Hong Kong: Hong Kong Institute of Asia-Pacific Studies, The Chinese University of Hong Kong), 175–205.

Chapter 2

Overview of Hong Kong Advertising

Ernest F. Martin, Jr.
Chris Fei Shen

Introduction

Hong Kong has long been a key center of commerce and a focal point of Southeast Asian business development. It remains one of the world's most dynamic economies. A special administrative region of China, Hong Kong is also one of the least regulated free-enterprise systems in the world, one of the world's largest container ports, and a major international financial center.

Hong Kong's communication and transportation infrastructures are well developed. The legal system is designed for business and trade. As the largest port of entry to Mainland China, Hong Kong is the trade conduit between Taiwan and China; the economic interdependence among the three places continues to increase. Additionally Hong Kong continues to be the center of Western business interests in East Asia. The people of Hong Kong are culturally disposed toward business and English is the official second language, making it highly accessible to Westerners. Overall Hong Kong is the prime business, communications, and marketing center in the region.

Economy

Throughout history Hong Kong has been a key center of commerce and one of the least regulated free-enterprise systems in the world.

According to the findings of the "Economic Freedom of the World: 2004 Annual Report," which was released on July 15, 2004 by the Cato Institute and Canada's Fraser Institute (Cato Institute and the Fraser Institute 2004), it remained for eight consecutive years the world's freest economy. Hong Kong was ranked the world's freest economy for the tenth consecutive year by the Heritage Foundation and Wall Street Journal with the release of the "2004 Index of Economic Freedom" (Heritage Foundation and Wall Street Journal 2004) dated January 9, 2004. The advertising industry thrives in the environment of economic freedom.

What makes Hong Kong a great economic center? InvestHK, an organization established in 2000 to promote Hong Kong's many advantages as an investment and business hub in Asia, describes the advantages as follows: "Executives identify a combination of factors: its location in the heart of East Asia on China's southern coast; its low tax regime; its transparent common law legal system and impartial judiciary; state-of-the-art infrastructure; free flow of information; its entrepreneurial spirit; and a truly international lifestyle." (InvestHK 2004)

Hong Kong is a resilient as well as a dynamic center. Gross domestic product (GDP) per capita compares favorably with the big economies of the world. After GDP growth averaged a strong 5% in the years 1989–1997, Hong Kong suffered two recessions in the ensuing six years because of the Asian financial crisis in 1998 and the global downturn of 2001–2002. After a marked slowdown from 10.2% in 2000 to 0.5% in 2001, the Hong Kong economy staged a moderate rebound to 2.3% in 2002 (Information Services Department 2002).

The SARS (Severe Acute Respiratory Syndrome) outbreak then battered Hong Kong's economy. By late 2003 strong growth nevertheless resumed as tourism from the Mainland boomed with China's relaxation of individual travel to Hong Kong. This period also witnessed a return of consumer confidence and a solid rise in exports. During the first quarter of 2004, tourism and other factors boosted Hong Kong's economic growth and the latter surged to 6.8%, the highest growth rate for three years (*China Daily* 2004).

Consumer Population

The population is approximately 6.8 million (Information Services Department 2002). According to the population census, around 60% of the population was born in Hong Kong and 36% in China.

Annual growth rate has remained fairly constant at 1% for over a decade. Births dropped from 16 per 1,000 people in 1983, 12 per 1,000 in 1993, to 7 per 1000 in 2001. There has been a stable death rate of 5 per 1,000 since the 1980s (Information Services Department 1994). Despite a decrease in the birth rate the population grew at about the same rate thanks to a larger net inflow of persons into the territory.

Market Segmentation

Although a predominantly Chinese community, Hong Kong is a culturally diverse city reflecting a wide range of attitudes and behaviors. The marketing challenge in Hong Kong is to classify the population into meaningful groups of consumers. Market segmentation, in essence, lays the foundation on which a group will be targeted in advertising or more general marketing efforts (Martin 1995). Many attributes can be used to divide a population into segments. Historically in Hong Kong, as well as in much of the rest of the world, demographics (age, sex, race, income, education) and geographics (areas of residence) have been the building blocks for defining market segmentation. More recently, psychographics (lifestyle and value segmentation) have been added to the mix (Michman 1991). The following discussion describes the segmentation of the Hong Kong population based on geographics, demographics, and psychographics respectively.

Density

With a land area of only 1,078 square kilometers, 6.8 million citizens and 11.3 million tourists, Hong Kong is one of the most densely populated places in the world. A considerable part of the population is shifting out of the urban areas. In the past ten years the proportion of the population in the New Territories has increased from 44.5% to 50%.

Table 2.1: **Hong Kong population distribution by district, 2001**

District	Region	Population
Central and Western	HK Island	261,884
Eastern	HK Island	616,199
Islands	New Territory	86,667
Kowloon City	Kowloon	381,352
Kwai Tsing	New Territory	477,092
Kwun Tong	Kowloon	562,427
North	New Territory	298,657
Sai Kung	New Territory	327,689
Sham Shui Po	Kowloon	353,550
Sha Tin	New Territory	628,634
Southern	HK Island	290,240
Tai Po	New Territory	310,879
Tsuen Wan	New Territory	275,527
Tuen Mun	New Territory	488,831
Wan Chai	HK Island	167,146
Wong Tai Sin	Kowloon	444,630
Yau Tsim Mong	Kowloon	282,020
Yuen Long	New Territory	449,070
18 districts' total		6,708,389

Source: *Hong Kong Population Census 2001* (Census and Statistics Department 2001)

Overall the 2001 Census reflected a distribution of 20% on Hong Kong Island, 30% in Kowloon, and 50% in the New Territories (Census and Statistics Department 2001).

Housing

The revised estimate of public expenditure on housing in 2002–2003 was HK$29.1 billion, or 11% of total public expenditure. Total housing stock in December 2002 amounted to 2,305,680 flats, comprising 684,500 public rental-housing flats, 373,370 subsidized home ownership flats and 1,245,820 flats in the private sector (Information Services Department 2002).

Sex

In 2001 Hong Kong had 3,285,344 males and 3,423,045 females. The ratio of males to females in the population has been in decline during the past decade.

Table 2.2: Hong Kong population by sex: 1991, 1996, 2001

Sex	1991		1996		2001	
	Number	% of total	Number	% of total	Number	% of total
Male	2 811 991	50.9	3 108 107	50.0	3 285 344	49.0
Female	2 710 290	49.1	3 109 449	50.0	3 423 045	51.0
Total	5 522 281	100.0	6 217 556	100.0	6 708 389	100.0
Gender Ratio	1 038		1 000		960	

Source: *Hong Kong Population Census 2001* (Census and Statistics Department 2001)

Table 2.3: Hong Kong population by ethnicity

Ethnicity	Number	% of total
Chinese	6 364 439	94.9
Filipino	142 556	2.1
Indonesian	50 494	0.8
British	18 909	0.3
Indian	18 543	0.3
Thai	14 342	0.2
Japanese	14 180	0.2
Nepalese	12 564	0.2
Pakistani	11 017	0.2
Others	61 345	0.9
Total	6 708 389	100.0

Source: *Hong Kong Population Census 2001* (Census and Statistics Department 2001)

Ethnicity

Close to 98% of Hong Kong residents are Chinese. Non-Chinese include, in descending order of proportions in the population, Filipinos, Indonesians, British, Indians, Thais, Japanese, and many others.

Age

The consumers of Hong Kong are "aging." Although compared with most Western markets Hong Kong is a "youth" market, the demographic skew has changed over the past ten years. The population aged under 35 has fallen while that of those aged 35 or above has risen.

Table 2.4: Hong Kong population by age group

Age Group	1991		1996		2001	
	Number	% of total	Number	% of total	Number	% of total
0–14	1 151 916	20.9	1 151 038	18.5	1 109 417	16.5
15–24	839 841	15.2	869 511	14.0	920 445	13.7
25–34	1 178 288	21.4	1 188 424	19.1	1 108 529	16.5
35–44	891 032	16.1	1 178 522	19.0	1 360 487	20.3
45–54	487 658	8.8	683 569	11.0	960 417	14.3
55–64	491 506	8.9	516 937	8.3	502 042	7.5
65+	482 040	8.7	629 555	10.1	747 052	11.1
Total	5 522 281	100.0	6 217 556	100.0	6 708 389	100.0

Source: *Hong Kong Population Census 2001* (Census and Statistics Department 2001)

The projected age structure of the Hong Kong population continues to show an "ageing" trend. By the year 2025, 15.4% will be under 15 years of age, 61.4% between 15 and 64, and a significant 23.2% will be over 64, compared with only 9.1% in 1991 (Genzberger et al. 1994).

Education

The education system in Hong Kong has expanded steadily over the years to meet the needs of an ever-growing population. The enrollment in 2002 exceeded 1.2 million: 143,000 kindergartens, 483,000 primary schools, 465,000 secondary schools, and 142,000 tertiary institutes. Approved recurrent public expenditure and aggregate public expenditure on education in the 2002–2003 financial year amounted to 49.3 billion and 59.4 billion dollars respectively, representing 23.8% of government expenditure (Information Services Department 2002).

About one fifth of Hong Kong's residents are studying full-time. All children aged between 6 and 15 are required by law to be in full-time education or to complete Secondary 3. After Secondary 3, most of them

Table 2.5: Hong Kong population aged 15 or above by educational attainment (highest level attended)

Educational Attainment	1991		1996		2001	
	Number	% of total	Number	% of total	Number	% of total
No schooling/ Kindergarten	557 297	12.8	480 852	9.5	469 939	8.4
Primary	1 100 599	25.2	1 146 882	22.6	1 148 273	20.5
Lower Secondary	837 730	19.1	958 245	18.9	1 060 489	18.9
Upper Secondary	1 169 271	26.7	1 403 211	27.7	1 473 681	26.3
Matriculation[1]	214 577	4.9	308 808	6.1	528 090	9.4
Tertiary						
Non-degree course	234 912	5.4	243 004	4.8	209 878	3.7
Degree course	255 979	5.9	525 516	10.4	708 622	12.7
Total	4 370 365	100.0	5 066 518	100.0	5 598 972	100.0

Source: *Hong Kong Population Census 2001* (Census and Statistics Department 2001)

stay on for a two-year senior secondary course, proceeding to the first public examination. Others enroll full-time in vocational training. A small number quit formal education.

The educational level in Hong Kong is rising with fewer people having only primary education and an increasing proportion receiving tertiary degree qualifications.

Literacy

Ninety-three percent of the Hong Kong population is literate. The official languages are Chinese (Cantonese) and English. Cantonese is the major medium of daily communication.

Income

Per capita income was US$23,800 in 2002 (Information Services Department 2002). In 2004 the estimated per capita income increased to US$28,700. By contrast, the average per capita earning in 1991 was US$13,430 (Genzberger et al. 1994). However, because of inflation, the pressure on family income is still great.

Table 2.6: **Hong Kong population aged 5 or above by usual language**

Usual Language	1991		1996		2001	
	Number	% of total	Number	% of total	Number	% of total
Cantonese	4 583 322	88.7	5 196 240	88.7	5 726 972	89.2
Putonghua	57 577	1.1	65 892	1.1	55 410	0.9
Other Chinese Dialects	364 694	7.0	340 222	5.8	352 562	5.5
English	114 084	2.2	184 308	3.1	203 598	3.2
Others	49 232	1.0	73 879	1.3	79 197	1.2
Total	5 168 909	100.0	5 860 541	100.0	6 417 739	100.0

Source: *Hong Kong Population Census 2001* (Census and Statistics Department 2001)

A significant proportion of per capita income, however, does not come from the main employment. The median wages from the main employer was approximately 61% (Census and Statistics Department 2001).

Hong Kong is a community of contrasts in everything, including income distribution. Almost one third of all income is earned by 10% of the population. In other words, one out of ten people control one out of three of the dollars.

The income stratification in 2003 in Hong Kong dollars is shown in Table 2.7.

Other Population Indicators

Other population indicators and projects shed light on the demographic composition of Hong Kong (Census and Statistics Department 2001). Marriage rates dipped slightly from 1997 through 2002 but have generally remained stable since the 1980s, and divorce rates are low. In the population as a whole in 2001, 32% were single, 59% married, and 9% separated, divorced, or widowed.

Average household size has declined in the past decade, down from 3.4 persons in 1991 to 3.1 persons in 2003. The number of women of childbearing age increased but the fertility rate dropped. The fertility rate plunged from 1.5% in 1991 to 0.94% in 2003. Life expectancy at

Table 2.7: Hong Kong monthly income, 2003

Monthly Personal Income (HK$)	%
Under $8,000	27
$8,000–9,999	15
$10,000–14,999	30
$15,000–19,999	14
$20,000–29,999	9
$30,000 and over	5
Median Monthly Income	$10,792
Monthly Household Income (HK$)	%
Under $10,000	20
$10,000–12,999	16
$13,000–14,999	5
$15,000–19,999	21
$20,000–24,999	15
$25,000–29,999	7
$30,000–39,999	9
$40,000 and over	6
Median Monthly Household Income	$16,001

Source: ACNielsen Hong Kong (2003)

birth increased to 81 in 2003 from 78 years of age in 1990, compared with 64 years of age in 1960.

Individual Modernity and Western Orientation

Psychographic segmentation is useful for segmenting the world of consumers in the wake of modernization and Western influence in Hong Kong.

Despite the modern, deceptively Western look of the Hong Kong society, the ethnic Hong Kong Chinese maintain a strong cultural identity (Bond et al. 1985; Bond and Hwang 1986). In summarizing previous findings in the field, Bond (1991) and Yang (1986) contend that individual traditional and modern attitudes do not necessarily stand in opposition to each other, especially when mediated with Chinese values. In various studies in North America, Taiwan, Hong Kong, and China, a "Modern Chinese" is a person who retains the essential Chinese virtues (especially family, achievement, and moderation) in a creative amalgam with Western technical mastery; while a "Traditional Chinese" is one who values traditional characteristics like thrift and filial piety, as well as traits of non-competitiveness, superstition, and authoritarianism (Bond 1991).

To summarize the findings from literature dealing with the Chinese personality, individuals who consider themselves modern tend to develop a greater concern about self-expression, self-assertion, independence, personal achievement, dominance, tolerance, as well as less inhibition in associating with the opposite sex. They are also less prone to conforming to customs, achieving organization and orderliness, blaming and belittling self, helping or giving sympathy to others, persevering in a task or activity until finished, seeking approval or admiration from others or society, and striving to achieve goals set by others or society (Martin 1995).

A series of research studies on Chinese market segmentation have been conducted. Martin and others (1993; 1994a; 1994b), Martin and Wilson (1993), and Martin and Tsui (1993) found the combined concepts of individual modernity/traditionalism and Chinese/Western value orientation are desirous in segmenting the Hong Kong Chinese population with its very diverse backgrounds, status, and life experiences.

Five clusters are identified to segment the Hong Kong population. The "Middle–Middle" cluster is the largest, taking up 51.4%; "Modern–Western" cluster 20.9%; "Traditional–Chinese" 13.9%; "Modern-Chinese" 7.9%; and "Traditional-Middle" is the smallest with only 5.9% (Martin et al. 1994a).

The demographics of the clusters indicate a significant age skew with Modern–Western being youngest, Modern–Chinese, Middle–Middle, Traditional–Middle progressively older, and Traditional–Chinese with the oldest age skew. The educational attainment of the respondents within clusters is highest among Modern–Western, Middle–Middle, and Modern–Chinese clusters, and lowest among Traditional–Chinese and Traditional–Middle clusters. Family income demographics indicate that the Modern–Western cluster is more affluent than the Traditional–Chinese cluster.

Media usage also varies with each cluster. Television usage is the heaviest among the Traditional–Chinese and Traditional–Middle segments, with Modern–Western and Modern–Chinese segments being the lightest television viewers. Newspaper usage weighs the most within the Middle–Middle segment. The Modern–Chinese segment respondents are the lightest newspaper readers. Radio usage is most common in the Traditional–Middle cluster. Magazine usage is most prevalent for Modern–Western and lightest for Traditional–Chinese.

Hong Kong respondents are generally supportive in their attitude towards advertising. The Modern–Western and Modern–Chinese segments show the strongest support, whereas the Traditional-Chinese segment is the most critical (Martin et al. 1994a).

Advertising Industry

The advertising and related industries in Hong Kong are sophisticated, fast-paced, and money-driven. The intense competition is unrivaled in the neighboring region and even worldwide. Advertisers are demanding and cut-throat business maneuvers among competitive agencies prevail.

Advertising and market research are two of the fastest growing service industries in Hong Kong, in line with the development of Hong Kong into a high-income economy and the rising prominence of the Chinese mainland as a big market for consumer products and other goods and services.

There are 4,529 advertising agencies and related services in Hong Kong, employing approximately 17,000 people, according to a research conducted in March 2003 (InvestHK 2004). In 2003 Hong Kong's overall advertising expenditure totaled HK$35.8 billion, posting a moderate growth of 8% over 2002.

Historical Context of Advertising

Early Hong Kong advertising was closely linked with painting and fine arts. Companies hired artists who practiced the traditional style of painting, mainly brought in from Guangdong province. Calendars, matchbox covers, newspapers, magazines, painted signs, and posters reflected the adaptation of traditional Chinese painting for product promotion. Many of the painters who are prominent in Hong Kong art history enhanced advertising creativity in the early days.

Along with establishment of local agencies in the late 1920s one multinational agency, D'Arcy Masius Benton & Bowles (DMB&B), began operating in Hong Kong in 1927 (Euromonitor 1993). Throughout the 1930s small agencies and freelance artists provided advertising support for companies. Although radio broadcasting began in 1928, no advertising was allowed until the commencement of commercial radio in 1959. Commercial television broadcasting began in 1967 (Everest 1978). Two multinational agencies were established in the 1940s and 1950s, four more in the 1960s, and most of the remaining multinational agencies that are still in operation today were established in Hong Kong in the 1970s (Euromonitor 1993; Dun & Bradstreet 1993; Sin and Cheng 1984).

Importance of Mainland China

Advertising in Hong Kong is dramatically impacted by the rest of China. The mainland is responsible for an increasing share of advertising spending with tremendous growth potential.

Hong Kong is situated at the hub of a huge economic powerhouse called "Greater China," which includes the combined economic resources of China, Taiwan, Hong Kong, Singapore, Macau, and other overseas Chinese communities in Southeast Asia. Greater China transcends geopolitical borders, and the places are bound together by a common cultural tradition. As Greater China further develops it will be an economic bloc as powerful as, if not more powerful than, North America, Europe, or Japan. Beyond dispute, Hong Kong is the capital of Greater China.

Structure of the Industry

Most of the major international advertising agencies are based in Hong Kong, either as wholly owned, majority owned, or joint-venture arrangements with local companies.

The agencies are divided into the "4As" membership, which is limited to the larger multinational agencies, and the "2As" composed primarily of smaller, Chinese-owned agencies. Formally, the 2As is the Hong Kong Advertisers Association and the 4As is The Association of Accredited Advertising Agents of Hong Kong.

The majority of total advertising billings are placed by the 4A agencies (Table 2.8).

In addition to the advertising agencies themselves, the infrastructure for advertising is as complete as anywhere in the world with a massive selection of graphic and photographic services, film/video production houses, translation, and other services.

Direct response agencies, expanding rapidly during the past few years, offer integrated promotion techniques to clients marketing throughout Asia. There are several dozens available, many of which spring out of full service agencies. Hong Kong vies with Singapore as a center for Asian direct marketing (Davis Direct Worldwide 2004).

Table 2.8: 4As Agency Hong Kong income report 2001

Name of Agency	Total Billings (million HK$)
Ogilvy & Mather	21.2
DDB Worldwide	18.2
McCann-Erickson Guangming	13.6
Bates Hong Kong	13.1
JWT	12.4
FCB Hong Kong	12.1
Grey Hong Kong	11.7
Leo Burnett	8.0
Euro RSCG Partnership	7.2
BBDO Hong Kong	5.6
DY&R	5.4
Saatchi & Saatchi	5.1
D'Arcy	3.8
Publicis AD-Link	3.6
Dentsu Hong Kong	3.3
TBWA Hong Kong	3.2
Lowe Lintas & Partners	2.6
Draft Worldwide	0.7
M&C Saatchi	—
Total	151.0

Source: The Association of Accredited Advertising Agents of Hong Kong (2004)

Another group of service companies provides sales promotion specialty, over a hundred companies provide public relations consultancy, and at least two dozen companies provide market research services to an international standard.

Weekly TV ratings (sample of 100+, 4 years of age and older) use people meters. Radio listening habits (sample of 1,400, 12 years of age and older) use a diary. An annual media index of demographics and media habits (sample of 8,000+, 9 years of age and older) is conducted through personal interviews.

Hong Kong has world standard production and creative services which are on a par with other major international centers.

Advertising Agency Rate Structure

Hong Kong agencies generally follow international standards for compensation for services. Agencies charge a negotiated 15% commission on media space and time. Production work is billed at cost plus.

Advertising Personnel

Agency employment in Hong Kong, like the rest of the world, generally parallels the billings and number of clients. Based on a survey by the Vocational Training Council (VTC) of Hong Kong in 2003, in agencies, around 50% of employees are in managerial and supervisory functions (see Table 2.9).

Overall employment in Hong Kong advertising agencies is still disproportionately dominated by males. In the VTC survey in 2001, in the sector overall, employment is 53% male, 47% female. In advertising agencies and services, 62% are male. This pattern is reflected throughout the whole organization. In the managerial ranks, 63% of advertising agency employees are male compared with 55% in the sector overall. At the supervisory level, 69% are male compared with 59% in the sector. Among executional workers, 58% in ad agencies are male compared with 49% overall (see Table 2.10). On the other hand, salaries of agency personnel continue to be attractive (Table 2.11).

Table 2.9: **Number of workers employed by the mass communications industry (Advertising and public relations)**

	Managerial	Supervisory	Editorial/ Production/ Executive	Supporting Technical	Total
Public Relation Services	311	319	391	7	1028
Advertising Sales/PR/ Marketing Department in Media Organizations	252	460	754	0	1466
Advertising Company, Agency & other Advertising Services	1528	2720	5157	100	9505
Corporate Communica- tions/PR/Advertising/ Marketing Department in Company/Institution	228	228	327	13	806
Total	2329	3727	6629	120	12805

Source: Vocational Training Council (2003)

Advertising Expenditure for Product Categories

Skin care, entertainment, and health are leading product categories in terms of advertising expenditure. Real estate, overseas travel, and mobile communication were strong, but they weakened in relation to other categories (Table 2.12).

Hong Kong Creative Advertising

On January 8, 2003, the Chief Executive, Mr. Tung Chee Hwa, devoted a whole paragraph in his annual Policy Address (Chapter 19) to the importance of the creative industries. His points are summarized as follows:

- Creative industries were important elements of a knowledge-based economy.
- New dimension and vigor would be added to the economy by actively promoting creative industries.

Table 2.10: Mass communications industry manpower statistics
(Advertising and public relations)

Managerial Level	Male	Female	Total
Public Relations Service	135	168	303
Advertising Sales/PR/Marketing Department in Media Organizations	116	88	204
Advertising Companies, Agencies and other Advertising Services	1062	617	1679
Corporate Communications/Public Relations/ Advertising/Marketing Department in Companies/Institutions	92	217	359
Subtotal	1405	1140	2545
Supervisory Level			
Public Relations Services	88	300	388
Advertising Sales/PR/Marketing Departments in Media Organizations	197	257	454
Advertising Companies, Agencies and other Advertising Services	2046	925	2971
Corporate Communications/Public Relations/ Advertising/Marketing Departments in Companies/Institutions	60	208	268
Subtotal	2391	1690	4081
Executional Level			
Public Relations Services	71	309	380
Advertising Sales/PR/Marketing Departments in Media Organizations	297	607	904
Advertising Companies, Agencies and other Advertising Services	2625	1898	4523
Corporate Communications/Public Relations/ Advertising/Marketing Departments in Companies/Institutions	79	345	424
Subtotal	3072	3159	6231
Supporting/Technical Level			
Advertising Companies, Agencies and other Advertising Services	4	7	11
Grand total	6872	5996	12868

Source: Vocational Training Council (2001)

Table 2.11: Hong Kong sector salaries

Monthly salary HK$	All sectors %	Advertising agencies only %
$10000 or below	17.9	21.1
$10001–20000	45.0	48.7
$20001–30000	14.8	14.8
$30001–50000	9.0	6.4
$50001–70000	2.6	2.3
$70001–90000	1.2	1.0
$90001 or above	1.3	1.1
Unspecified	8.2	4.6

Source: Vocational Training Council (2003)

Table 2.12: Hong Kong top 10 product categories
(January 2004 vs. January 2003)

Category	Year to Year Change	Ranking based on Ad Spend Jan 2004	Ranking based on Ad Spend Jan 2003
Skin Care	+80%	1	5
Tonic	+31%	2	4
Restaurants/Clubs	+16%	3	2
Overseas Travel	–4%	4	1
Supermarkets	+29%	5	6
Movie/Entertainment	+46%	6	10
Residential Estates-Sales/ Rental	+1%	7	3
CDs & Tapes	+192%	8	27
Department Stores	+67%	9	17
Mobile Communication Services & Equipment	–3%	10	8

Source: ACNielsen Hong Kong (2003)

- Priority would be given to the performing arts, film and television, publishing, art and antique markets, music, architecture, advertising, digital entertainment, computer software development, animation production, fashion and product design.
- Government departments and bureaus would work together to devise a concrete plan and create the necessary favorable environment to promote and facilitate the development of these creative industries.

Hong Kong Advertising Expenditures by Medium

Television in Hong Kong provides the interaction of sight, sound, motion, and emotion—with choices of language or combinations of languages. There are now two free commercial operators—Television Broadcasts Limited (TVB) and Asia Television Limited (ATV). Each operates one Cantonese channel and one predominantly English channel. Radio Television Hong Kong (RTHK) shares the use of all four channels for program presentation at various times.

Television remains the medium with the highest advertising expenditure.

Forty-nine percent of expenditure goes to television (up from 44% 10 years ago), 34% to newspaper, 12% to magazines, 2% to radio, 2% to Mass Transit Railway (MTR), and 1% to other (ACNielsen Hong Kong 2003).

Television

Television viewing is the most popular leisure time activity with more than 98% of households owning one or more television sets. Ninety-six percent tune in during any 24-hour period. The average person (aged 9 years and older) watched almost 4 hours of television per day.

Table 2.13: **Advertising spending by medium**

Hong Kong's Spending on Advertising by Medium	Jan 2004 (HK$000)	Jan 2003 (HK$000)	Year to Year Change
TV	1,558,617	1,241,169	25%
Newspapers	1,086,869	1,054,167	3%
Magazines	377,792	343,127	10%
Radio	73,207	79,953	−8%
Cinema	1,764	7,235	−76%
MTR	65,245	68,575	5%
Other	45,846	25,335	81%
Total	3,209,339	2,819,560	14%

Sources: ACNielsen Hong Kong (2003); InvestHK (2004)

Each of the private television broadcasters, Television Broadcasts Limited (TVB) and Asia Television Limited (ATV), provides one Chinese and one English-language channel. Broadcasters use translators to provide a high-quality over-the-air signal to all parts of the territory.

Competition is keen with each trying to strengthen their audience share by diversifying and enriching program content. A variety of movies, variety shows, continuing comedies and dramas, magazine shows, sports and horse racing, and news programs are aired. On the Chinese channels, locally produced serialized dramas (and some from other parts of Greater China, dubbed into Cantonese) are the programming cornerstone. Feature films retain strong popularity. Game/contest shows, beauty pageants, musical specials, fund-raising charity, and musical variety programs are also prevalent.

TVB Jade dominates the Chinese TV station share with slightly over three fourths of the viewers. Viewers of ATV Home, the competing Cantonese channel, have increased from several years ago. Cantonese and Mandarin audiences, both in Hong Kong and in Guangdong Province, account for 1.6 million viewers per day.

English-language programming has a niche market of about 250,000 viewers per day. On the English channels feature films, imported comedies and drama, nature programming, documentaries, sports, and cartoons are strong programming elements. News and information programs are an important part of the programming on all channels. TVB Pearl generally enjoys significantly higher ratings than ATV World but for specific feature films, ATV World at times surpasses TVB Pearl. Viewing of the English channels is much more fragmented, unlike the Chinese-language channels where many loyal "single channel" partisans are in favor of TVB Jade.

Broadcasting is in bilingual format, thanks to the use of multi-channel sound with NICAM. This has enabled the English services to attract more Cantonese-speaking viewers and similarly has also enabled Putonghua speakers to enjoy the Cantonese programs.

The majority of Hong Kong television programs on TVB Jade and ATV Home are locally produced. Over 90% of the top 100 programs are local.

Pay TV

Cable or subscription television was introduced in Hong Kong with the franchise award in June 1993. With the high population density and high-rise residential communities making cable installation a relatively painless task, Hong Kong is ideally suited to pay-TV services. Over three quarters of all households now have broadband network access, while nearly 60% have fiber-optic cable running to their building.

After the launching and scrapping of plans in the early 2000s, four pay-television operators are now competitors: exTV, I-Cable Communications, NOW Broadband TV and City Telecom. I-Cable, the territory's no. 1 sector operator, charges a monthly fee of $298 for its service while City Telecom's service costs $88.

Digital TV

There is a reluctance to introduce digital technology and programming although Hong Kong Cable TV began digital broadcasting in early April 2002. The HKSAR Government has indicated its willingness to proceed with the UK system, but the key private broadcasters hesitate until they know which system mainland China decides to choose.

Radio Television Hong Kong (TV)

Radio Television Hong Kong (RTHK) produces 10 hours of public affairs television programs, each generally half an hour in duration. Five hours are allotted for RTHK programs during prime time on TVB Jade and ATV Home. The programs are mainly about current affairs, drama, information and community services, variety and quiz shows, children's programs, and general educational programs.

Radio

Hong Kong has 15 different radio channels broadcasting in English, Cantonese, and Mandarin. The major commercial radio stations are Radio Television Hong Kong (RTHK) with seven stations; Hong Kong Commercial Broadcast Company Limited (Commercial Radio) with three; and Metro Broadcast Corporation Limited (Metro Broadcast), also with three.

Table 2.14: Hong Kong TV reach analysis, 2003

	% of people watched yesterday			
	TVB Jade	ATV Home	TVB Pearl	ATV World
All aged 9+	90	59	16	10
Sex				
Male	90	60	16	11
Female	91	58	16	11
Age				
9–14	97	61	15	7
15–24	93	52	19	10
25–34	82	49	23	16
35–49	91	57	18	12
50+	91	70	9	6
Education				
Tertiary	69	45	37	27
Post secondary	87	55	23	18
Secondary	94	59	15	8
Primary or under	91	70	9	6
Monthly personal income				
Under $8,000	84	56	19	13
$8,000–$9,999	91	56	17	12
$10,000–$14,999	89	54	19	13
$15,000–$19,999	85	55	20	13
$20,000–$29,999	89	48	20	13
$30,000 or over	71	49	38	25
Occupation				
Managers & Administrators	74	46	31	24
Professionals	77	48	37	27
Associate Professionals	88	51	21	11
Clerks	93	50	16	12
Service workers & Shop sales workers	90	54	16	12
Craft & related workers	94	65	11	7
Plant & machine operators & assemblers	94	63	15	11
Elementary occupations	80	52	20	14
Student	96	58	17	8
Full-time housewife	96	67	10	5
Unemployment	91	66	15	11
Retired	89	78	4	3

Source: ACNielsen Hong Kong (2003)

RTHK operates seven channels with 24-hour service. Government-funded and under the Information Technology and Broadcasting Bureau (ITBB), RTHK is nevertheless editorially independent, operating more along the lines of a private broadcaster than a government department. Its radio broadcasting division dates back to 1928.

Radio 1, 2, and 5 are Cantonese channels, while Radio 3 is in English. Radio 4 provides bilingual presentations of fine music, while the Mandarin channel offers music programs, talk shows, and hourly news reports. Radio 6 relays the BBC World Service 24 hours a day.

Commercial Radio has been in operation since 1959. It runs two Cantonese services on FM (CR1 and CR2) and one music and news service on AM (Quote 864), all on a 24-hour basis. One of the most popular stations in Hong Kong, CR1 offers programs mainly in the form of public affairs, magazine, drama, sports, music, and talk shows. CR2 puts emphasis on Chinese pop music, much of it sponsored by HMV. Quote 864 broadcasts all-Western pop music programs, punctuated by spot news programs at regular intervals.

Through a subsidiary since mid-2000, the Commercial Radio Production Co Ltd, Commercial Radio also runs a joint venture with PCCW that produces an audio/archive channel with is own internet site (www.881903.com). The site provides interactive broadcasting to Chinese listeners around the world.

Metro Broadcast operates two FM channels (FM Select and Hit Radio) and one music and news service on AM (Metro Plus), all on a 24-hour basis. FM Select targets older listeners while Hit Radio, a Chinese pop music channel, targets younger listeners. The English-language Metro Plus broadcasts current affairs and musical programs with hourly news reports. Advertising is accepted on all Commercial Radio and Metro Broadcast channels. Program sponsorships are accepted on RTHK.

Audience composition for each station in Hong Kong tends to follow its programming format and identity (Table 2.15).

Newspapers

There are 52 daily newspapers in Hong Kong, including 25 Chinese-language dailies, 4 English-language dailies, 8 English-language

Table 2.15: **Hong Kong listener composition profile, 2003**

| | \% of people listened yesterday | | | | | |
	Any CR	CR1	CR2	Any RTHK	RTHK1	RTHK2
All aged 9+	19	14	7	15	6	6
Sex						
Male	22	16	7	13	5	5
Female	17	11	6	17	7	8
Age						
9–14	10	5	6	6	2	3
15–24	21	6	16	6	2	4
25–34	17	9	10	12	5	8
35–49	21	18	4	17	7	8
50+	20	18	3	20	9	5
Education						
Tertiary	19	11	8	15	5	5
Post secondary	22	13	10	11	4	6
Secondary	21	13	10	11	4	6
Primary or under	16	14	3	17	7	5
Monthly personal income						
Under $8,000	18	13	6	16	7	6
$8,000–$9,999	22	15	8	15	5	9
$10,000–$14,999	25	17	9	13	6	7
$15,000–$19,999	23	17	6	10	4	6
$20,000–$29,999	19	13	6	14	7	3
$30,000 or over	18	17	2	19	9	4
Occupation						
Managers & Administrators	16	12	4	12	4	5
Professionals	23	19	6	16	6	5
Associate Professionals	21	13	9	13	7	5
Clerks	21	13	9	14	4	9
Service workers & Shop sales workers	19	11	8	12	6	5
Craft & related workers	20	16	6	10	3	4
Plant & machine operators & assemblers	46	40	12	21	12	10
Elementary occupations	17	13	4	15	6	6
Student	15	4	11	6	2	4
Full-time housewife	17	14	3	20	8	8
Unemployment	23	17	8	16	9	6
Retired	19	17	2	22	8	4

Source: ACNielsen Hong Kong (2003)

newspapers publishing 5 or 6 days a week, 7 bilingual dailies, and 5 newspapers in other languages. Intense competition is evident in Hong Kong newspapers (Fact Index 2004). About three fourths of the Chinese language dailies cover mostly general local and overseas news, with a few covering primarily financial news and the remaining ones covering entertainment and gossip, especially movie and TV personalities. The larger papers are distributed to overseas Chinese communities, with some having editions printed in the Australia, Canada, United Kingdom, and the United States.

The leading Chinese-language newspapers are the *Oriental Daily News, Sing Pao Daily News, Ming Pao, Hong Kong Commercial Daily, Hong Kong Economic Journal, Hong Kong Economic Times, Sing Tao Daily, Apple Daily, Sun Daily, Ta Kung Pao*, and *Wen Wei Po*. The English-language newspapers are the *South China Morning Post* and *The Standard*. Readership composition for various newspapers in Hong Kong is shown in Table 2.16.

Magazines

Periodicals provide Hong Kong magazines for every taste. The coverage of weekly magazines is the highest, with monthly and biweekly also contributing. Readership of weekly magazines is 30% of all people nine years of age or older.

Magazine titles include general-interest magazines, business/finance weeklies and monthlies, Hong Kong editions of business and regional magazines, women's monthly magazines, and leisure magazines. There is also a range of auto, sports, TV guides, electronics, computer, hi-fi, photography, interior design, club, and trade magazines. Titles include *East Week Weekly, Sudden Weekly, 3 Weekly, Yes, Next Magazine, East Touch, HK Magazine, Eat & Travel Weekly, The Mirror, Cheng Ming Magazine, Far Eastern Economic Review, Jessica Hong Kong, Elle Hong Kong, Marie Claire Hong Kong, Beat Magazine, Breakthrough, Penthouse Hong Kong, HIM Hong Kong, Hong Kong Nightlife*, and *Esquire*.

Magazine readership for several magazines is shown in Tables 2.17 and 2.18.

Table 2.16: **Hong Kong newspaper readership composition profile, 2003**

	Oriental Daily News	Apple Daily	The Sun	Ming Pao	South China Morning Post	Sing Pao	HK Economic Times
				% of people read yesterday			
All aged 9+	34	23	8	6	4	3	1
Sex							
Male	35	24	9	6	5	3	1
Female	33	22	7	6	4	2	1
Age							
9–14	23	14	7	6	2	2	0
15–24	37	27	9	8	5	2	1
25–34	33	29	7	4	8	2	1
35–49	38	25	9	6	4	2	1
50+	32	18	8	5	2	4	1
Education							
Tertiary	21	28	6	11	21	2	3
Post secondary	36	28	8	10	10	3	3
Secondary	39	25	9	5	2	2	1
Primary or under	29	15	7	3	0	3	0
Monthly personal income							
Under $8,000	34	17	7	3	4	3	1
$8,000–$9,999	36	28	8	10	10	3	1
$10,000–$14,999	39	25	9	5	2	2	1
$15,000–$19,999	35	30	7	9	9	1	2
$20,000–$29,999	34	35	4	9	11	2	3
$30,000 or over	18	30	1	18	27	2	6
Occupation							
Managers & Administrators	30	27	5	5	18	2	3
Professionals	21	38	6	18	22	3	5
Associate Professionals	35	35	7	9	7	2	2
Clerks	38	32	7	7	2	2	3
Service workers & Shop sales workers	43	28	6	4	5	2	0
Craft & related workers	43	24	12	2	0	1	2
Plant, machine operators & assemblers	47	22	9	1	0	3	0
Elementary occupations	34	17	10	2	4	2	1
Student	27	18	9	8	4	2	1
Full-time housewife	33	19	8	4	0	2	1
Unemployment	43	18	7	4	4	3	1
Retired	29	13	9	4	1	8	1

Source: ACNielsen Hong Kong (2003)

Table 2.17: **Hong Kong magazine readership (weekly magazine past week readership), 2003**

	Audience '000	9+ Past Week %
Any Weekly	1,823	30
Sudden Weekly/Eat & Travel Weekly	537	9
Next Magazine	464	8
Easy Finder	298	5
TVB Weekly	168	3
New Monday	161	3
Yes	131	2
East Touch	118	2
Express Weekly	117	2
Milk	114	2
Ming Pao Weekly	103	2
Weekend Weekly	87	1
Oriental Sunday	80	1

Source: ACNielsen Hong Kong (2003)

Mass Transit Railway and Kowloon Canton Railway

Hong Kong has a very complete and well-utilized rail public transportation system. The MTR and KCR provide additional advertising coverage for Hong Kong commuters.

The MTR operates in the urban area. The system began operation in 1979. The MTR carries almost two and a half million passengers a day. On a cumulative basis, approximately 85% of Hong Kong consumers use the MTR in an average month, 50% in an average week, and 20% in an average day.

The KCR began operation in 1910 and was electrified and double tracked in the early 1980s. The railway provides suburban service to the new towns and northeastern New Territories and a freight service to China. The KCR also owns and operates Light Rail Transit (LRT) in the northwest New Territories. The KCR carries over a million passengers a day (KCR 2003 Annual Report). Cumulatively, over one third of Hong Kong consumers use the KCR during an average month, 15% in the last week, and 5% on an average day.

Table 2.18: Hong Kong magazine readership composition profile, 2003

	% of people read in past week				
	Sudden Weekly/ Eat & Travel Weekly	Next Magazine	Easy Finder	TVB Weekly	New Monday
All aged 9+	9	8	5	3	3
Sex					
Male	5	7	6	1	1
Female	12	8	3	4	4
Age					
9–14	5	2	1	3	4
15–24	12	6	13	4	11
25–34	14	13	10	3	1
35–49	10	9	3	3	1
50+	4	5	1	1	0
Education					
Tertiary	9	11	6	2	3
Post secondary	12	9	7	6	4
Secondary	11	9	6	3	3
Primary or under	4	3	1	2	0
Monthly personal income					
Under $8,000	8	5	5	3	2
$8,000–$9,999	11	9	8	2	2
$10,000–$14,999	10	10	8	3	1
$15,000–$19,999	10	13	7	1	0
$20,000–$29,999	7	15	7	3	1
$30,000 or over	8	16	2	1	0
Occupation					
Managers & Administrators	5	13	4	3	1
Professionals	8	14	8	0	0
Associate Professionals	14	13	11	2	1
Clerks	16	12	5	4	3
Service workers & Shop sales workers	10	9	11	3	3
Craft & related workers	3	7	6	1	1
Plant & machine operators & assemblers	9	8	9	1	0
Elementary occupations	6	6	2	2	1
Student	6	3	4	4	0
Full-time housewife	10	6	2	4	9
Unemployment	7	7	5	5	2
Retired	2	2	0	0	1

Source: ACNielsen Hong Kong (2003)

Other Transportation and Outdoors

In addition to the rail services, franchised bus services provide advertising availability including whole bus painting. Hong Kong minibuses carry 16 passengers. There are private light buses offering advertisers side panels and seat back availability. Taxis offer limited advertising availability.

Outdoor panels and neon signs are evident throughout Hong Kong. Panels popular with advertisers include the Star Ferry, Wilson Car Park locations, Pacific Place, Hong Kong International Airport, electronic display boards at Causeway Bay, Tsim Sha Tsui, and the Cross Harbor Tunnel.

Advertising Industry Regulation

Hong Kong has a laissez-faire approach to the advertising industry. However, there are numerous codes of practice relating to advertising and programming content.

The main points of the *Advertising Industry Code of Practice* (HKSAR Government 2000) are that advertisements must be clean, honest, and truthful. Comparisons between products should be substantiated and supportable by research or other statistical evidence. Comparative superlatives such as "the best" and "the most successful" should not be adopted without backup evidence.

Table 2.19: Hong Kong outdoor advertising reach, 2003

Outdoor Ads Reach (Past Month Reach)	% of people noticed the ad		
	All aged 9+	Male	Female
Bus Body Advertisements	83	84	81
Bus Shelter Advertisements	74	76	72
Bus TV	62	62	61
Advertisements in MTR	59	64	55
Mini-Bus Body Advertisements	29	29	28
Taxi Advertisements	17	17	17
Tram/Tram-stop Advertisements	16	17	15

Source: ACNielsen Hong Kong (2003)

Provisions set out in the *Satellite Television Code of Practice on Advertising Standards* (1997) and the *Subscription Television Code of Practice on Advertising Standards* (1997) deal with matters of good taste and unacceptable products and services, such as firearms, tobacco products, escort services, fortune tellers, or undertakers. This code is applicable to license holders for subscription television only, but it is a good guide to standards that are generally considered to be acceptable in Hong Kong by regulatory authorities.

Specific statutory prohibitions include advertising of tobacco products in broadcast (Baker and McKenzie Hong Kong 2000).

References

ACNielsen Hong Kong. 2003. Asia Target Market Survey, Hong Kong, October.

Association of Accredited Advertising Agents of Hong Kong, The. 2004. http://www.aaaa.com.hk/ (accessed February 2005).

Baker and McKenzie Hong Kong. 2000. E-com legal guide Hong Kong. http://www.bakerinfo.com/apec/hongkong_main.htm#2.2 (accessed February 2005).

Bond, M. H. 1991. *Beyond the Chinese face: Insights from psychology.* Hong Kong: Oxford University Press.

———, K. C. Wan, K. Leung, and R. Giacalone. 1985. How are responses to verbal insult related to cultural collectivism and power distance? *Journal of Cross-Cultural Psychology* 16: 111–27.

———, and K. K. Hwang 1986. The social psychology of the Chinese people. In M. H. Bond, ed. *The psychology of the Chinese people.* Hong Kong: Oxford University Press.

Cato Institute and the Fraser Institute's official website. Economic freedom of the world: 2004 annual report. http://www.cato.org (accessed February 2005).

Davis Direct Worldwide's official website. http://www.davisdirect.com/newsletter/2v01/hong_kong.html (accessed February 2005).

Census and Statistics Department, Government of Hong Kong SAR. 2001. *Population Census 2001.* http://www.info.gov.hk/censtatd/eng/news/01c/01c_index.html (accessed February 2005).

China Daily's official website. 2004. Hong Kong witnesses strong economic growth. August 19, 2004. http://www.chinadaily.com.cn/english/doc/2004-08/19/content_366658.htm (accessed February 2005).

Dun & Bradstreet. 1993. *Dun's guide to Hong Kong businesses 1993.* Hong Kong: Dun & Bradstreet Information Services.

Everest, F. A. 1978. Hong Kong. In J. A. Lent, ed. *Broadcasting in Asia and the Pacific: A continental survey of radio and television.* Philadelphia: Temple University Press.

Euromonitor. 1993. *The world directory of advertising agencies 1993.* Chicago: Euromonitor.

Fact Index's official website. 2004. Media in Hong Kong. http://www.fact-index. com/m/me/media_in_hong_kong.html (accessed February 2005).

Genzberger, C. A., E. G. Hinkelman., D. E. Horovitz, W. T. LeGro, J. W. Libbey, C. S. Mills, J. L. Nolan, S. S. Padrick, K. C. Shippey, K. X. Wang, C. B. Wedemeyer, and A. Woznick. 1994. *Hong Kong Business.* San Rafael, CA: World Trade Press.

HKSAR Government. 2000. *Advertising Industry Code of Practice.* http://www. info.gov.hk (accessed February 2005).

Heritage Foundation and Wall Street Journal's official website. 2004. Index of economic freedom. http://www.heritage.org (accessed February 2005).

Information Services Department, HKSAR Government. 1994. *Hong Kong 1994.* Hong Kong: Government Printing Department.

———. 2002. *Hong Kong 2002.* Hong Kong: Government Printing Department.

InvestHK's official website. 2004. http://www.investhk.gov.hk (accessed February 2005).

Martin, E. F. Jr. 1995. The interviewing process in communicating change: An Asian perspective. In D. P. Cushman, ed. *Communicating organizational change.* Albany: SUNY Press.

———, and Y. W. Tsui. 1993. Hong Kong Chinese opinions toward the portrayal of women in advertising. Paper presented at the University Women of Asia (UWA) Triennial Conference, November, Hong Kong.

———, Y. M. Cheng, G. B. Wilson, and Y. W. Tsui. 1993. Advertising images among Hong Kong Chinese: A preliminary study of individual modernity and western orientation. Paper presented at Asian Mass Communication Information Centre Conference on Communication, Technology and Development: Alternatives for Asia, June, Kuala Lumpur.

———, and G. B. Wilson. 1993. Hong Kong Chinese individual modernity and western orientation related to job and educational expectations: A preliminary study. Paper presented at the 4th International Intercultural Conference, March, San Antonio, TX.

———, Y. M. Cheng, G. B. Wilson, and Y. W. Tsui. 1994a. Advertising images among Hong Kong Chinese: Use of individual modernity and western orientation clusters in determining market segmentation. *Asian Journal of Communication* 4(1): 12–32.

———, G. B. Wilson, and Y. M. Cheng. 1994b. Attitudes toward media freedoms in Hong Kong: A prelude to 1997. *Gazette: The International Journal of Mass Communication Research* 54 (2):103–20.

Michman, R. D. 1991. *Lifestyle market segmentation.* New York: Praeger.

Satellite Television Code of Practice on Advertising Standards. 1997. http://www. washlaw.edu/forint/asia/hongkong/sattvadv.htm (accessed February 2005).

Sin, Y.M.L., and D.W.L. Cheng. 1984. *Advertising in Hong Kong: The consumer view.* WP-84-08. Hong Kong: Faculty of Business Administration, The Chinese University of Hong Kong.

Subscription Television Code of Practice on Advertising Standards. 1997. http://www. washlaw.edu/forint/asia/hongkong/subtvadv.htm (accessed February 2005).

Vocational Training Council. 2001. 2001 manpower survey. http://www.vtc.edu. hk (accessed February 2005).

Vocational Training Council. 2003. 2003 Manpower survey. http://www.vtc.edu. hk (accessed September 2005).

Yang, K. S. 1986. Chinese personality and its change. In M. H. Bond, ed. *The psychology of the Chinese people.* Hong Kong: Oxford University Press.

Acknowledgements

Part of this chapter is updated from Ernest F. Martin Jr. (1996), "Advertising in Hong Kong." In K. T. Frith, ed. *Advertising in Asia: Communication, Culture and Consumption* (Ames, IA: Iowa State University Press), 39–72.

Chapter 3

Political Ideology in Hong Kong's Public Service Announcements

Wendy Siuyi Wong

Introduction

On June 30, 1997 Hong Kong's sovereignty was returned from Britain to China. The former British colony is now renamed the Hong Kong Special Administrative Region (HKSAR). The constitutional document governing Hong Kong—The Basic Law of the Hong Kong Special Administrative Region (The Basic Law)—was coproduced by Britain and China together with an exclusive group of representatives from Hong Kong. Under Deng Xiaoping's policy of "one country two systems" (OCTS), the Basic Law is the "mini-constitution of Hong Kong after its reversion to China" (Lau 2000, 73–89). The Basic Law is not just the symbol of China resumption of the exercise of sovereignty over Hong Kong; it is also "the blueprint for [the] HKSAR's future development" (Basic Law Promotion Steering Committee, n.d.). In order to promote such an important document to the Hong Kong public, both the British colonial rulers and the HKSAR government carried out different communication and information strategies in different periods before and after 1997.

Although the two governments might have had different promotional objectives, the broadcast of Basic Law Public Service Announcements has always been the responsibility of the Information Services Department (ISD, formerly Hong Kong Government Information Service). Public Service Announcements (PSA) of publicity messages in the mass media are also known as public service advertising or advertisement. PSA are known as Announcements in the Public Interest (API) in Hong Kong (Information Services Department 2003a). API in Hong Kong provide publicity support for government policy and departments "to arouse greater public awareness of matters in the public interest." (Information Services Department 2003b). Such API messages often entail ideological messages as in advertising, and reflect a set political position. The promotion of the Basic Law exemplifies a campaign imbued with a political ideological subtext.

This study investigates how political ideology is portrayed through PSA in Hong Kong under the campaigns conducted by the two different government regimes. This chapter begins with a review of the operation and production of PSA in Hong Kong over the years. It focuses on the different political ideologies emphasized and represented in the APIs from two different periods: pre-1997 and post-1997. Examples from the pre-1997 Human Rights campaign and post-1997 Basic Law Promotion campaign (included under the Civic Education campaign) will be used to illustrate the different ideological positions of the two governments. The Human Rights campaign represented the information and messages that the colonial government *needed* the people to know in order to empower them for the post-handover period. The Civic Education–Basic Law campaign represented materials that the HKSAR government thought its residents *ought* to know in order to further the agenda of the new regime. This chapter argues that the political ideologies represented in the APIs mark the political changes that the Hong Kong society is already facing post-1997, flying in the face of the idea of "remaining unchanged for fifty years" (Lau 2000, 89) as promised by the OCTS policy.

The Operation and Production of Public Service Advertising

The Government Information Services (GIS), a government department in the colonial Hong Kong, was responsible for organizing and producing

PSAs and campaigns systematically for various government departments since the 1950s (Hacker 1989, 2). The now renamed Information Service Department (ISD) serves as public relations consultant, publisher, advertising agent, and news agency of the HKSAR government. The ISD also provides the link between the Administration and the media through various channels in order to facilitate "public understanding of government policies, decisions and activities." (Information Services Department 2003c) The department is structured into four divisions—Local Public Relations, Publicity and Promotions, Public Relations Outside Hong Kong, and Administration. Among them the Publicity and Promotions Division is in charge of the planning and implementation of large-scale government publicity campaigns. The Division has three subdivisions: Local Promotions, Creative, and International Promotions.

Since the early 1990s, based on a recommendation made by the Broadcasting Review Board, publicity messages handled by the ISD are termed Announcements in the Public Interest (APIs). Prior to that, API used to stand for Announcements of the Public Interest. This minor change in name was made in order to emphasize that "such announcements are to provide information which the public needs to know" (Information Services Department 1998, 1). The Broadcasting Authority divides API messages into four categories:

a) to inform the public of important health and safety measures, or legislative changes affecting their interest;

b) to educate the public as to their rights and responsibilities as citizens;

c) to enlist public co-operation in tackling important social and environmental problems;

d) to seek recruitment to the auxiliary services which require public support in carrying out duties of benefit to society (Information Services Department 1998, 1–2).

Most API campaigns produced by the ISD are carried out in collaboration with other government departments and publicity programs. Major government publicity campaigns cover a wide range of "public interest" as defined by the Administration. Among the major campaigns, the "Clean Hong Kong" campaign has the longest history. It can be traced back to the early 1960s when Hong Kong was faced with an influx of new immigrants from Mainland China. There was an urgent need to convey information on personal and public hygiene to the general public. Miss Ping On 平安小姐 [Miss Safety] was a highly successful public service advertising character created by the GIS creative department. She appeared in posters, which were the most popular medium at that time (Hacker 1989). Before Miss Ping On, Mr. Zebra 斑馬線先生 [Mr. Zebra Crossing] was the first public advertising character created by the GIS in the late 1950s to educate the public about road safety. The Clean Hong Kong campaign created the Lap Sap Chung character in 1972 (Hacker 1989). Lap Sap Chung was a great hit and is still remembered by many people in Hong Kong. Decades after it was first introduced, the Clean Hong Kong campaign continues to be one of the major ongoing publicity campaigns.

The Promotion subdivision of the Public Division works closely with client departments, relevant working groups, and steering committees for the campaign themes and communication strategies. The subdivision also handles API work for non-government organizations such as the Independent Commission Against Corruption (ICAC) and the Community Chest. Publicity campaigns often employ different media such as "TV and radio commercials and special programs, exhibitions, community involvement activities and a host of printed materials" (Information Services Department 2003c). Of the mass media, the television API is the most popular and effective medium for delivering a message to the public. According to the regulations of the Television and Entertainment Licensing Authority it is mandatory for television stations to allocate not more than two minutes free airtime per two clock hours without charge for government and non-government APIs (Information Services Department 1998). TV APIs have been enjoying free systematic broadcasting over the decades, and represent a familiar government publicity medium recognized by a large majority of Hong Kong people.

The duration of each TV API ranges from 15 to 60 seconds, with the average length being 30 seconds. There are an average of 30–35 government APIs and 10–12 non-government APIs scheduled for broadcasting each month. The frequency of broadcast of each API may vary from one to four times per month, depending on the nature or importance of different campaigns and the audience's need for the information. The Promotion subdivision produces a monthly TV API priority list for all English and Chinese channels on TVB, ATV, and Cable TV in advance. The priority list is compiled based on requests from and consultation with individual departments and organizations (Information Services Department 1998).

The PSA campaigns have been systematically organized and produced by both the British Hong Kong government and the HKSAR government. This chapter attempts to study the different political ideologies represented by the TV APIs. Like most scholars (Phelan 1991; Salmon 1989; Watson and Hill 1994) who have studied PSAs, this chapter considers Hong Kong APIs as another form of advertising embedded with ideological messages along with information that the government wants to convey to the pubic. Through the study of APIs we can understand what "messages" the government wants to convey to the public in different periods of time and political environments. Among the various publicity campaigns, the pre-1997 Human Rights (HR) campaign and the post-1997 Civic Education (CE) campaign with the Basic Law promotion campaign are the best examples to use in order to illustrate the ideological differences between the two governments. With these two examples we can see how APIs on television are used as a tool, or an attempt to "enlist public co-operation" (Information Services Department 1998, 2) by the Administration.

Ideological Issues and Focus of Study

As many scholars have pointed out, advertising is one of the most important forms of social communication in modern world development. PSAs are an advertising form with similar objectives to commercial advertising. Both public service advertising and commercial advertising are persuasive, trying to convince the audience to conform to a set agenda or underlying messages. This study takes the position that advertising is a mirror reflecting society and helps shape public discourse. Here I consider public service advertising a "privileged discourse" (see Leiss,

Kline and Jhally 1986/1990). Like commercial advertising, public service advertising is a form of discourse that reaches a mass audience and plays a role in projecting images of ideological life, while on the surface it aims simply to convey information and messages.

In spite of the significance and breadth of public advertising there are not many published studies on public advertising produced and broadcast by local government. Cuklanz and Wong (1999, 105) conducted a historical textual analysis on the ideological themes in the Fight Crime API campaign from the 1970s to the 1990s in Hong Kong. The authors concluded that "the civic person is nearly absent from the Fight Crime campaign," and that the campaign APIs rarely "focus on the benefits and rights of citizens with respect to police and government protection." However, with the introduction of the HR campaign in 1996, the authors are confident that "Hong Kong will have to develop its own conception of human rights." This chapter will aim to pick up what has been left out by this study on the HR campaign and to further investigate the ideological aspects of Hong Kong public service advertising following the HR campaign. Following political development after 1997, the CE campaign has became one of the active ongoing campaigns. The selection of the CE campaign is based on its political and ideological content that contrasts with that of the HR campaign. This study undertakes an examination of the underlying texts of these two campaigns covering the pre-1997 and post-1997 periods, which represent two different political ideologies. It argues that the pre-1997 APIs provide information which the audience *needs* to know, and the post-1997 period APIs deliver information the authorities deem the audience *ought* to know. A conclusion can be drawn as to how the new government altered the definition of API messages over the passage of time to provide information which the public ought to know.

Review of the Development of the Civic Education Campaign and the Human Rights Campaign

One of the purposes of an API is to "educate the public as to their rights and responsibilities as citizens" (Information Services Department 1998, 2). To carry out this function, the ISD cannot work alone. The steering committee, the Committee on the Promotion of Civic Education (CPCE), is the client of both the HR and CE campaigns, collaborating closely with the ISD. The CPCE was established in 1986 "to liaise with related Government departments and community organizations in promoting civic education outside schools and encourage all sectors of the community to actively promote civic awareness and assume civic responsibility" (Committee on the Promotion of Civic Education 2004). The committee members were representatives from all types of professionals and businesses, as well as from government departments such as the Home Affairs Bureau, Education and Manpower Bureau, Hong Kong Police Force, Social Welfare Department, etc.

The production of CE TV APIs has not been constant since its inception. From 1986 to 2001 the CE campaign had an average of two to seven TV APIs produced every year. Among those APIs, many were the routine information messages concerning annual or special public activities organized by the CPCE. The activities of the CPCE have been wide-ranging, including the Community Participation Scheme, Civic Education Day, and the Computer Design Competition in 1994. The CE campaign also covered the announcement of changes in government structures, for which the CPCE took responsibility for notifying the public. For example, APIs about the District Board, Legco, Urban Council, and Regional Council were launched in 1986. The CE campaign sometimes even responded to political crisis by producing uplifting announcements to encourage the general public. An API entitled "Hong Kong's Future is Right in Your Hands" was produced after the Tiananmen Incident in 1989, when the people of Hong Kong completely lost their confidence in their future under the reign of the People's Republic of China (PRC).

To restore the confidence of the people in their future the government started introduce the concept of human rights to society. In 1992 the CE campaign launched an API entitled "Community Participation Scheme for Human Rights Projects." It gave a preview of the introduction of a human rights law to the territory. The International Covenant on Economic, Social and Cultural Rights ("The Covenant") was finally endorsed by the PRC government on June 20, 1997 and it is guaranteed that the agreement will remain effective after July 1, 1997 (United

Nations Centre for Human Rights 1989/2004, 25). To educate the Hong Kong public about their human rights, an area in which PRC has a poor international record, the CPCE introduced a series of HR campaigns in 1996. However, this series of TV API HR campaigns was not listed under as a CE campaign although the announcements were credited to the CPCE. The campaign, mainly produced in 1995 and 1996, introduced topics covered by the Convenant such as the fundamental principles of equality, human rights, and the rights of a child. It comprised only a few versions and was short-lived, gradually fading out from public screening after 1998. Since 1997 no new TV API project on human rights issues has been produced.

Before the handover in July 1997, the CE campaign made a last effort to introduce the Basic Law with four different versions of TV APIs. In 2002, after the Seventh National People's Congress (NPC) of the PRC adopted the Basic Law 12 years after April 4, 1990, the CE campaign finally boosted publicity of the Basic Law. Instead of simply giving out the information on the existence of the Basic Law (as in its first TV API launched in 1997), the CE campaign created a series of nine different versions of TV APIs with different content, exemplifying the details of the Basic Law. The new TV APIs covered various themes ranging over economic freedom, creative freedom, civil rights, and other major issues in the Basic Law. Another 20 TV APIs were produced in 2002 and 2003. Among them 16 APIs were on promotion of the Basic Law (Information Services Department 2004). Obviously the increased exposure to and budget for promoting the Basic Law as part of civic education may be the result of the establishment of the Basic Law Promotion Steering Committee (BLPSC) in November 1998 with the Chief Secretary for Administration, Donald Tsang, as the Chairman.

From a brief review of the historical development of the CE and HR campaigns it is easy to distinguish the differences in promotional approaches and strategies of APIs after 1997 under the new government. The following section analyses the textual messages presented in the two campaigns reviewed above. We can distinguish how the two different governments inform the public of the information that they *need* to know from the ideology of information that they *ought* to know.

Information that the Public *Needs* to Know:
Promotion of Community and Individual Rights

In a section of Benjamin Leung's book *Perspectives on Hong Kong Society* (1996) he notes that the mass media in pre-1960 Hong Kong conveyed traditional Chinese values and ideals. The 1960s witnessed significant changes. Leung points out that "Hong Kong was modernizing by copying the culture and lifestyle of the Western capitalist countries." (65) This copying included Western political ideological values. This is illustrated by Kuan and Lau (2002, 305) who found in their study that in Hong Kong "[a] small minority of the respondents accept paternalism whereas over 40% of them agree with elitism" when compared to other two traditional Chinese societies, i.e., Mainland China and Taiwan. This phenomenon can be traced back to the 1960s. An observer of the development of Hong Kong culture, Matthew Turner, states that "by the end of the sixties the idea of 'community' was no longer an irrelevance to the majority of the population (Turner 1995/2003, 26). For alongside the official discourse, a local, and largely unarticulated sense of identity had begun to emerge in Hong Kong." In Turner's study he notes that the colonial government "first deployed on a grand scale as anti-Communist counter-propaganda" the rhetoric of "citizenship," "community," and "belonging" in their policy after the 1967 riots. Public service campaigns such as Clean Hong Kong and Fight Crime were launched in the 1970s "in order to instill solidarity among the Hong Kong people" (Lo 2001,132). The concept of community in Hong Kong was formed and shaped in the 1980s although the colonial government's laissez-faire policy did little to impose a moral model for the development of the society.

In the 1980s the CE campaign served as a channel to deliver government messages that the public needed to know. The APIs under this campaign (hereinafter as "CE APIs") such as the "Community Participation Project," "Theme Song," "District Board," "Regional Council," "Omelco 1998," and so forth, launched in 1996 and 1997, met the set objective purely on the information level. Rarely did any of these APIs try to establish a moral model. Instead they simply reflected the factual reality of the lifestyle of Hong Kong at that time and projected an image of the community along with hard-sell messages. Like most public service announcements, the CE APIs were boring and unmemorable (Andsager, Austin, and Pinkelton 2001). However, the introduction of the HR campaign in 1995 broke through the boredom barrier of the previous CE APIs. The HR campaign can be seen as a product of the Tiananmen Incident in 1989. As Lo points out: "the British administration itself—responding to the fears among Hong Kongers triggered by the Tiananmen massacre—quickly attempted to shore up confidence in the colony." A "rights-regarding" citizenry was given a major boost. In 1990, a Bill of Rights was enacted to protect Hong Kongers after the transfer of sovereignty" (Lo 2001, 133). The Tiananmen Incident in 1989 contributed to the "breakdown of Sino-British cooperation in the transitional period created immense instabilities, uncertainties and disruption in Hong Kong" (Lau 2000, 90), forcing the CPCE to look into the issue of the "future" after the handover.

As a result, the CE API entitled "Hong Kong's Future is Right in Your Hands" was launched in November 1989. This API takes an encouraging tone in order to reduce the insecurity of the public. Like the Fight Crime campaign, the CE campaign was used for the needs of government administration and policy. In the twenty years of Fight Crime campaign, a civic person was "defined exclusively in terms of duties and responsibilities" and the stress on "citizen duty has increased over time" (Cuklanz and Wong 1999, 95). The empowerment strategy of an individual's rights over one's future in a 1989 CE API was a response to the breakdown of Sino-British cooperation in the transitional period. The human rights project promotion by the CPCE in the 1990s reflected the alternative solution of the British "political agenda to leave with glory" (Lau 2000, 89). Under the 1992 political reforms brought in by Chris Patten, the last governor of colonial Hong Kong, "the citizens of Hong Kong were to be empowered" and "would enjoy political as well as civil rights" (Lo 2001, 135). Once again, this API functions as a tool to inform and educate the people in what they *need* to know as wished by their government. The information in the APIs under the HR campaign was designed to empower the people about their basic human rights—to gird them against what was to happen after the handover. In a sense the British authorities hoped that the message of the HR campaign would resonate with the citizens of Hong Kong, helping them to fight for their rights after the handover.

The first TV API under the HR campaign, entitled "Fundamental Principles of Equality," was launched in September 1995. The HR campaign included a total of six different versions of TV APIs. The last version, entitled "Rights of the Child," was produced in February 1997. Unlike most of the APIs under the Fight Crime campaign, the HR campaign presented more creative and interesting messages. Most of them were produced in either two- or three-dimensional animation. The exception was an API showcasing the theme song by popular singer, Hacken Lee. These APIs stood out for being well planned with a creative concept and an appealing visual execution. The first API opens on a three-dimensional globe, then the camera zooms into the map of Hong Kong with the text of "Hong Kong Bill of Rights Ordinance" in both Chinese and English rotating around the Hong Kong Island. Then the image cuts to a family of four while a male voice-over begins the narration and a female voice-over provides a supportive role. The content of the script explains the Human Rights Bill in detail by giving examples such as liberty of movement, protection of privacy, freedom of thought, conscience and religion, enjoyment of one's own culture, religion and language, and the protection of children. The API ends with the male voice-over saying "we can protect our rights, and respect the rights of the others. Hong Kong will be a better place for home." Finally, the superimposition reads: "Human Rights are Every Human's Right" with the CPCE's logo. The colonial government needed its audience, i.e., the people of Hong Kong to know that they have rights—a message that they should not forget. Although they might be already familiar with that concept the API reinforces the idea; and its message might hopefully stay with the citizens long after the handover.

Unlike other CE campaigns with general community participation messages, this HR API aimed at teaching the audience about their individual rights. Such rights were merely mentioned in most API campaigns in the past. Unlike other campaigns, this one does not emphasize the "responsibilities as citizens" but rather the rights of the individual. In one of the scenes, as the voice-over compares the individual right to protection for children, the pictures show a little girl was sitting on the floor reading a book with blue cover. But a big hand takes away her blue-covered book and gives her a red-covered book. The girl is unhappy with the new red-covered book and ends up crying. The symbolic meaning of this sequence clearly represents the underlying political ideology. The blue colour represents the capitalist system that Hong Kong was enjoying at the time, contrasting sharply with the red colour implying the communist ideology. This API made the abstract concept of human rights easy to understand by using a simple visual device complementing the key words and embodying the essence of universal rights.

In March 1996 a new TV API entitled Equal Opportunity III explored a similar theme in order to remind people of their individual rights. This time the gender rights of a boy and girl were clearly spelled out in the 30-second message under "Human Rights are Every Human's Right." This three-dimensional animation API was even better visually and more creatively executed than all the previous ones. The main characters in this announcement are a boy and a girl composed using three-dimensional animation techniques. The girl is ambitious and wants to be a professional—a doctor, or CEO of a big company. But the boy keeps telling her that she cannot do those kinds of things because she is a girl. Finally the male voice-over says: "If we all enjoy our same rights, we can make an equal contribution." The ideology behind this API is clearly a Western liberal one espoused by the departing British government. Chris Patten commented on the achievements of Britain in Hong Kong in his interview to the foreign press in October 1996, saying that: "I think that Britain had provided a framework of liberal values which has enabled Chinese men and women to thrive and excel and to keep the benefits of their work and excellence." (quoted in Wong 1998/2003, 227) This can explain why Hong Kong has always been considered as enjoying the highest rate of gender equality in Asia. Before the retreat of British, this HR API repeatedly reminds the public not to forget and to protect their liberal rights.

Without doubt, the human rights policy pursued in the HR APIs were the last attempt of the British colonial government to give the people of Hong Kong a taste of democracy and political freedom before the return to the Communist Chinese system. The human rights policy pursued by the British in the final days of colonial Hong Kong was a result of the progressive breakdown of Sino-British cooperation shortly before 1997. As Lau reminds us, the Chinese government did not want to see Britain introduce political reforms in Hong Kong shortly before the handover, and "[d]uring the transitional period, China had failed to build rapport between itself and the people of Hong Kong." It is foreseeable that it will be challenging for the Chinese government to acquire the trust of the citizens of Hong Kong, who are trying to maintain the *status quo*. Chinese officials do not want to see the Hong Kong people turn "the place into a 'political city'," (Lau 2000, 90) and the advocacy of a new policy of human rights by the colonial government was not in the interests of the future boss of Hong Kong—the Chinese Communist government. It is no surprise then that shortly after the handover the new government deemed that the Hong Kong people no longer *needed* to know the "information" contained in the HR campaign. The new Communist government had different priorities and the HR campaign gradually faded out and was replaced by stronger and more politically focused API campaigns. These new campaigns stood out from the previous ones because their content was determined by what the new government thought its residents *ought* to know.

Information that the Public *Ought* to Know: Education in Patriotic Ideology

While the HR campaign was fading away from airtime scheduling after 1997, a new major CE campaign focused on The Basic Law began emerging on the main screen. Although the Seventh National People's Congress (NPC) of the PRC adopted the Basic Law on April 4, 1990, promotion of the content in the mass media on a large scale in Hong Kong under the rule of the British colonial government never took off before July 1997. The content of the promotion of the Basic Law campaign represented what the HKSAR government thinks its residents *ought* to know. While the previous APIs in the HR campaign were intended to empower the citizenry, the new campaign was designed to inform the population about their duties as citizens in a new political era. As such the campaign does more than just inform—it aimed at influencing the political ideology of its audience. The first TV API on the promotion of Basic Law entitled "Know more about Basic Law" was launched before the handover, in January 1997. This pre-handover Basic Law API stands in sharp contrast to the post-handover Basic Law APIs. This Basic Law API opens on the red-covered booklet of the Basic Law, with a male voice-over informing the audience about the importance of this constitutional document for Hong Kong. The verbal content is very general, giving key areas of what the Basic Law covers such as protection of lifestyle, economic system, citizens' duties and responsibilities, political and legislative system, etc. The visuals are a montage images of daily life in Hong Kong such as a wedding scene, a view of the stock market, and faces of people from all walks of life. This API is like just another normal, straightforward, and boring government announcement.

However, after the handover in July 1997, the new HKSAR government determined to push a little harder to promote the Basic Law. In this later series of the Basic Law campaign two APIs, entitled "Dolphin" and "Seagull," highlighted the key components of the Basic Law. The "Dolphin" series emphasizes Hong Kong as a place with a high degree of autonomy enjoying independent judicial power, final judicatory power, legislative power, executive power, and protection of the rights and freedom of all Hong Kong people. In the "Seagull" series the message is focused on the Basic Law guarantees of Hong Kong's economy as a free port, to manage its own finances, to issue its own currency, and so forth. The information has an interesting visual presentation using a three-dimensional animated dolphin and seagull respectively in each API. This campaign series ends with the slogan: "Understand the Basic Law, Care for Hong Kong." Unlike the previous APIs launched before July 1, this campaign series not only familiarizes the audience with the contents of this important document but also manages to make the content seem more interesting to the audience.

Shortly after the handover in July 1997 the Asian financial crisis hit Hong Kong and the HKSAR government. The unemployment rate of Hong Kong had been around 5–6% since 1998 (Lau 2003) without any sign of dropping in the following few years. When numerous economy recovery plans failed effectively to benefit the general public, the HKSAR government's standing dropped in the public survey polls, hitting its lowest point during the SARS crisis in 2003. Sociologist Lau Siu-Kai (2003, 386) observes that "[s]ocial discontent is on the rise" in the post-1997 era. People were not happy with the HKSAR government under the leadership of Tung Chee-hwa, but they were stuck with him. Under the Basic Law, they cannot directly elect their own Chief Executive of Hong Kong.

Between 2002 and 2003, 16 TV APIs were produced to promote the Basic Law of Hong Kong. In the heat of public criticism of the performance of the HKSAR government, the attention that the government put on promotion of the Basic Law was in retrospect an unwise one. It drew people's attention to examine the origin of their problems in this financial downturn. Among the 16 TV APIs, some were targeted at education in specific Articles of the Basic Law. Although they were carefully selected, some of the Articles that the TV APIs covered were sensitive topics. The Articles that have been covered in the promotion of the Basic Law series APIs include numbers: 37, 14, 114, 149, 34, 9, 28, 31, 106, 155, 111, 23, 27, 32, 140, and 10 to date..

Among the Basic Law TV APIs, the one on Article 23, entitled Insurance, is the most sensitive one. It covered very important information that Hong Kong people *ought* to know according to the HKSAR government. The TV API was launched after the outbreak of the SARS crisis in February 13, 2003. Although the launch version of this TVAPI has been revised, the message is one which Hong Kong people are not ready to accept. According to the Basic Law's Article 23 The Hong Kong Special Administrative Region shall enact laws on its own to prohibit any act of treason, secession, sedition, subversion against the Central People's Government, or theft of state secrets, to prohibit foreign political organizations or bodies from conducting political activities in the Region, and to prohibit political organizations or bodies of the Region from establishing ties with foreign political organizations or bodies.

Indeed, as Lau (2000, 86) points out, Hong Kong's "anti-Communist sentiments were well-known to the CCP." The existence of Article 23 in the Basic Law served as a mechanism to prevent Hong Kong from turning into a base of subversion against the Communist regime in

Mainland China. The HKSAR government's intention to "enact laws" according to this Article led to a great deal of dissension among the citizens of Hong Kong in 2003. To sell the concept of this Article to the public, the Insurance API employs the metaphor of acquiring insurance. This API opens on an insurance company supervisor training a new batch of insurance agents. The new agents eagerly show off their aggressiveness by competing against each other in correctly answering a series of questions from the supervisor. They successfully identify the different scenarios where there is a need to protect a family ("ga" in Cantonese Chinese) with the appropriate type of insurance. Then, the supervisor asks "And … for the nation ("kwok-ga")?" A good-looking young woman agent answers instantly, "National Insurance!" Everyone looks at her and waits to see how she is going to explain that answer. Within a second, she explains, "Ah … according to Article 23 of the Basic Law, we should enact laws to protect national security. That's our Insurance for national security." The supervisor praises her at the end of the class for giving out such smart answer.

This campaign simplifies the nature of Article 23 by assuming a patriotic position, which is signified with clear use of the word of "kwok-ga" in the text. "Kwok-ga" is the PRC nation to which Hong Kong now belongs. Cultural critic Ackbar Abbas (1997/2004, 284) states that "Hong Kong culture does not express the hopes and aspirations of a people or nation. In a society of migrants, immigrants, and urban nomads, 'the people' is hardly a unified concept." Ho, Chau, Chiu, and Peng (2003, 404) also point out in their study that the majority of Hong Kong people see themselves as "solely or primarily as Hongkongers rather than as Chinese. Furthermore, they do not trust Mainlanders and prefer to maintain a marked distinction between themselves and Mainlanders." Over decades, Hong Kong has had a long history of anti-Communist sentiments, and the word of "kwok-ga" is a negative one. This is especially true if it touches on the political issue, conjuring up bad memories for people who have been persecuted by the Communists.

Given their history, Hong Kong people are sensitive to the concept of "treason, secession, sedition, subversion" as included in Article 23. With the dismal human rights record of the PRC, any future law enacted under Article 23 is perceived as endangering their freedom of expression. During the colonial period and thus far since the handover, Hong Kong people have been able to freely express their political opinions including demanding the resignation of any Chinese official leaders or HKSAR officers. The fear is that once there are laws enacted under Article 23, the free expression enjoyed today will be interpreted as subversion under the Communist regime. In the Insurance API, through the young woman agent, the HKSAR government is trying to arouse the patriotic feelings of Hong Kong people, hoping that they will accept laws enacted under Article 23 as simply as they acquire an insurance policy for things "just in case." Article 23 has been strongly opposed by the public and was one of the main reasons for the July 1 demonstration in 2003. Once again, the HKSAR government overestimated "the political passivity of the people of the place" (Lau 2000, 89), as the Chinese government did in the early 1980s. The enactment of any Article 23 laws was finally postponed, partly in response to the 1 July 2003 rally.

After a long history of separation under colonial rule it is now clear that the HKSAR Government want the general public gradually to learn more about their "ancestral country" ("jo-kwok") through the Civic Education campaigns. Abbas (1997/2004, 284) once commented on the identity of Hong Kong people, writing "… Hong Kong, caught between the not-quite-there (it is Chinese but not quite) and the more-than-there (it is too open to other influences). Its relation to tradition then is an often frustrating game of hide-and-seek." To play this hide-and-seek game, time is needed for Hong Kong people to accept the concept of the PRC as their "jo-kwok" after decades of anti-Communist sentiments. As far as the pro-Chinese HKSAR Government is concerned such anti-Communist sentiments should no longer exist, and what the people *ought* to know is their concept of love of "jo-kwok" (ancestral country). Thus they have to do something for and contribute to their "jo-kwok."

The public dissension created by Article 23 was far beyond the expectation of the HKSAR government. In the Basic Law promotion series, the TV API entitled "Breakfast" was launched on February 26, 2003. My analysis of the function of this campaign is to ease the anxiety of Hong Kong people about laws enacted in the future that might endanger their individual freedoms. This API covered Article 32 of the Basic Law which states:

> Hong Kong residents shall have freedom of conscience.
> Hong Kong residents shall have freedom of religious belief and freedom to preach and to conduct and participate in religious activities in public.

In this API, a family of four is having breakfast. While the father is reading his newspaper with his Chinese breakfast, and the daughter is having her Western style breakfast, the son and the mother are rushing off to the church and to the temple respectively. The father tells them goodbye while he is reading his newspaper and having his breakfast, and at the same time the daughter trying to talk to him. The father tries to shut the daughter down, saying: "Look, according to Article 32 of the Basic Law, we all have freedom of religious belief and freedom to participate in religious activities.… The freedom of religion won't be affected by any new law in the future." Finally the daughter gets a chance to tell him he is dipping his Chinese breakfast in her ketchup. When the daughter moves over to the father, the camera shifts to the back of the father and we can see he is reading the newspaper with the headline of "How much do you know about Article 23?" Is such an arrangement accidental or is it suggesting to the audience an association with what the father just said? Is the line "won't be affected by any new law in the future" said by the father referring to Article 23 or he is talking about Article 32? Perhaps such ambiguities are deliberate because the comments of the father referring to Article 23 are to what the Government hopes the public will pay attention.

Most of the Promotion of the Basic Law TV APIs are available on the website of the Basic Law Promotion Steering Committee (BLPSC) (n.d.), but the "Insurance" and "Breakfast" APIs are excluded for some unknown reason. Obviously with the set up of the BLPSC, the promotion of the Basic Law became more accessible to the general public. The people of Hong Kong have to be cautious about the freedoms and rights that they used to enjoy, and they now have to adjust their ideology to be more in line with the new Government. As sociologist Renita Wong (2002, 152) comments, under the "one country, two systems" policy "individual Hong Kongers experienced a split in their return to their

ancestral country: 'going back' to China and yet resisting 'going in'."
Indeed "[b]ecause of the radically different historical experiences they
have gone through in a century, one would expect to find significant
divergence in their respective contemporaneous political cultures,
concerning the role of government, legal institutions, freedom of the
press, and so forth.... Thus, questions about the future of Hong Kong
may be traced largely to underlying tensions originating from a collision
of political culture" (Ho et al. 2003, 412). The example of Article 23
demonstrates the differences in political ideology between the Hong
Kong people and the current Government. APIs are becoming a
propaganda tool as a "means to disseminate or promote particular ideas"
(Jowett and O'Donnell 1986, 15) specifically and openly. Unlike the
APIs of the colonial period, which sought to empower the people, the
new government APIs selectively inform the population about initiatives
it thinks people *ought* to know. The new generation of APIs is inherently
political. Ironically, Hong Kong people can only hope that they continue
to be entitled to the freedom and autonomy written into the Basic Law.

Conclusion

The pre-1997 HR campaign contained information on a topic that its
audience generally agreed upon, and these APIs are announcements that
the public *needs* to know. The political ideology in that era was a "'rights-
regarding' citizenry" (Lo 2001, 133) and a pro-democracy one. In
contrast, the post-1997 Basic Law Promotion campaign delivered
information on a topic that its audience does not have unified agreement
on. Here, I argue that such APIs are public announcements that the
government insists the public *ought* to know about the rules of the new
regime, which are already in place. A new pro-China political ideology
is emerging and is reflected in the Basic Law campaign. Under the new
regime the prodemocratic HR campaign has faded from the scene. Such
disagreement is predictable because the colonial government and
the new HKSAR government represent "two antagonistic ideological
orientations. In one orientation, the emphasis is placed on the
maintenance of the political culture that has emerged from Hong Kong's
unique political history. The other orientation, however, emphasizes

the assimilation of the Hong Kong political culture into that of mainland China" (Ho et al. 2003, 412).

As Kuan and Lau (2002, 316) put it, the "post-colonial politics has opened up a new vista in terms of state building, fostering the idea of a moral state under a new mantel." However, faced with Hong Kong's unprecedented economic downturn since the Asian financial crisis in 1998, Hong Kong people have already "become less confident of the economic future of the next generation" (Lau 2003, 384) and troubled by the poor economy. The Basic Law campaign in 2002–2003 was an example of how much the HKSAR government wants to build up Hong Kong as a pro-China "moral state." In hindsight, it is a campaign based on a wrong focus and wrong timing. What the government missed is the most important factor that made Hong Kong successful in the past while trying to drag themselves and Hong Kong into becoming a "political city." Also the government has ignored the fact that "since 1982, the people of Hong Kong have gradually asserted themselves politically" and "assuming the qualities of both a 'rights-regarding' and 'monitorial' citizenships" (Lo 2001, 139). The unveiling of Article 23 as an issue for discussion during difficult economic times was not a good strategy and was an unpopular idea.

The "one country, two systems" policy will never be able to ensure that Hong Kong "remains unchanged for fifty years" even in the materialistic sphere let alone at the political ideological level. At a time when Hong Kong is still dealing with the effects of the Asian financial crisis and facing emerging competition from the numerous cities in Mainland China, a survey shows "31% of respondents saw fewer opportunities," and only "37% on the other hand expected the next generation to enjoy more opportunities" (Lau 2003, 385). What the people want is to see a rebound of Hong Kong's economy. Currently the government, with the assistance of the central Chinese government, has introduced the Closer Economic Partnership Arrangement (CEPA) and various economic recovery plans to help the economy. However, the current government will not abandon their "state building" will. It will be interesting to monitor how the HKSAR government makes further use of APIs as a channel to educate the public about the information and messages that they think the public ought to know. It is foreseeable that "the pressures of modernization will continue to challenge elitist, paternalist, anti-democratic, and anti-pluralism positions" (Kuan and Lau 2002, 316) in the future Hong Kong.

Reference

Abbas, Ackbar. 1997/2004. Hong Kong: Other histories, other politics. In M.K.E. Cheung and Y. W. Chu, eds. *Between home and world: A reader in Hong Kong cinema*, 273–96. Hong Kong: Oxford University Press.

Andsager, J., E. W. Austin, and B. Pinkleton. 2001. Questioning the value of realism: Young adults' processing of messages in alcohol-related public service announcements and advertising. *Journal of Communication* (March): 121–42.

Basic Law Promotion Steering Committee, HKSAR Government. n.d. Welcome message. http://www.info.gov.hk/basic_law/welcome/index.htm (accessed August 31, 2004).

Committee on the Promotion of Civic Education, HKSAR Government. 2004. Terms of reference. http://www.cpce.gov.hk/eng/cpce/tor.htm (accessed August 31, 2004)

Cuklanz, L., and W. S. Wong. 1999. Ideological themes in Hong Kong's public service announcements: Implications for China's future. In R. Kluver and J. Powers, eds. *Civic discourse, civil society, and Chinese communities*, 93–110. Stamford, CN: Ablex Publishing.

Hacker, A. 1989. *Hong Kong in posters: A history of public service advertising*. Hong Kong: Hong Kong Printer.

Ho, D.Y.F., A.W.L. Chau, C. Y. Chiu, and S. Q. Peng. 2003. Ideological orientation and political transition in Hong Kong: Confidence in the future. *Political Psychology* 24(2): 303–14.

Information Services Department, HKSAR Government. 1998. *Information Paper on Announcement in the Public Interest (API)*. Hong Kong: Cuklanz & Wong.

———. 2003a. Publicity and promotion division. http://www.isd.gov.hk/eng/pub. htm (accessed August 31, 2004).

———. 2003b. Major government publicity campaigns. http://www.isd.gov.hk/ eng/pubcam.htm (accessed August 31, 2004).

———. 2003c. Home. http://www.isd.gov.hk/eng/index.htm (accessed August 31, 2004).

———. 2004. *TV APIs on Civic Education (1996–present)*. Hong Kong: Arthor.

Jowett, G. S., and V. O'Donnell. 1986. *Propaganda and persuasion*. Newbury Park, CA: Sage Publications.

Kuan, S. C., and S. K. Lau. 2002. Traditional orientations and political participation in three Chinese societies. *Journal of Contemporary China* 11(31): 297–318.

Lau, S. K. 2000. The Hong Kong policy of the People's Republic of China, 1949–1997. *Journal of Contemporary China* 9(23):77–93.

———. 2003. Confidence in Hong Kong's capitalist society in the aftermath of the Asian financial turmoil. *Journal of Contemporary China* 12(35):373–86.

Leiss, W., S. Kline and S. Jhally. 1986/1990. *Social communication in advertising: Persons, products and images of well-being.* 2nd ed. London & New York: Routledge.

Leung, B. 1996. *Perspectives on Hong Kong society.* Oxford: Oxford University Press.

Lo, S. H. 2001. Citizenship and participation in Hong Kong. *Citizenship Studies* 5 (2):127–42.

Phelan, J. M. 1991. Selling consent: The public sphere as a televisual marketplace. In P. Dahlgren and C. Sparks, eds. *Communication and citizenship*, 75–93. New York: Routledge.

Salmon, C. T. 1989. Campaigns for social "improvement": An overview of values, rationales, and impacts. In C. T. Salmon , ed. *Information campaigns: Balancing social values and social change*, 19–53. Newbury Park, CA: Sage.

Turner, M. 1995/2003. 60s/90s: Dissolving the people. In N. Pun and L. M. Yee, eds. *Narrating: Hong Kong culture and identity*, 24–51. Hong Kong: Oxford University Press.

United Nations Centre for Human Rights. 1989/2004. *International covenant on economic, social and cultural rights.* Hong Kong: The Government Logistic Department.

Watson, J., and A. Hill. 1994. *A dictionary of communication and media studies.* 3rd ed. New York: Edward Arnold.

Wong, T.W.P. 1998/2003. Colonial governance and the Hong Kong story. In N. Pun and L. M. Yee, eds. *Narrating: Hong Kong Culture and Identity*, 219–51. Hong Kong: Oxford University Press.

Wong, R.Y.L. 2002. Going "back" and staying "out": Articulating the postcolonial Hong Kong subjects in the development of China. *Journal of Contemporary China* 11(30):141–59.

Acknowledgements

The author would like to thank the Information Services Department of the HKSAR Government for its assistance in the completion of this study.

Chapter 4

Criticism and Public Opinion of Advertising

Kara Chan

Introduction

*I*n this chapter we review major criticism of advertising, why it is accused, and summarize a few surveys about Hong Kong's public opinion about various types of advertising, including advertising in general and television advertising in particular.

Richard Pollay, a history professor at the University of British Columbia, publishes a classical article titled "The Distorted Mirror: Reflections on the Unintended Consequences of Advertising," that summarizes the major criticism of advertising. He argues that any culture is a mosaic of multiple values and a culture is characterized in substantial measure by the relative importance of these values. He states that advertising is a "distorted" mirror that fails to give a true reflection of symbols and cultural values that are readily understood and accepted by the target audience. Advertising reflects cultural values "on a very selective basis, echoing and reinforcing certain attitudes, behaviors, and values far more frequently than others" (Pollay 1986, 18). It reinforces only certain lifestyles and philosophies that serve sellers' interest (Pollay and Gallagher 1990).

Advertising is often being the focus of criticism, because of: (1) its pervasiveness, it penetrates into all aspects of people's life. It occurs in various forms on television, broadcast, newspapers, magazines, transportation vehicles, outdoor places, shopping malls, and now in the internet and other computer-mediated communication media; (2) its repetitive nature, reinforcing the same or similar ideas over and over again; (3) it was professionally developed and executed, with all the sophisticated market research tools and creative talents in the production of the messages; and (4) its audience is increasingly detached from traditional sources of cultural influence, including families, churches, and schools (Pollay 1986). The institutions of family, religion, and education have declined in authority. Advertising has replaced these socializing agents to become a new kind of social guide by providing ideas about consumption style, morality, and behavior (Berman 1981).

It is argued that the impact of advertising can be readily underestimated because of its environmental nature and is therefore hard to detect. McLuhan and Fiore (1967, 184) stated that, "Environments are invisible. Their ground rules, pervasive structure, and overall patterns elude easy perception." As advertising is environmental, people do not take it very seriously. People think that they are personally immune to the influence of advertising. This myth will make people even more vulnerable to the hidden works of advertising (Barnouw 1978).

Criticism of Advertising

The criticism of advertising comes from scholars of different fields. There are psychologists who view advertising as a source of learning or conditioning, with cognitive and affective results. There are sociologists who focus on the role modeling aspects of advertising and its impact on social behaviors. There are anthropologists who consider advertising as rituals and symbols that give meaning to material objects. There are educators who are particularly interested in the influence of advertising on child development. There are communication scholars who view advertising as persuasive forms of communication and are interested in its effects. The criticism of advertising originates also from general public and parents, which will be covered in the later part of this chapter.

The following paragraphs summarise and elaborate each of the criticisms from scholars in Pollay's (1986) article.

1. Encouraging materialism

Because advertising promotes goods, it encourages materialistic values, the belief that consumption is the route to happiness, meaning, and the solution of most personal problems. Advertising is seen as inducing people to keep working in order to be able to keep spending, to keep productive in order to keep consuming. Advertising keeps people on a treadmill, chasing new and improved carrots, even though our basic needs may be well met. Advertising romanticizes goods. It displaces feeling from people to objects and displaces spiritual development with secular hedonism (Leiss 1976). Advertising people now abuse highly emotional expressions that used to be applied to human beings, to objects. People become more and more emotionally involved with objects and less and less involved with people. Goods become superior to love, friendship, and other human relations (Skolimowski 1977). It distorts political priorities; private goods vs. public goods; gross economic goal vs. justice, peace. It encourages ecological wastefulness and damage to the nature environment.

2. Encouraging irrational consumption

Advertising is repetitive, fantastic, one-sided, and exhortative. It will therefore blur the distinction between reality and fantasy, producing hypnoid states of uncritical consciousness. People's mind become "jammed with bits and pieces of jingles, buzz words, products, ad images, brand names, and slogans so there is no room for mediation and little room for self-confrontation" (Schrank 1977, 90). A majority of advertising uses emotional appeals. It repeats. It attracts audience attention by using sexual images. It threatens people and then provides them with daydreams about a sudden change in one's life. All these methods are irrational. The have nothing to do with the qualities of the products. They suppress the critical thinking of the audience and make them irrational (Fromm 1976).

3. Idealizing "the good life"

Advertising models a pattern of behavior that is held out to be "the good life." The lifestyles displayed are ideal from a consumption point of view. Imitation of the ideal life creates frustration and the feeling of dissatisfaction of the existing lifestyles. Advertising seeks to "create needs, not to fulfill them; to generate new anxieties instead of allaying old ones. By surrounding the consumer with images of the good life, … the propaganda of commodities simultaneously makes him acutely unhappy with his lot" (Lasch 1978). It also creates new forms of unhappiness, i.e., personal insecurity, status anxiety, and envy (Lasch 1978).

4. Reinforcing social stereotypes

A particular concern about modeling is that advertising reinforces social stereotypes, for example, gender portrayal in advertising. Advertising portrays the ideal women, who are slim, beautiful, charming, have perfect skin, take good care of children and families, and master a successful career, etc. Advertising instills a sense of inadequacy with respect to women's self-concept when she cannot achieve the ideal image. Women spend time "worrying over the gray streaks or the extra pound or the dry skin instead of our minds, our hearts, and our fellow men." (Mannes 1964, 31) Advertising, using "ideal types," can lead the audience to be dissatisfied with the realities of his or her everyday world. "Fantasies are a loaded gun. They *may* sweeten life and advance culture; they *may* also destroy life in a reckless pursuit of impossible accomplishments" (Toronto School of Theology 1972, 22). A typical advertising is short, 30 seconds on television or one single page on a magazine. Simplistic, symbolic stereotypes are often used, for clarity and appealing to a mass audience. The stereotyped models fail to take care of individual differences. Advertising reinforces stereotypes for gender, as well as for races, ages, occupations, and family relations.

5. Encouraging undesirable values

Some of the criticisms are about specific appeals used in advertising will encourage undesirable values. For example, because advertising often targets a mass market using popularity theme, it encourages conformity. The use of modernity value will enhance disrespect for experience, tradition, and history. The glorification of youth will reduce family authority and suppress respect for age. The use of sexual appeal will encourage sexual preoccupations and pornography. Sexual ads represent a challenge to standards of decency and pornography.

In the recent literature, people also criticize that advertising encourages comparative and competitive consumption (Schor 2000). Advertising encourages people to engage in conspicuous consumption by portraying the image of owners of status goods, upscale lifestyles, and the enjoyment of expensive goods. Individuals constantly try to keep up with the norms of the social groups with which they identify. In the past, people may look into their neighbors and try to keep up with those other households of similar background and income levels. However, people now are increasingly looking into the upper middle class and the rich for identification (Schor 2000).

The following paragraph is a summary of criticism of advertising provided by UNESCO:

> Regarded as a form of communication, it [advertising] has been criticized for playing on emotions, simplifying real human situations into stereotypes, exploiting anxieties, and employing techniques of intensive persuasion that amount to manipulation. Many social critics have stated that advertising is essentially concerned with exalting the materialistic virtues of consumption by exploiting achievement drives and emulative anxieties, employing tactics of hidden manipulation, playing on emotions, maximizing appeal and minimizing information, trivializing, eliminating objective considerations, contriving illogical situations, and generally reducing men, women, and children to the role of irrational consumer. Criticism expressed in such a way may be overstated but it cannot be entirely brushed aside (MacBride 1980, 154).

Public Attitudes

To the general public, do they agree with the criticisms suggested by scholars? The general audience is usually more concerned about specific creative execution such as sex appeal and immediate consequences of advertising, such as pestering parents to buy the products advertised. In this chapter, we are going to discuss the public opinion about advertising and television advertising in Hong Kong. Offensive advertising, advertisement that generates high level of discomfort or dislike from audience, will be discussed in Chapter 5.

Advertising is a highly visible force in the Hong Kong society. Assessment of public opinion about advertising has interested both the advertising industry and academic scholars. It is a common belief that attitudes toward advertising in general will affect audience attitudes toward a particular advertisement, which will in turn affect advertising effectiveness and liking of the brand advertised.

Public opinion toward advertising and television advertising has been studied in United States since the 1960s. Poll data consistently shows that the public is appreciative of the usefulness of advertising on one hand, while is wary and skeptical of the claims and undesirable consequences of advertising on the other (Calfee and Ringold 1994). In two surveys from a 1990 Chicago sample of over 200 viewers and a 1991 consumer panel of about 800 respondents conducted by Alwitt and Prabhaker (1992; 1994), television advertising was perceived by a majority to be less useful, less enjoyable, and less credible than advertising in general. In a study of a consumer panel of about 200 respondents from a southern U.S. city conducted by Mittal (1994), television advertising has been seen as a contaminant of social mores and as an impediment to informed consumer decision-making. The result has been "faint praise and harsh criticism" (Mittal 1994). Such criticism has been characterized by diminished overall consumer attitudes and recommendations for stricter governmental regulations.

In the surveys mentioned in the above paragraphs, attitudes toward advertising are measured by asking respondents whether they agree on certain attributes and by asking respondents attitudes toward specific beliefs about advertising. Such beliefs consist of the following underlying factors:

Perceived functions   Whether advertising is perceived to contain information values by telling consumers about product features and uses; whether advertising can build buyer confidence; whether advertising is perceived to contain entertainment values; and whether advertising provides consumers with information about social images.

Perceived consequences   Whether advertising is encouraging materialism; whether advertising is having impact on audience' gender perception; whether advertising is harmful to children by promoting irrational consumption and unhealthy products; and perception about the economic cost and benefits of advertising (e.g., if the consumer pays higher prices because of advertising or whether advertising encourages competition and results in lower prices).

Previous Studies on Public Opinion of Advertising in Hong Kong

Some research has been conducted in the 1980s and 1990s on the public opinion of advertising in Hong Kong. In 1982, AGB McNair (a market research company) conducted a study of attitudes towards television advertising for the Television and Entertainment Licensing Authority. In 1984, faculty members of The Chinese University of Hong Kong conducted a survey of 1,152 Hong Kong residents (Sin and Cheng 1984) using a scale comprising 10 attitudes statement. It was found that people strongly agree that most advertising encourages materialism in the society (3.0 on a four-point scale), the frequency of advertising is too high (3.0 on a four-point scale), and most advertising did not provide sufficient information (3.0 on a four-point scale). Faculty members of the Hong Kong Baptist University conducted a survey of 1,019 Hong Kong Chinese residents in April 1993 using face-to-face intercept interviews (Martin et al. 1994). It was found that people strongly agree that advertising is a good way to learn about products and services (3.8 on a five-point scale) and advertising helps economic development (3.8 on a five-point scale). They also strongly agreed that most advertising encourages materialism in the society (3.7 on a five-point scale). People perceived that the contents of advertisements are interesting and enjoyable (3.4 on a five-point scale). They placed doubts about the credibility of advertising as they agreed that products don't perform as well as the advertisements claim and advertisements don't present a true picture of the product advertised (both 3.4 on a five-point scale). They agreed that advertising has a bad influence on children and advertising often portrays women as sex objects (both 3.3 on a five-point scale).

The study also segments the respondents according to their individual modernity/traditionalism and Chinese/Western orientations. Traditional Chinese segment respondents criticized advertising the most, especially about the encouragement of materialism in society. They were also most skeptical about the credibility of advertising. On the other hand, Modern Western and Modern Chinese segments were most positively disposed toward advertising.

A survey on a sample of 691 Hong Kong residents was conducted to investigate the public attitudes toward television advertising in Hong Kong (Chan 1995). The questionnaire used was based on Mittal's (1994) study. Students at the Hong Kong Baptist University were asked to distribute questionnaires according to a preset quota on sex and occupation. Results indicated that respondents endorsed the market information and entertainment functions of television advertising. However, they did not endorse the buying confidence and social image information functions of television advertising. They agreed that advertising improved people's standard of living. They worried that television advertising would increase the cost of the products.

An Updated Study on Television Advertising

Television advertising accounts for over 50% of Hong Kong's total advertising media expenditures. So public attitudes towards advertising in general can be reflected by the public attitude toward television advertising. A study was conducted in Hong Kong using a structured questionnaire in Chinese in April 2002. The study was an update of Chan's (1995) study. Communication Studies students at the Hong Kong Baptist University were asked to recruit respondents through personal sources to answer a self-administered questionnaire. Attitudes toward television advertising were measured.

Respondents were asked to indicate whether they considered television advertising to be good or bad; and whether they liked or disliked it. Averaging the scores on these three questions generates an overall attitude score toward television advertising. The questionnaire followed with statements on functions and perceived consequences of television advertising and on opinions on the regulation of television advertising. Respondents were asked to rate these statements on a five-point scale (5 = strongly agree to 1 = strongly disagree). Altogether 692 questionnaires were collected. Fifty-eight percent of the respondents were females and the remaining 42% were males. Two thirds of the sample was aged 20–29. The sample profile is detailed in Appendix. The sample contained 60% students. As a result, it has limitation in projecting to a general population. We have compared the results of the updated survey with that obtained in Chan's (1995) survey. It was found that public attitudes were very similar in both studies. It can be interpreted as either one of the following scenarios: (1) public attitudes did not change significantly over the time period; or (2) attitudes toward television advertising of college students were similar to that of the general public.

Overall attitude

Hong Kong consumers have positive overall attitude toward television advertising (see Table 4.1). Fifty percent of the respondents consider television advertising very good or somewhat good. Seventeen percent of the respondents consider it very bad or somewhat bad. Fifty-five percent of the respondents strongly or somewhat like television advertising. Fourteen percent of the respondents strongly or somewhat dislike it.

The mean score on the bad/good scale is 3.4 which are slightly higher than the mean score of 3.5 on the dislike/like scale.

Table 4.1: Overall attitude toward television advertising

Item	%	Mean	S.D.
Overall, do you consider TV advertising a good or a bad thing?		3.4	1.0
Very good	11		
Somewhat good	39		
Neither good nor bad	33		
Somewhat bad	15		
Very bad	2		
Overall, do you like or dislike TV advertising?		3.5	0.9
Strongly like it	10		
Somewhat like it	45		
Neither like nor dislike	31		
Somewhat dislike it	12		
Strongly dislike it	2		

Perceived functions of television advertising

The frequency distribution, the mean and standard deviation of consumers' perceived functions of television advertising are summarized in Table 4.2. Offering market information about goods and services is considered to be the basic function of advertising. Results indicate that the knowledge function is well known among Hong Kong consumers. A majority of the sample say television advertising helps them keep updated about new products and is a main source of product information. They also perceive that television advertising provides information about brand features and benefits.

Hong Kong consumers least agree with the buying confidence function of television advertising. They are skeptical about trustworthiness of commercials. About 40% of the respondents disagree that one can put more trust in advertised brands. About 40% of respondents disagree that consumers have more difficulty making purchase decisions if there was no television advertising. One third of respondents disagree that television advertising helps them to get the best buy.

Hong Kong consumers are neutral about the social image function of television advertising. Over 40% of the respondents reported neutral position to the three statements about social image function of television advertising. Over one third of respondents do not think that television advertising tells them what people like them are buying and using or helps them select products that reflects their lifestyles.

The entertainment function of television advertising is well received by respondents. A majority of the consumers finds some commercials enjoyable and takes pleasure in thinking about them. Nearly half of the respondents agree that sometimes commercials are even more enjoyable than television programming.

Perceived consequences of television advertising

The frequency distribution, the mean and standard deviation of consumers' perceived consequences of television advertising are summarized in Table 4.3. One major area of criticism about advertising concerns its negative social effects. A majority of the respondents agrees that television advertising makes people to go after things as well as

Table 4.2: Perceived functions of television advertising

Function	Mean	S.D.	Disagree %	Neutral %	Agree %
Knowledge					
TVA helps me keep up-to-date about products and services.	3.6	0.9	13	23	63
TVA is a main source of information about products and services.	3.4	0.9	18	32	50
TVA tells me which brands have the features I am looking for.	3.2	0.9	23	32	45
Buying confidence					
TVA helps the consumer buy the best brand for the price.	2.9	0.9	34	43	23
If there were no TVA, deciding what to buy would be difficult.	2.8	1.0	39	33	28
One can put more trust in products seen in TVA than in those not in TVA.	2.8	0.9	39	40	21
Social image					
TVA helps me know which products will reflect my personality and taste.	2.9	0.9	34	44	23
From TVA, I learn what is in fashion and what I should buy for keeping a good social image.	2.9	0.9	31	46	23
TVA tells me what people like me are buying and using.	2.8	0.9	36	43	21
Entertainment					
I enjoy some TV commercials.	3.8	1.0	13	20	68
Sometimes I take pleasure in thinking about what I saw in TVA.	3.6	1.0	15	22	64
Sometimes TV commercials are even more enjoyable than TV programs.	3.3	1.0	26	27	48

Notes:

TVA = television advertising

All items are in five-point scale with larger number indicating agreement to the statement.

Table 4.3: Perceived consequences of television advertising

Consequence	Mean	S.D.	Disagree %	Neutral %	Agree %
Materialism					
TVA is making us to go after things.	3.4	1.0	18	26	56
TVA sometimes makes people live in a world of fantasy.	3.2	0.9	22	35	43
TVA encourages materialistic values and creates people's desire in buying and owning things.	3.1	1.0	24	37	39
TVA makes people buy unaffordable products just to show off.	3.0	1.0	31	36	33
Adverse effect on children					
TVA leads children to make unreasonable purchase demands on parents.	3.3	0.9	19	34	47
TVA takes undue advantage of children.	3.0	0.9	25	50	25
Economic costs					
TVA increases the cost of products.	3.7	1.0	16	16	69
It would be better to save money on TVA and invest it on product improvements instead.	3.2	1.0	22	38	40
If TVA was eliminated, consumers would be better off.	2.8	0.9	43	38	19
Economic benefit					
We need TVA to support TV programming.	3.5	1.0	15	32	53
Manipulation					
TVA encourages people to buy what they do not need.	3.2	0.9	21	37	42

Notes:

TVA = television advertising

All items are in five-point scale with larger number indicating agreement to the statement.

makes people live in a fantasy world. There are roughly equal numbers who disagree or agree that television advertising makes people buy unaffordable products.

A majority of the respondents accuses television advertising of having adverse effects on children. They agree that television advertising leads children to pester their parents. However, there are equal numbers who disagree or agree that television advertising takes undue advantage of children.

Respondents perceive strongly about the economic costs of television advertising on consumers. They generally believe that television advertising increases the costs of products and agree that some advertising money could be reserved for product improvements. However, respondents do not favor the complete elimination of television advertising.

Despite the perceived undesirable economic costs of television advertising, respondents seem to accept the legitimacy and economic contributions of it. A majority recognizes that television advertising supports free programming.

Do Hong Kong people think that television advertising manipulate consumers? The answer is yes. Over 40% of respondents agree that television advertising encourages people to buy what they do not need.

Call for government regulation

Respondents strongly object to the proposition that television advertising content should be free from government control. They strongly urge some control over the content of television advertising. Respondents do not support regulation to limit the number of times a commercial is run. Despite the strong perception that television advertising has adverse effects on children, 45% of respondents disagree that advertising should be banned from children's programming (see Table 4.4).

Prediction analysis

The predicted variable is the overall attitudes toward television advertising. It is compiled by taking the mean of the respondents' perception of television advertising on the good/bad and the like/dislike

Table 4.4: **Public opinion on regulation of television advertising**

Regulation	Mean	S.D.	Disagree %	Neutral %	Agree %
TVA should be free from government control so that advertisers may say what they want to. [R]	3.8	1.1	67	19	14
The content of TVA should be more closely regulated by the government.	3.0	1.0	24	40	36
There should be a limit on how many times a TV commercial may be repeated.	2.8	1.0	41	34	25
TVA should be banned on children's programs.	2.7	0.9	45	36	19

Notes:
TVA = television advertising
[R] Reversed coding in the compilation of mean.
All items are in five-point scale with larger number indicating agreement to the statement.

scales. The Pearson correlation between the two scales is 0.4. This indicates that a good evaluation of television advertising is positively related with a liking for it. The high correlation coefficient also justifies the compilation of an overall attitude score toward television advertising. The predictors are perceived functions and consequences of television advertising. To aid the interpretation, composite scores for each of the four functions of television advertising are compiled by taking the mean of the constituent items. Likewise, the mean scores on the constituent items for perceived consequences on materialism, adverse effect on children and economic costs are also computed. For the economic benefit and manipulation effects of television advertising, no composite scores are compiled because both are single-item variables.

Result of regression analysis is summarized in Table 4.5. For the prediction of overall attitude toward television advertising, a statistically significant R square value of 0.25 is obtained. This indicates that 25% percent of the total variation of the overall attitude is explained by perceived functions and consequences of television advertising. Five out of nine predictors are significant. Among these predictors, perceived entertainment, perceived economic benefit of free television

Table 4.5: Regression analysis for predicting overall attitude toward television

Advertising Perceived functions and consequences	Parameter estimate	Standard error	Standardized estimate
Knowledge	0.09	0.05	0.08
Buying confidence	0.04	0.05	0.03
Social image	0.13	0.05	0.10*
Entertainment	0.35	0.04	0.36***
Materialism	0.06	0.05	0.05
Adverse effect on children	−0.16	0.04	−0.14***
Economic costs	−0.16	0.05	−0.13***
Economic benefit	0.09	0.03	0.11***
Manipulation	0.03	0.03	0.04

Multiple regression R square = 0.25
Notes:
* $p < 0.05$
** $p < 0.01$
*** $p < 0.001$

programming, and perceived social image function of television advertising are correlates of a favorable overall attitude. Perceived adverse effect on children and perceived economic costs are correlates of unfavorable overall attitudes.

The three out of the nine predicting variables with the highest standardized estimates are perceived entertainment function, perceived adverse effect on children, and perceived economic costs of television advertising. It suggests that these three perceptions act as a set of core beliefs that affects respondents' overall attitudes toward television advertising.

Past research often concerns itself with evaluating the effects of demographic and psychographic profiles of viewers. Four demographic variables including sex, age, education, and monthly personal income, are added as possible source of influences.

The additional contribution in multiple regression R square values for overall attitudes is 2%. This suggests that after the effects of perceived functions and consequences of television advertising are controlled, the demographics characteristics yield little additional predictive power.

Conclusion

The survey reveals that Hong Kong consumers hold positive attitudes toward television advertising. This contradicts many research findings in the West that consistently report increasing distaste of television advertising (Alwitt and Prabhaker 1992; Mittal 1994).

The entertainment and knowledge functions of television advertising are well received while the buying confidence and social image functions are not readily accepted among respondents. This suggests that Hong Kong consumers are rational and pragmatic. They enjoy watching television advertising and utilize it to gain market information about products, services, brands, and features. However, they place a healthy skepticism on advertising claims and they do not put more trust on advertised brands. For the consequences of television advertising, the perceived economic benefits including free television programming are well received by respondents. On the other hand, the major criticisms are its economic costs, encouragement of materialism, and perceived adverse effects on children. Perception on manipulation of consumer decisions is weak among respondents. This indicates that Hong Kong consumers are practical. Their major concerns are about economic costs and benefits of television advertising. Overall attitude toward television advertising is affected mainly by the perceived entertainment function of television advertising, the perceived adverse effect on children, and the perceived economic costs of television advertising.

Appendix: Sample Profile (N=692)

Demographic	%
Sex	
Male	42
Female	58
Age	
19 or under	13
20–29	64
30–39	11
40–49	8
50 or above	4

Education
Elementary school or below	5
Secondary School	30
College or University	65

Residence
Public housing	34
Home Ownership Scheme housing	23
Private housing	43

Occupation
Students	60
Clerical and services	12
Professional and sub-professional	10
Managerial and administrative	5
Housewives	5
Production and construction	4
Retired or unemployed	4

Personal monthly income
No	23
HK$1,000 or below	23
HK$1,001–2,500	21
HK$2,501–5,000	12
HK$5,001–7,500	12
HK$7,501 or above	9

References

Alwitt, L. F., and P. R. Prabhaker. 1992. Functional and belief dimensions of attitudes to television advertising: Implications for copytesting. *Journal of Advertising Research* (September / October): 30–42.

———. 1994. Identifying who likes television advertising: Not by demographics alone. *Journal of Advertising Research* (November / December): 17–29.

Barnouw, E. 1978. *The sponsor: Notes on a modern potentate.* New York: Oxford University Press.

Berman, R. 1981. *Advertising and social change.* Beverly Hills, CA: Sage.

Calfee, J. E., and D. J. Ringold. 1994. Public assessment of TV advertising: Faint praise and harsh criticism. *Journal of Advertising Research* (January / February): 35–53.

Chan, K. 1995. *Hong Kong television advertising: The good, the bad, and the ugly.* Hong Kong: Department of Communication Studies, Hong Kong Baptist University.

Fromm, E. 1976. *To have or to be?* New York: Harper.

Lasch, C. 1978. *The culture of Narcissism: American life in an age of diminishing expectations.* New York: Norton.

Leiss, W. 1976. *The limits of satisfaction.* Toronto: University of Toronto Press.

MacBride, S. 1980. *Many voices, one world: Communication and society, today and tomorrow.* New York: Unipub (UNESCO).

Mannes, M. 1964. *But will it sell?* New York: Lippincott.

Martin, E. F. Jr., Y. M. Cheng, G. B. Wilson, and Y.W.L. Tsui. 1994. Advertising images among Hong Kong Chinese: Use of individual modernity and western orientation clusters in determining market segmentation. *Asian Journal of Communication* 4(1): 12–32.

McLuhan, M., and Q. Fiore. 1967. *The medium is the message: An inventory of effects.* New York: Random House.

Mittal, B. 1994. Public assessment of TV advertising: Faint praise and harsh criticism. *Journal of Advertising Research* (January / February): 35–53.

Pollay, R. W. 1986. The distorted mirror: Reflections on the unintended consequences of advertising. *Journal of Marketing* 50(2): 18–36.

———, and K. Gallagher. 1990. Advertising and culture values: Reflections in the distorted mirror. *International Journal of Advertising* 9: 359–72.

Schor, J. 2000. The new politics of consumption. In J. Cohen and J. Rogers, eds. *Do Americans shop too much*, 3–36. Boston: Beacon Press.

Schrank, J. 1977. *Snap, crackle, and popular taste: The illusion of free choice in America.* New York: Delacorte.

Sin, Y.M.L., and W.L.D. Cheng. 1984. *Advertising in Hong Kong: The Consumer view. WP-84-08.* Hong Kong: Faculty of Business Administration, The Chinese University of Hong Kong.

Skolimowski, H. 1977. The semantic environment in the age of advertising. In T. H. Ohlbren and L. M. Berk, eds. *The new languages: A rhetorical approach to the mass media and popular culture*, 91–101. Englewood Cliffs, NJ: Prentice-Hall.

Toronto School of Theology. 1972. *Truth in advertising: A symposium.* New York: Harper.

Acknowledgements

The updated study on television advertising reported in this chapter was conducted by students taking the course COMM2320 at Hong Kong Baptist University in 2001/2002. The data was given to the author by Mr. Charles C. W. Man.

Chapter 5

Offensive Advertising

Gerard Prendergast
Benny Ho

Introduction

*I*n order to draw the audience's attention to a product or service advertisement, there has been an increasing use of controversial advertising in recent years (Lyons 1996; Matthews 1997; Waller 1999). This trend has occurred in Hong Kong as well (Schwartz 2001; Tilles 1998; Wong 2000; "Thirteen complaints" 1999). A distinctive advertisement may enhance brand awareness and recall, but the effect on brand liking and purchase intention may be either positive or negative. Some consumers, as a form of protest against advertising which they find offensive, have put pressure on advertisers to change their advertisements, encouraged the media to stop accepting the advertisements, or even boycotted the company and its products (Schwartz 2001; Tilles 1998; Wong 2000).

Western research on offensive advertising is extensive, with the foundation work being done by Aaker and Bruzzone (1985) and Barnes and Dotson (1990). But in an Asian context, research in the area is limited. This chapter throws more light on offensive advertising in Hong Kong. Hong Kong, a unique place where East meets West, has a modern Western look, yet ethnic Hong Kong Chinese have also maintained a strong cultural identity (Bond et al. 1985). There is an increasing awareness and adoption of offensive advertisements in Hong Kong (Schwartz 2001; Tilles 1998; Wong 2000; "Thirteen complaints" 1999). However, not much is known about the attitudes and responses of Hong Kong consumers to offensive advertising. This chapter answers the following questions:

- What are the products and services that consumers find offensive in advertising (i.e., the *matter* of advertising)?
- What are the appeals that consumers feel are offensive in advertising (i.e., the *manner* of advertising)?
- What is the degree of tolerance to offensive advertisements compared in different media?
- What are the effects of offensive advertising on purchase intention?

Offensive Products/Services: The Matter of Advertising

Unmentionable products are those that are considered to be offensive, embarrassing, harmful, socially unacceptable, or controversial to some significant segment of the population. According to Wilson and West (1981), unmentionables are products, services, or concepts that for reasons of delicacy, decency, morality, or even fear, tend to elicit reactions of distaste, disgust, offence, or outrage when mentioned or when openly presented through the media. Katanis (1994) furthered this research and redefined unmentionables as "offensive, embarrassing, harmful, socially unacceptable, or controversial to some significant segment of the population." The examples of unmentionables that he presented were: "products" such as items used in personal hygiene, birth control, warfare, and drugs for terminal illness; "services" such as abortion, sterilization, the treatment of veneral disease and mental illnesses, funeral services, and artificial insemination; and "concepts" such as political ideas, palliative care, unconventional sexual practices, racial/religious prejudices, and terrorism.

Geographic location is a factor affecting the perceived levels of offensiveness of the products/services. In Western countries, Aaker and Bruzzone (1985) found that the three most disgusting commercials in the United States were those encouraging consumers to purchase the following products: feminine hygiene products, women's undergarments, and hemorrhoid treatment. Waller (1999) disclosed that the three most offensive products/services in Australia were those related to racially extremist groups, religious denominations, and feminine hygiene products. Recent research carried out in Singapore (Phau and Prendergast 2001) found that the three most offensive products were chat-line services, veneral diseases treatments/prevention, and dating services. Phau and Prendergast (2001) also found that these attitudes vary according to demographics, particularly in terms of gender and education. The above research suggests that consumers' attitudes towards offensive advertising might vary across cultures and demographic groups.

Offensive Appeals: The Manner of Advertising

If an advertisement is found to be offensive, it does not just depend on the product and the service itself, but also on the type of appeal and the manner of presentation. Objections include use of sex or fear, and silliness of presentation (Greyser 1972). These emotions can lead to general consumer irritation. Sexuality in advertising creates high attention value (LaTour et al. 1990); but sometimes excessively offensive advertisements will generate negative feelings (Blech et al. 1981; La Tour 1990), especially towards those advertisements that adopt sexual appeals or nudity.

Several studies have found that advertisers can maximize the involvement and persuasiveness of an advertisement via the use of a fear appeal (Neal et al. 1999). But the use of a fear appeal may "expose a person against one's will to harmful or seriously offensive images" (Henthorne et al. 1993). Products such as deodorants, dandruff shampoos, and mouthwash are criticized for attempting to create anxiety and using fear of social rejection to increase sales (Belch and Belch 2001). In the Hong Kong context, slimming products in particular often use fear appeals in their advertising, although such advertisements are now under scrutiny as a result of the Government issuing a public consultation paper relating to the regulation of health claims in advertising (Department of Health 2003).

Potential Effects on Purchase Behavior

Experiencing offensive advertising may negatively effect the consumer's buying decisions. Ford et al. (1997) hypothesized a model to examine female response to offensive sex role portrayals in advertising. The model suggested that potentially offensive advertisements damaged company image and are proportional to the purchase intention of the consumer. Once the customer feels uneasy or has a negative impression of the advertisement, he or she might not buy the products of the companies that are perceived of as using offensive advertisements. Phau and Prendergast (2001) found that while Singaporean consumers with tertiary education may find the advertisements for one product offensive, this offending image does not spill over to other products from the same company.

The Hong Kong Context

The Hong Kong Chinese have maintained a strong cultural identity (Bond et al. 1985). Hong Kong consumers are generally supportive of advertising, but the modern Western and the modern Chinese segments give a greater support than the traditional Chinese segment. Because Hong Kong is a place where there is a close interaction between Eastern and Western values, and because it is basically an international society, it is an interesting location to explore consumer perceptions of offensive advertisements. Hong Kong is a source of social influence to neighboring countries in Southeast Asia (Tse et al. 1989), yet there has been no previous study of Hong Kong consumers' perception of offensive advertising.

Presumably, not all Hong Kong consumers will have the same attitudes towards offensive advertising. It is usually believed that a person's background is a crucial determinant of his/her attitudes. For example, Cheung (1982) has suggested that women are often portrayed as sex objects. In addition, sexual discrimination against women is believed to be part of traditional Chinese culture. Considering these factors, it is possible that women will be more offended by certain advertisements. Sin and Cheng (1984) have found that there is a positive correlation between the level of educational attainment of the interviewees and concern over the potential negative effects of advertising. Therefore, the educational level may also affect perceptions of offensive advertising. Age is another factor that might affect perceptions of offensive advertising, because younger people tend to be more open-minded.

A Study Examining Hong Kong Consumers' Perceptions of Offensive Advertising

The main objective of this study was to compare differences in perceptions of offensive advertising across demographic variables, especially education and gender (since these two variables are found in previous studies to be significantly related to perceptions of offensive advertising).

The questionnaire was originally developed in an earlier Singapore study (Phau and Prendergast 2001). This questionnaire was based on a combination of the literature and focus groups held in Singapore with a cross-section of consumers. Then, this questionnaire was brought to Hong Kong, and slight amendments were made based on feedback from focus groups held with a cross-section of Hong Kong consumers.

The questionnaire had five sections, and each section used of a six-point Likert scale for responses. A six-point Likert scale was used instead of a five-point Likert scale to avoid central tendency and for higher discriminatory power. The first section was comprised of a list of products/services while the second section consisted of a list of reasons for offensive advertising, where 1 = "not at all offensive" and 6 = "extremely offensive." This section of the questionnaire borrowed items from Wilson and West (1981), Katsanis (1994), and Waller (1999). As cigarette advertisements are banned in Hong Kong, this item was removed from the list that was originally developed by Phau and Prendergast (2001) for research in Singapore. However, from the focus group, funeral services were considered to be somewhat offensive in the Chinese culture and this item was added to the list. The final list of products/services was as follows:

1. Alcohol
2. Chat-line services

3. Condoms
4. Dating services
5. Female contraceptives
6. Feminine hygiene products
7. Female underwear
8. Funeral services
9. Gambling
10. Hair replacement products
11. Male underwear
12. Pharmaceuticals
13. Sexual diseases (AIDS, STD [sexually transmitted disease] prevention)
14. Weight-loss programs

The second section of the questionnaire listed seven possible reasons for an advertisement to be seen as offensive. The main literature input for these items was by Belch and others (1981), as well as La Tour (1990). Following the focus group sessions, the final list of reasons included:

1. Sexual connotations
2. Evoking unnecessary fear
3. Sexist
4. Cultural insensitivity
5. Indecent language
6. Subject too personal
7. Nudity

In Section 3, nine media were listed to determine the different levels of tolerance to offensive advertisements in different media. This scale was based on prior research (Boddewyn 1989) on sexism and decency in advertising. A six-point Likert scale measuring the level of tolerance to offensive advertisements in different media, where 1 = "very tolerant" and 6 = "very conservative," was listed in this section. The list of media were as follows:

1. Broadcast Television
2. Cable Television
3. Posters/Billboards

4. Newspapers
5. General Magazines
6. Women's Magazines
7. Men's Magazines
8. Direct Mail
9. Radio

The fourth section consisted of three statements regarding the effect of offensive advertising on consumers' purchase intentions. The scale was adopted from Ford and others (1997). The three questions examined the purchase behavior of the respondents in response to an offensive advertisement—whether the respondent would still purchase the product if the product offered attractive benefits, discontinue using it, or even boycott the company. In addition, the following question was added to investigate further the effect of offensive advertisements on consumers' purchase behavior: *"When two companies offer the same products with similar benefits, I will not buy from the one using an advertisement that I find offensive."*

Finally, Section 5 of the questionnaire consisted of questions regarding respondents' demographic information.

In consideration of the time frame and unavailability of a suitable sampling frame, a non-probabilistic quota sample of 200 (100 male and 100 female Hong Kong consumers, from both tertiary and non-tertiary educated groups, aged over 16) was selected as respondents. The questionnaire was translated into Chinese and then back translated for accuracy. It was then pilot tested on 20 people before administering it to the full sample. The 200 interviews took place during a two-week-period near the entrance of shopping malls on the Kowloon side of Hong Kong, as these shopping malls draw large volumes of customers of different age groups and social backgrounds.

Of the 200 respondents, the majority was aged between 20 and 29 years old and single. Around 70% were employed full time. According to the quota criteria, around half the respondents were male and half were female. In addition, around half of the respondents had university or higher education level and half did not. Details of the profiles of the respondents are presented in Table 5.1.

Table 5.1: Profile of respondents

Gender	N	%
Male	100	50.0
Female	100	50.0
Age		
Below 19	21	10.5
20–29	131	65.5
30–39	40	20.0
40 or above	8	4.0
Marital Status		
Single	148	74.0
Married, without child	28	14.0
Married, with child	21	10.5
Divorced/Widowed	3	1.5
Education Level		
Non-tertiary	90	45.0
Tertiary	110	55.0
Occupation		
Clerical and service workers	66	33.0
Managers and executives	23	11.5
Production and construction workers	9	4.5
Professionals (e.g., teacher, engineer)	39	19.5
Students	50	25.0
Homemaker	9	4.5
Others (e.g., self-employed and unemployed)	4	2.0
Monthly Personal Income (HK$)		
$10,000 or below	68	34.0
$10,001–20,000	64	32.0
$20,001–30,000	21	10.5
$30,001–40,000	10	5.0
$40,001 or above	4	2.0
Not applicable	33	16.5

Offensive products

In the first section of the questionnaire, respondents were asked to indicate their level of personal offensiveness with respect to a list of products/services commonly advertised. Table 5.2 presents the details of the results (mean scores and standard deviations).

Table 5.2: Perceived offensiveness of products and services

Product/Services	Total N=200		Gender		Education Level	
			Male N=100	Female N=100	Non-tertiary N= 90	Tertiary N=110
Chat-line services	3.20	(1.50)	3.20	3.19	1.55	1.45
Funeral services	2.86	(1.54)	2.82	2.90	1.57	1.51
Gambling	2.76	(1.50)	2.87	2.64	1.64	1.37
Condoms	2.44	(1.32)	2.26	2.62	1.45*	1.17*
Dating services	2.42	(1.30)	2.39	2.44	1.35*	1.21*
Female contraceptives	2.36	(1.34)	2.24	2.48	1.48	1.21
Feminine hygiene products	2.26	(1.32)	2.26	2.26	1.38*	1.25*
Weight loss products	2.25	(1.31)	2.34	2.16	1.32	1.29
Female underwear	2.25	(1.29)	2.28	2.22	1.39	1.20
Sexual diseases	2.22	(1.27)	2.30	2.15	1.30	1.25
Male underwear	2.18	(1.20)	2.16	2.20	1.25	1.16
Hair replacement products	2.13	(1.36)	2.21	2.06	1.41	1.32
Pharmaceuticals	2.13	(1.28)	2.15	2.12	1.40	1.17
Alcohol	2.03	(1.25)	2.09	1.97	1.31	1.20

Key: * $p < 0.05$
1 = "not at all offensive" and 6 = "extremely offensive"
Figures in bracket represent the standard deviation of the mean values

Of the 12 items, chat-line services were regarded as most offensive to the respondents. Funeral services, the item added in this survey, ranked second, followed by gambling, condoms, and dating services. Female underwear (mean = 2.25) was considered slightly more offensive than male underwear (mean = 2.18). Alcohol was regarded as the least offensive product/service to be advertised.

The list of offensive products with respect to gender is quite consistent with the overall results. Chat-line services were regarded as the most offensive while gambling and funeral services could be found at the top of both the women's and men's lists. Similar to the overall list, both males and females ranked alcoholic beverages as the least offensive product in the list. According to the results of *t*-tests comparing males results to females, no products were significantly less or more offensive.

In terms of education, both tertiary and non-tertiary groups ranked chat-line services, funeral services, and gambling as the most offensive. Meanwhile, alcoholic beverages remained as the least offensive product in the list with respect to the two groups.

Offensive appeals

As shown in Table 5.3, respondents generally found advertisements offensive due to sexist attitudes (mean = 4.20) displayed in the advertisement, followed by indecent language (3.99) and nudity (3.95). Prior research (Phau and Prendergast 2001) indicated that sexual connotation was regarded as an important reason for respondents to find advertisements offensive. However, sexual connotations (2.97) in this research ranked sixth, followed by cultural insensitivity (2.73) ranking at the bottom of the list.

With respect to gender, the results were generally consistent with the overall findings. Female respondents ranked nudity in advertisements to be most offensive, while nudity ranked fourth for male respondents (*t*-test results indicate that this difference was significant).

Media tolerance

In Section 3 of the questionnaire, respondents were asked to rank their personal level of tolerance with regard to potentially offensive advertisements shown in nine different listed media, with 1 for "very tolerant" and 6 for "very conservative." By using the mid-point 3.5 as a test value, media with a mean significantly greater than 3.5 were regarded as producing lower levels of tolerance in consumers while media with a mean significantly lower than 3.5 were regarded as producing higher levels of tolerance in consumers, as presented in Table 5.4.

Generally, the nine media had means ranging from 3.20 to 3.92. Men's magazines and women's magazines were regarded as media producing higher levels of tolerance in consumers not only in general, but also with respect to gender and education level. On the other hand, direct mail, posters/billboards, and newspapers were classified as media producing lower levels of tolerance in consumers.

With respect to gender, male respondents showed a lower level of tolerance to potentially offensive advertisements in direct mail while female respondents showed lower levels of tolerance to potentially offensive advertisements not only in direct mail but also on radio and posters/billboards. The *t*-test showed that the differences between males and females in this context, however, were not significant. Respondents

Table 5.3: Reasons for finding advertisements offensive

Reasons	Total N=200		Gender		Education level	
			Male N=100	Female N=100	Non-tertiary N= 90	Tertiary N=110
Sexist	4.20	(1.48)	4.15	4.25	4.27	4.15
Indecent language	3.99	(1.42)	3.86	4.12	4.14	3.86
Nudity	3.95	(1.56)	3.61*	4.29*	4.04	3.87
Evoking Unnecessary fear	3.94	(1.43)	3.85	4.03	3.90	3.97
Subject too personal	3.52	(1.35)	3.39	3.65	3.60	3.45
Sexual Connotations	2.97	(1.25)	2.82	3.11	3.00	2.94
Cultural Insensitivity	2.73	(1.28)	2.68	2.78	2.80	2.67

Key: * $p < 0.05$

1 = "not at all offensive" and 6 = "extremely offensive"

Figures in bracket represent the standard deviation of the mean values

Table 5.4: Level of tolerance in media

Media	Total N=200		Gender		Education level	
			Male N=100	Female N=100	Non-tertiary N= 90	Tertiary N=110
Direct mail	3.92*	(1.48)	3.80	4.04	3.89	3.95
Posters/billboards	3.69*	(1.25)	3.66	3.82	3.47***	3.88***
Newspapers	3.67*	(1.24)	3.66	3.73	3.41***	3.88***
Radio	3.65	(1.38)	3.54	3.68	3.56	3.73
Broadcast television	3.58	(1.34)	3.48	3.62	3.51	3.64
General magazines	3.53	(1.22)	3.47	3.59	3.38	3.65
Cable television	3.43	(1.31)	3.36	3.50	3.54	3.34
Men's magazines	3.21**	(1.22)	3.17	3.29	3.27	3.15
Women's magazines	3.20**	(1.19)	3.12	3.23	3.19	3.21

Key: * Mean > 3.5, $p < 0.05$

　　** Mean < 3.5, $p < 0.05$

　　*** $p < 0.05$

1 = "Very Tolerant" and 6 = "Very Conservative"

Figures in bracket represent the standard deviation of the mean values

with tertiary levels of education, on the contrary, were found to have significantly higher levels of tolerance to offensive advertisements shown in newspapers and posters/billboards than respondents with non-tertiary levels of education.

Effect on Purchase Intention

In the final section of the questionnaire, respondents were asked whether their purchase intention would be affected by offensive advertising. Table 5.5 shows the mean values of the four scales on purchase intentions in detail. For the first statement: "*If a new product is introduced with advertisements that I find offensive, I might still buy the product if it offers me benefits that I find attractive,*" respondents were somewhat likely (mean = 3.90) to buy products with offensive advertisements if the product offered attractive benefits. According to *t*-test results, gender and education did not produce any significant differences.

For the second statement: "*If the product or service that I use adopts an advertisement campaign that I find offensive, I will discontinue using it,*" generally, respondents were somewhat likely (mean = 3.92) to discontinue the usage of products when the product or service they used adopted an offensive advertisement. Once again, the *t*-test showed that gender and education did not produce any significant differences in the results.

For the third statement: "*Even though I may see an advertisement that is offensive for one product, I would continue to purchase other products that I have been using from the same company,*" the overall result showed respondents were somewhat unlikely to continue purchasing under this situation. With respect to gender, the *t*-test indicated that male respondents were significantly more unlikely to continue purchasing than female respondents.

For the last statement, "*When two companies offer the same products with similar benefits, I will not buy from the one using an advertisement that I find offensive,*" the mean value of this statement (mean = 4.48) was higher than that of the previous three statements. Overall, respondents were generally unlikely to buy products from the company using an offensive advertisement, if given a similar alternative from a "non-offending" company. Similar means were found with respect to gender and educational level.

Looking at the overall results from this study, compared to chat-line services other products/services were generally ranked with lower levels of offensiveness among Hong Kong subjects. One can only

Table 5.5: Mean values of purchase intention

1. If a new product is introduced with advertisements that I find offensive, I might still buy the product if it offers me benefits that I find attractive.

Total	Male	Female	Non-tertiary	Tertiary
3.90	3.95	3.85	3.69	4.07
(1.45)	(1.48)	(1.42)	(1.50)	(1.39)

2. If the product or service that I use adopts an advertisement campaign that I find offensive, I will discontinue using it.

Total	Male	Female	Non-tertiary	Tertiary
3.92	3.93	3.91	3.77	4.05
(1.37)	(1.37)	(1.39)	(1.39)	(1.35)

3. Even though I may see an advertisement that is offensive for one product, I would continue to purchase other products that I have been using from the same company.

Total	Male	Female	Non-tertiary	Tertiary
3.35	3.15*	3.55*	3.29	3.40
(1.20)	(1.10)	(1.27)	(1.26)	(1.16)

4. When two companies offer the same products with similar benefits, I will not buy from the one using an advertisement that I find offensive.

Total	Male	Female	Non-tertiary	Tertiary
4.48	4.44	4.53	4.42	4.54
(1.36)	(1.44)	(1.27)	(1.45)	(1.28)

Key: * $p < 0.05$
1 = "most unlikely" and 6 = "most likely"
Figures in bracket represent the standard deviation of the mean values

speculate as to why chat-line services were found to be so offensive. It may be because chat-line services in Hong Kong, unofficially, basically mean phone sex. It is not as innocent as the name "chat-line" suggests.

Mean scores with respect to offensive products were generally lower than those for the reasons for finding advertisements offensive. As the focus groups suggested, whether the audience will feel offended by the advertising may depend more on the appeal than the product itself.

Compared to Phau and Prendergast's (2001) Singapore study, advertisements related to veneral diseases, dating services, and male underwear were found to be less offensive in Hong Kong than in Singapore. Looking specifically at underwear, male underwear was found to be more offensive than that of females in Singapore, yet female underwear was found to be slightly more offensive than that of males in Hong Kong.

Moving on to the manner of advertising, sexist themes, indecent language, and nudity were found to be the major reasons for respondents to find advertisements offensive in Hong Kong. Chat-line services were found to be the most offensive product from the list probably because advertisements for these services are usually presented in poor taste and with double meanings. However, this cannot explain the reasons why participants found advertisements regarding funeral services and gambling offensive. Phau and Prendergast's (2001) found in their Singapore study that sexist themes, nudity, and indecent language were the least offensive "advertising manner" in Singapore. Instead, Singaporeans were most offended by advertisements with sexual connotations, with subjects that were too personal, and with subjects evoking unnecessary fear. Phau and Prendergast (2001) also found that female audiences were more sensitive to advertisements for chat-line services, male underwear, and condoms, than were male audiences. However, no differences in levels of offensiveness to any of the products/ services were found to be significantly different between male and female respondents in this Hong Kong study.

Respondents with higher education level generally perceived lower levels of offensiveness towards potentially offensive products and appeals, such as condoms, dating services, and feminine hygiene products than did those with lower education levels. On the contrary, Phau and Prendergast's (2001) Singaporean respondents with higher education levels indicated a higher level of offensiveness towards products like condoms, female underwear, and chat-line services, than did respondents with lower education levels.

With respect to gender, the perception towards offensive advertising was generally consistent except on the level of offensiveness elicited by advertisements illustrating nudity. The *t*-test showed that female participants expressed a significantly higher level of offensiveness towards this type of advertisement than did males.

Consistent with the findings of Phillips (2001), interviewees were more tolerant of offensive advertising if it was placed in men's magazines and women's magazines. Advertising contents in magazines in Hong Kong have in the past faced less legal restrictions than advertisements in the broadcast media. Therefore, Hong Kong people may "expect" to be more offended by print magazines. They have become somewhat conditioned to it.

Phau and Prendergast (2001) found that although consumers in Singapore with tertiary education may find the advertisements for one product offensive, this offending image did not spill over to other products of the same company. The current study showed no such relationship for Hong Kong respondents. Instead, female respondents showed a higher likelihood of boycotting a company using offensive advertising than did male respondents. In addition, respondents were unlikely to buy products from a company using offensive advertising if a similar alternative was available from a "non-offending" company.

This study showed that the manner of advertising is more crucial than the matter of advertising. Advertisers should try to downplay sexist themes, indecent language, and nudity in their execution if they do not wish to offend the public or cause controversy. However, for adventurous marketers who wish to run controversial campaigns to gain public awareness, execution associated with sexual connotations, instead of nudity and sexist themes, may be considered as a less offensive means "to cut through the clutter."

Apart from the execution and the message, selection of media is also an important element affecting the offensiveness of advertisements. Men's and women's magazines not only enable the message to be more targeted, but the audiences of these media are also less sensitive to potentially offensive advertisements. Adventurous marketers may use male- or female-oriented fashion or hobby magazines to try out their controversial approaches to market their products. Sex appeals like nudity, which create more sensitivity in female consumers, may be considered less risky if they appear in male-oriented magazines.

Although controversial advertising campaigns can help generate consumer attention, consumers in this study were generally unlikely to purchase the product promoted by advertisements they found offensive. They would rather choose products with the same features and with similar benefits from companies without offending advertising. Balances, as well as trade-offs, have to be found while "cutting through the clutter," so as not to offend customers who might look elsewhere for a similar product. While it could be argued that the word "offensive" (as used in the purchase intention questions) is not a neutral term, and that it carries negative connotations, the fact is that the results reported in this paper suggest offensive advertising negatively differentiates a product which, in all other aspects, is identical to a competing offer. In other words, offensive advertising can sway consumers away from purchasing a particular product, even though that product meets the consumer's needs in a utilitarian and/or hedonic sense.

It is common practice to produce more creative and more controversial campaigns to target one product at more liberal consumers while producing less offensive advertising for another product targeted at more conservative consumers. However, this survey shows that the offending image of one product may spill over to the company's image. Adventurous marketers and brand managers should, therefore, consider not only the target audience of one product, but also other important customers of the company.

Limitations and Conclusions

The single study reported here cannot answer all the questions raised by offensive advertising and it has a number of limitations. The first limitation relates to the scope of the research. Other than gender and education, age, income level, and marital status may also be of pertinent influence on perceptions of offensive advertising. Also, the research did not examine consumer involvement and usage of the products under study. Furthermore, whether different value orientations will have an effect on the perception of offensive advertising is also not revealed in this research. For example, will people with a non-traditional value orientation have higher levels of tolerance to offensive advertisements, or are ethnic Chinese more sensitive to offensive advertisements than those who are more Western-minded? Further research should be carried out to investigate whether the above-mentioned factors constitute any effect on perceptions of offensive advertising.

The second limitation of this study relates to the list of media used to examine the tolerance to offensive advertising in different media. Absent from this list of media was the Internet. Future research may include this as a mass-market media that also has the potential to carry offensive advertisements.

The third limitation of this study relates to the generalizability of the results. The sample in this study was not purely random, and therefore may not be completely representative of all Hong Kong consumers.

Despite the limitations, the research is useful in that it has clearly demonstrated the extent to which the matter and manner of advertising offend Hong Kong consumers, how this relates to the media carrying the offensive message, and how the offensiveness of the advertising relates to consumers' purchasing behavior. Conventional wisdom in the advertising industry holds that a certain amount of irritation or so-called "creativity" enhances the effectiveness of advertising. This assumption, however, seems not to be valid. The research reported here shows that for certain demographic groups offensive advertising may be negatively perceived, to the extent that it effects their purchase behavior.

References

Aaker, D., and D. E. Bruzzone. 1985. Causes of irritation in advertising. *Journal of Marketing* 12(2):47–57.

Barnes, J. H., and M. J. Dotson. 1990. An exploratory investigation into the nature of offensive television advertising. *Journal of Advertising* 19(3):61–69.

Belch, M. A, and B. E. Belch. 2001. *Advertising and promotion: An integrated marketing communications perspective*, 5th ed. New York: McGraw-Hill.

Belch, M. A., G. E. Belch, B. E. Holgerson, and K. Jerry. 1981. Psychophysiological and cognitive response to sex in advertising. In A Mitchell, ed. *Advances in consumer research*, vol. 9, 424–27. Provo, UT: Association for Consumer Research

Boddewyn, J. J. 1989. *Sexism and decency in advertising: Government regulation and industry self-regulation in 47 countries*. New York: International Advertising Association.

Bond, M. H., K. C. Wan, K. Leung, and R. Giacalone. 1985. How are responses to verbal insult related to cultural collectivism and power distance? *Journal of Cross-Cultural Psychology* 16:111–27.

Cheung, O. 1982. Advertising and consumer. *Hong Kong Manager (June)*: 30–31.

Ford, J. B., M. S. LaTour, and E. D. Honeycutt, Jr. 1997. An examination of the cross-cultural female response to offensive sex role portrayals in advertising. *International Marketing Review* 14(6):409–23.

Department of Health, Government of the HKSAR. 2003. *Regulation of health claims in Hong Kong: A consultation document.* Hong Kong: Department of Health.

Greyser, S. A. 1972. Advertising: Attacks and counters. *Harvard Business Review* (March):22–28

Henthorne, T. L., M. S. LaTour, and R. Nataraajan. 1993. Fear appeals in print advertising: An analysis of arousal and ad response. *Journal of Advertising* 22(2):59–68.

Katsanis, L. P. 1994. Do unmentionable products still exists? An empirical investigation. *Journal of Product & Brand Management* 3(4):5–14.

LaTour, M. S. 1990. Female nudity in print advertising: An analysis of gender differences in arousal and ad response. *Psychology and Marketing* 7(1):44–53.

LaTour, M. S., R. E. Pitts, and D. C. Snook-Luther. 1990. Female nudity, arousal, and ad response: An experimental investigation. *Journal of Advertising* 19(4): 51–62.

Lyons, K. 1996. Offensive, titillating, outrageous? *Australian Professional Marketing*, 8–10. Sydney: Australian Marketing Association.

Matthews, T. 1997. Lost causes in advertising. *B&T* (July 11):21.

Neal, C., P. Quester, and D. Hawkins. 1999. *Consumer behavior: Implications for marketing strategy.* New York: McGraw-Hill.

Phau, I., and G. Prendergast. 2001. Offensive advertising: A view from Singapore. *Journal of Promotion Management* 7(1):1–21.

Phillips, H. 2001. Too sexy perfume poster cut. *South China Morning Post*, January 29, 5.

Schwartz, S. 2001. Sexy Dior billboard to vanish. *Hong Kong iMail*, February 8, A05.

Sin, L., and D. Cheng. 1984. Advertising in Hong Kong: The consumer view. Unpublished manuscript, Faculty of Business Administration, The Chinese University of Hong Kong.

Thirteen Complaints Made to CTI's TVC (1999). *Apple Daily*, March 26, A06. (In Chinese)

Tilles, D. 1998. DDB France pulls religious VW ads. *Adweek* 39(7):5.

Tse, D. K., R. W. Belk, and N. Zhou. 1989. Becoming a consumer society: Longitudinal and cross-cultural content analysis of print ads from Hong Kong, the People's Republic of China, and Taiwan. *Journal of Consumer Research* 15 (4):457–72.

Waller, D. 1999. Attitudes towards offensive advertising: An Australian study. *Journal of Consumer Marketing* 16(3):288–94.

Wilson, A., and C. West. 1981. The marketing of unmentionables. *Harvard Business Review* (January/February):91–102.

Wong C. K. 2000. Sexual connotations in advertising. *Next Magazine*, June 1, 162–63. (In Chinese)

Acknowledgements

Part of this chapter has been published in the *Journal of Marketing Communications*, vol. 8, no. 3 (2002), 165–77.

Chapter 6

Advertising Regulation and Ethical Issues

Chao-wai Wong
Susanna Wai-yee Kwok

Introduction

*I*n a recent survey the position of advertising regulation in Hong Kong was concluded to be "industry self-regulation" (Sawant and Bandyopadhyay 2002).

It is easy for a researcher to come to the same conclusion that the advertising industry in Hong Kong is mainly self-regulated. This is a statement which fails to pick up the whole picture. What is in place is continuous promotion by the government that the advertising industry regulate its own affairs; a better description would be paternalistic guidance in return for maximum commercial output. A feature of the regulatory mechanism upheld by the government is not regulation of the advertising industry but regulation of the media. There is surprisingly extensive legislation which governs the channels of advertising.

As a part of commercial activity, advertising in the commercial or private sector is always being encouraged (Petty 1992). The existing regulatory regime, however, provides no identifiable central policy or theme in the regulation of advertising. The law regulating advertising activities apart from the above passive feature of paternalistic guidance would seem less sophisticated than those of neighboring territories; for example, there is no competition law or antitrust law. The lack of any strict rule on the other hand provides the freedom that is required by the trade. However, there are various organizations and government departments which affect advertising through the enforcement of policy or the promotion of objectives.[1]

The difficulty in identifying any specific policy or any source of legal regulation or decorum in connection with advertising activities is a result of the common law system which Hong Kong inherited from the British. This is clearly in contrast with the North American situation, or the continental system as practiced in Mainland China. In the North American context, the First Amendment of its Constitution and the interpretation of it by the American Courts have classified advertising as a form of "commercial speech" which "does no more than propose a commercial transaction" (Richards 2000). The body of law that has been developed in the United States is therefore a development of rights under the constitution. In Mainland China there is specific legislation[2] promulgated to regulate advertising activities in the private sector. In Hong Kong the legal sources are dispersed in legislation and case law. There has been no attempt to compile them into a single core catering for the activity of advertising.

The Regulatory Framework

Advertising is connected with the stimulation of sensations in order to draw attention (Petty 1992). Its true nature and function in society is a matter for the academics to discover. The question as to whether works by advertisers bear any responsibility towards society has always been the subject of discussion. Research into different aspects of advertising has been carried out abroad for years. Research into the local advertising industry, surprisingly, is still in its infant stage let alone in the area concerning the relationship between advertisement, law, and ethics.

In this article a conscious decision has been taken to exclude any discussion of the regulation of advertisements by means of private legal rights. By this we mean the rights of the private individual under the law of contract, the law of intellectual property, the law of defamation, the law of tort concerning product liability, landlord and tenant law, the law relating to buildings, and the law of tort. Readers who are interested in the extent of private rights relating to advertising are encouraged to consult the standard text for a full flavor treatment.[3] A decision was also taken not to cover policy and law regarding the installation and maintenance of advertisement signs in open areas.

However, we must stress that the decisions not to embark upon a discussion of these private rights and of advertisement signs were based on the allocation of resources and space, not on their significance. On the contrary, the nature and effect of private legal rights are themselves interesting and complicated.[4] The effect of private legal rights in the regulation of advertising campaigns and even the strategies for their implementation are very important. An interesting illustration for the reader to follow is the Andy Lau Tak Wah saga[5]—a case relating to the use of the famous celebrity to promote a bank's financial products. The case had an impact upon the notion of "image rights."

What is Social Decorum?

The regulation of advertisement in Hong Kong is in effect regulation of the media. The legal fabric exists primarily to allow market self-regulation through imposing restrictions upon use of the medium by advertisers. Interventions by legislators and legal enforcers have been in effect a parental role played by the government, which oversees that the decorum of society is maintained. This, however, begs the question: by whom and how decorum is being defined?

Advertising is an expression and every expression carries with it a value (Wright 1997; Gibbons 1998). The value may be expressed in terms of the esthetics of the advertisement, the choice of the topic, and the message to be conveyed. The legislature has passed laws from time to time which have had the cumulative effect of containing advertising activities. The recent survey conducted by Lo (2002) identified more than 40 legislative provisions which define illegal advertising or impose restrictions upon advertising activities.

It may be surprising to note that there is a legislative provision which classifies an advertisement for the recovery of lost property in specific circumstances to be illegal, and anyone who prints or publishes such advertisements with words to the effect that no questions would be asked or the finder be exempted from investigation is subject to penalties.[6]

Further, the legislature has left the powers to advertise in certain circumstances within the hands of administrators. For instance, advertising vehicles are subject to regulation under a permit which can only be issued by the Commissioner of Transport, and the administrative power extends to the granting of the right to advertise on or over any expressway.

The above seems to be the main philosophy of governmental regulation as far as advertising activities are concerned: the decision is left with the administrators to enforce policy. The Broadcasting Authority, for example, looks to the licence holders for compliance and therefore the duty to enforce the code of practice is in the hands of the media operators.

One of the functions of the Courts is to hand down precedents for future reference. However, in the area of advertising the cases that are reported are mainly concerned with private rights issues, although there are other classifications.[7] Most day-to-day matters which relate to the operations of advertisers are dealt with by tribunals or administrative bodies where there is no reporting system. Hence these bodies may not provide any guidance for the advertisers.

It is obviously that these administrators have no sympathy with and do not care about "standards" which advertising professionals in other areas have spent efforts to build up. Up to the present day we do not have a code of advertising applicable in a general sense. The standards being enforced vary according to the administrative bodies concerned.

This is not to say that no initiatives are taken in response to market forces or to promote professionalism, or incidentally to restrain competition (Calfee 1997). One example is the recent launch by the Hong Kong Internet Registration Corporation Limited (HKIRC) of a membership system to regulate the manner of doing business by traders providing internet services to the general public. This institution, which has since launched its mission under the title of Hong Kong Internet Service Providers Association (HKISPA), has taken a pro-active stance on many aspects of the industry including issuing various codes of practice to its members. Submission to the code of practice is on a voluntary basis and it is hoped that members will reach consensus on the manner of operation. A recent relevant release is the *Code of Practice in the Regulation of Obscene and Indecent Material* dated September 4, 2003.[8]

The Regulatory Bodies

The following is a general description of the administrative bodies which are essential to the regulation of advertisement activities.

The Broadcasting Authority[9]

The Broadcasting Authority has been set up to regulate licensed television and radio broadcasters in Hong Kong under the respective ordinances, namely the *Broadcasting Authority Ordinance* (Cap. 391 Laws of Hong Kong), the *Broadcasting Ordinance* (Cap. 562 Laws of Hong Kong), and the *Telecommunications Ordinance* (Cap. 106 Laws of Hong Kong). The Complaints Committee is responsible for considering complaints about broadcasts and making recommendations to the Broadcasting Authority regarding such complaints.

The role of the Broadcasting Authority is to set up yardsticks through its subcommittee. The Codes of Practice Committee is responsible for keeping various broadcasting standards under regular review and to set up standards for the trade. The *Broadcasting Ordinance* empowers the Broadcasting Authority to perform such functions. The Broadcasting Authority is empowered: i) to issue codes of practice on program and advertising standards relating to television program services transmission; ii) to issue codes of practice on program and advertising standards relating to sound broadcasting; and iii) to issue codes of practice on the technical requirements for television program services and sound broadcasting licensees on the advice of the Telecommunications Authority.

The Broadcasting Authority also deals with complaints about television and radio broadcasts and imposes sanctions on the broadcasters for contravening the various provisions and requirements. It enforces the anticompetition provisions and deals with complaints about contravention of the provisions.[10]

To enforce the provisions of legislation, licensing conditions, and the codes of practice, the Broadcasting Authority is empowered to impose sanctions on licensees for breaches. In most cases breaches will draw sanctions ranging in nature from a reprimand to a monetary penalty. The power to grant and review licence status remains the strongest measure for regulating licence holders. A feature of these codes is that there is no attempt to regulate the advertisers. It is for the licence holders to draw up standards with the advertisers. The value of the code is that it sets out guidelines as to how advertisers are expected to act. The current version of the *Generic Code on Practice on Television Advertising Standards* was issued on August 13, 2004 and the *Radio Code of Practice on Advertising Standards* was released also in August 2004.

There are nine specific categories of Advertisement that are regulated by the Rules, namely i) alcoholic beverages; ii) tobacco and tobacco-related products; iii) medical preparations and treatments; iv) claims relating to nutritional and dietary effects; v) personal products; vi) educational courses; vii) financial advertising; viii) real property advertising; and ix) film advertisements.

The Broadcasting Authority maintains a two-tier complaints system. A complaint made to the complaints division of the Broadcasting Authority will be subject to a preliminary enquiry[11]. If the complaint warrants further investigation then a formal investigation will be conducted. Upon finding a complaint to be substantiated then the appropriate sanction will be imposed upon the licence holder for an advertisement transmitted through its medium.

Apart from the specific codes of practice and guidelines issued, regulation by the Broadcasting Authority is backed by i) the *Telecommunication Ordinance* (Cap. 106 Laws of Hong Kong); ii) the *Broadcasting Authority Ordinance* (Cap. 391 Laws of Hong Kong); iii) the terms of the respective licences granted to the holders; and iv) other regulatory bodies such as the Commerce, Industry and Technology Bureau[12] and the Telecommunication Authority of Hong Kong.[13]

Features of the Generic Code of Practice on Television Advertising Standards[14]

Television is the most extensive medium in our society and it is therefore worth expanding on the coverage of the Generic Code of Practice on Television Advertising Standards ("the Generic Code").

Table 6.1: Salient features of the Generic Code of Practice on Television Advertising Standards

Chapter under the Generic Code	Conditions imposed on or expected from licence holders
Chapter 3 General Advertising Standards	(a) Presentation of advertisement with courtesy and good taste; (b) Advertisement should not disparage competitors; (c) Presentation must be candid and the licence holder is obliged to see that the claims in the advertisement are not untrue or misleading; (d) No permission for any imitation or unreasonable approximation of competitors; (e) No play on the element of fear; (f) Acceptance by the general public; (g) No insertion of advertisements during any religious service or other devotional program; (h) No insertion of advertisement within the Educational Television (ETV) time slot.
Chapter 4 Factual and Best-selling Claims	(a) All factual claims and best-selling claims should be capable of substantiation; (b) For all claims substantiated by research or tests, the source and date of the assessment or research should be indicated in the advertisement; (c) Best-selling claims should be substantiated by independently audited figures or probability sample surveys which are recognized or endorsed by the industry; (d) Best-selling claims should not be used unless there is adequate and explicit specification of the category of brand leadership, country, and the time period it covers; (e) Attention should be paid to presentation styles such as typeface, letter spacing, line spacing, background, and captions to ensure that the information supporting the claims is legible.
Chapter 5 Unacceptable Products or Services	(a) Advertisements of the following products are not accepted • firearms and associated equipment; • fortune-telling as distinct from pre-recorded information services; • undertakers or services associated with death or burial; • unlicenced employment services; • services providing betting tips; • betting, save those authorized under the Laws of Hong Kong, but such should not, *inter alia*, be shown between 4:00 p.m. and 8:30 p.m. each day on domestic free television;

Table 6.1 (Cont'd)

Chapter under the Generic Code	Conditions imposed on or expected from licence holders
	• program services and/or times where there may be exposure to young persons under the age of 18; • nights clubs or similar establishments in which hosts or hostesses are employed, or in which floor shows or other live performances or activities involving sexual behavior of whatever nature are presented; • escort services in general or dating services targeting young persons under the age of 18; • pay per call information offering adult material of a sexual nature save for the services allowed under a licence restricting viewing to adults. (b) Any indirect advertisement which in the opinion of the Broadcasting Authority is unacceptable will not be permitted.
Chapter 6 Specific Categories	(a) Alcoholic Beverages • targeted only at adults, and no children should be involved in the presentation of the advertisement; • not to be shown between the hours of 4:00 p.m. and 8:30 p.m. each day or in proximity to children's programs; • presentation as a desirable new experience is not permitted; • presentation as a gift in television contests is not permitted; • use as to portrait social status, course of achievement or other success, relieve stress or a solution to personal problems not permitted; • restriction of presentation similar to other non-alcoholic products which have particular appeal to children or young persons who are under the age of 18; • no suggestion that product should be preferred because of higher alcohol content or intoxicating effect; • choice of artist should be made with care; • restriction of presentation of use before sports or hazardous activities; • encouragement of manner of drinking prohibited; • drinks containing 1.2% or less of ethyl alcohol by volume and presented as a low or no alcohol version of an alcoholic liquor must not be advertised in or adjacent to children's programs. (b) Tobacco and Tobacco-related products • compliance with the *Smoking (Public Health) Ordinance* (Cap. 371 Laws of Hong Kong) is compulsory;

Table 6.1 (Cont'd)

Chapter under the Generic Code	Conditions imposed on or expected from licence holders
	• presentation as a prize for television contests should not be permitted;
	• advertisement of related products should pay attention to the effect on children and young persons under the age of 18.
	(c) Medical preparations and treatments
	• compliance with the Laws of Hong Kong including the *Undesirable Medical Advertisements Ordinance* (Cap. 231 Laws of Hong Kong);
	• no advertisements of products that falls within Part 1 of the *Poisons List in the Pharmacy and Poisons Ordinance* (Cap. 138 Laws of Hong Kong) and Schedule 1 of the Antibiotics Regulations, *Antibiotics Ordinance* (Cap. 137 Laws of Hong Kong) and which are classed as unacceptable products. For example, smoking cures, clinics for the treatment of hair and scalp, relief or cure of alcoholism and drug addiction, and procuration of miscarriage or abortion are not permitted;
	• unless it can be substantiated that professional advice or recommendation has been obtained from an acceptable organization in the relevant profession, advertisements giving the impression of rendering professional advice are not acceptable;
	• no use of fear or exploitation of credulity is allowed;
	• no general statements may be made which omit essential facts;
	• no general statements stating or implying that "all" diseases are due to a particular cause;
	• no statement stating that "all" of a certain group of diseases will be cured by the preparation;
	• patients receiving treatment are not to be shown;
	• no reference should be made to a prize competition or promotional scheme such as a gift, premium offers, and samples.
	(d) Claims relating to Nutritional and Dietary Effects
	• compliance with the provisions of the *Undesirable Medical Advertisement Ordinance* (Cap. 231 Laws of Hong Kong) and the *Public Health and Municipal Services Ordinance* (Cap. 132 Laws of Hong Kong);
	• support by sound scientific evidence for any specific claims;

Table 6.1 (Cont'd)

Chapter under the Generic Code	Conditions imposed on or expected from licence holders
	• no representation that dietary supplements are necessary as additions to a balanced diet, or that they are the only means to enhance good health; • no encouragement in patterns of behavior which are prejudicial to health; • advertisements for products, services, and establishments offering treatment aimed at the achievement of weight loss or reduction of body fat are acceptable if the advertisements state that the service/products is adjunct to a balanced/healthy diet in order to achieve its effect and provided the advertisements comply with five rules, namely they must not be addressed to persons under the age of 18, the effect of the products and services must be substantiated, the advertisement must not be directed at the obese and must not use case histories to show subjects who were or appeared to be obese lose weight and become slimmer after using the product or service advertised, there must be no suggestion or implication that being underweight is acceptable or desirable, and in the case of food products in this category it must be made clear that the product can assist weight loss only as part of a calorie controlled diet. (e) Personal Products • presentation must be in good taste and not overly graphic; • close-up shots of the crotch area for advertising female sanitary products are not allowed; • advertisements for condoms should be factual only and should not contain any claim that the product is capable of giving full protection against the transmission of Acquired Immune Deficiency Syndrome (AIDS); • advertisement of condoms on domestic free television programs services should not be shown between 4:00 p.m. and 8:30 p.m. except with the permission of the Broadcasting Authority. (f) Educational Courses • compliance with section 86A of the *Education Ordinance* (Cap. 279 Laws of Hong Kong), section 34 of the *Non-local Higher and Professional Education (Regulation) Ordinance* (Cap. 493 Laws of Hong Kong) and section 3

Table 6.1 (Cont'd)

Chapter under the Generic Code	Conditions imposed on or expected from licence holders
	of the *Non-local Higher and Professional Education (Regulation) Rules* (Cap. 493 sub leg.) (g) Financial Advertising • compliance with specific statutory provisions, for example, the Companies Ordinance (Cap. 32 Laws of Hong Kong) and the Rules Governing the Listing of Securities on the Stock Exchange of Hong Kong Limited and the Rules Governing the Listing of Securities on the Growth Enterprise Market of the Stock Exchange of Hong Kong Limited. (h) Real Property Advertising • advertisements are only allowed if there be satisfaction that the local property in question can be sold or let; • advertisements for property outside Hong Kong must be supported by (i) confirmation by legal representatives registered and recognized in the country where the property is situated confirming compliance with local regulations and laws, and that a housing loan is available, and (ii) a letter from a local firm of solicitors confirming the aforesaid legal representative is registered and recognized in the country where the property is situated; • the claims in property advertisements must be substantiated. (i) Film Advertisements • compliance with the provisions of the Film Censorship Ordinance (Cap. 392 Laws of Hong Kong) on, *inter alia*, displaying the appropriate symbol applicable to the film under the ordinance.
Chapter 7 Advertising and Children	(a) no product or service may be advertised and no method of advertising may be used in association with a program intended for children; (b) advertisement for products or services which are considered not suitable for children may not be shown within or in close proximity to programs targeting children; (c) advertisements which are frightening or provoke anxiety, or which contain depictions of violent, dangerous, or antisocial behavior, are not allowed to be shown within or in close proximity to programs targeting children; (d) the appearance of children in advertisements must pay heed to safety precautions, good manners, and behavior;

Table 6.1 (Cont'd)

Chapter under the Generic Code	Conditions imposed on or expected from licence holders
	(e) children should not be permitted in the presentation of advertisements for alcoholic liquor or tobacco-related products.

Source: Hong Kong Broadcasting Authority (2004)

The Generic Code is divided into nine chapters, namely 1) Preamble; 2) Definition of Advertisement; 3) General Advertising Standards; 4) Factual and Best-selling Claims; 5) Unacceptable Products or Services; 6) Specific Categories of Advertisement; 7) Advertising and Children; 8) Advertising Breaks; and 9) Program Sponsorship.

The guiding principle for all advertisement in the public arena is that the advertisement must be "legal, clean, honest, and truthful." Compliance with the code of practice is expected from all licence holders and necessitates that licence holders keep themselves abreast of the latest version of the code as well as with the specific laws relevant to the area the broadcast covers. It is, however, indispensable that all practitioners or readers refer to the complaints archives on the official website of the Broadcasting Authority in order to obtain an understanding of the enforcement of the Generic Code.[15]

Telecommunications Authority (OFTA)[16]

The Telecommunications Authority has an executive branch known as the Office of the Telecommunications Authority (OFTA). OFTA is the statutory body responsible for regulating the telecommunications industry in Hong Kong.

In order to attain and to maintain the policy objectives of the Telecommunications Authority, namely i) to enable Hong Kong to be recognized as a world-class telecommunications center for doing business; b) to ensure that Hong Kong has available high-quality telecommunications services at competitive prices; and iii) to ensure that Hong Kong has high performance in telecommunications as measured against the Organization for Economic Co-operation and

Development (OECD) economies, OFTA enforces the provisions in the *Telecommunications Ordinance* concerning anticompetitive practices and misleading conduct.

Because of the growing market and intensive competition in the telecommunications industry in Hong Kong, as well as in the region, the complaints board of OFTA has been deluged with complaints of misleading advertisement by traders as well as by their sale agents. Records of these complaints and the decisions of OFTA may be viewed on its website.

At present OFTA maintains guidelines and a Code of Practice, namely, A Guideline to Misleading or Deceptive Conduct in Hong Kong Telecommunications Markets. The Guideline is enforced under section 7M of the *Telecommunications Ordinance*, Cap. 106 Laws of Hong Kong, in which telecommunication operators are prohibited from engaging in conduct which is misleading or deceptive in providing or acquiring telecommunications networks, systems, installations, customer equipment or services. Section 7M of the *Telecommunications Ordinance* Cap. 106 Laws of Hong Kong replaced the voluntary Advertising Code of Practice issued in 1996.

The Code of Practice for Procedures for Handling Complaints against Senders of Unsolicited Fax Advertisements were being issued on January 2, 2004. Under the Code a junk-fax sender will be temporarily suspended for a period of 14 working days upon receipt of two complaints.

The Consumer Council[17]

The Consumer Council is a government body aimed at protecting consumer rights. With 11 centers open to the general public, the Consumer Council provides services which include the investigation of consumers complaints, prevention of anticompetition measures, and a Legal Action Fund to enable consumers' rights to be protected.

It is not clear from the figures provided in the annual reports of the Consumer Council the extent of complaints about advertisements. It is hard to believe that a complaint about a product would not involve how it is being marketed.

Professional Bodies

One of the rather less noticed areas in the regulation of advertisements is that of professional bodies. It is clear that professional bodies—for example, medical and the dental practitioners—have strict codes of practice which extend to the manner in which advertisements are to be placed. This includes displays at the venue of the practitioner's practice. Regulation of advertisement is through disciplinary regulation. The sanctions taken may even include disqualification.

From the judgement database provided on the Hong Kong Judiciary website, a handful of the decisions from these disciplinary proceedings were taken up with the appellant Courts, namely the Court of Appeal.

One also sees an increase in the relaxation of the professional code of practice in the area of advertisements. A notable example is the advertising rules for the solicitors and insurance professions.

Ethical Issues

The codes produced by the Broadcasting Authority propose general standards for advertisers. The guiding principle is that advertising materials must be presented with "courtesy and good taste." These rules, though never designed for use in all spheres of advertisement, provided the necessary model for other code of practices and it is believed to be good practice to follow the code.

Truthful Presentation

All factual claims and best-selling claims made in advertisements should be substantiated. The burden is on the advertiser to present information substantiating their advertising material.

It is not always easy for the general public to distinguish the subtle difference in the substantiation provided. A recent example is the claims made by a large supermarket chain that the price of its goods was the lowest in comparison with its competitor. The claim was supported by a research conducted by a notable market research company. Its competitor then launched a counter campaign by employing the same research company and claimed that the prices of specific goods offered by it were comparatively lower.

The effect of the two marketing campaigns suggested the respective supermarkets to be offering goods that were, at least in comparison with its competitor, at a lower price. The understatement of the two campaigns was that the claims were based on specific products only and the message in both campaigns was partially true. It does not follow that buying specific goods cheaper in one supermarket means that buying other products would be equally cheaper. In this example, the presentation may cause no harm because in practice consumers will follow the "weekly low price" when buying products offered by respective supermarkets. The problem arises where the consumer is in no way to judge but has to place total reliance upon the substantiation offered when making the choice of purchase.

Children

There are provisions catering for children and strict compliance is expected. None of the products or services intended to be advertised, or the method to be used for advertising, are allowed if there is a likelihood that it might harm the child physically, mentally, or morally. It is also stressed that no method of advertising may be employed which takes advantage of the natural credulity and sense of loyalty of children.

Disparagement

Although there are no competition laws in Hong Kong, the Code of Practice issued by the Broadcasting Authority discourages attempts to disparage competitors in terms of their products and services. It is also stressed that "imitation" of competitors is not allowed.

Recent Issues

Sexual Appeal

Over the past decade there have been developments in the promotion of adult entertainment services. This form of advertisement, formerly considered taboo, has now been accepted under the umbrella of "right to knowledge." In both of the most widely circulated Chinese newspapers in Hong Kong there is a column published on a daily basis directly and indirectly promoting adult entertainment services. This remains a gray area and has been manipulated by advertisers from time to time[18].

The main task of regulation of this issue falls to the Obscene Articles Tribunal, which implements the relevant provisions under the *Control of Obscene and Indecent Articles Ordinance* (Cap. 390 Laws of Hong Kong).[19] Regulation by the tribunals suffers one main problem: namely that these institutions of law are not a court of law and their determinations are not open to the public, nor are their decisions binding for future reference. Hence their regulatory or educational value is not great as far as advertisements are concerned.

Human Rights

Human rights activists have gained mileage in lobbying the Hong Kong Government over the passing of the *Sex Discrimination Ordinance* (Cap. 480 Laws of Hong Kong), *Disability Discrimination Ordinance* (Cap. 487 Laws of Hong Kong), and *Family Status Discrimination Ordinance* (Cap. 527 Laws of Hong Kong). These pieces of legislation provided for the setting up of the Equal Opportunities Commissions to oversee, *inter alia*, that advertisements published do not contravene provisions against discrimination.

The effect on advertisements is that information about i) sexual status; ii) marital status; iii) state of pregnancy; iv) state of health; and v) family status is now forbidden. Contravention will incur a fine.

Conclusion

The philosophy of self regulation means that any government policy is to cultivate an environment in which will be the most cost effective to administer whilst giving freedom to the community to operate. Advertising is by its nature creative. There will always be a problem with the government's regulatory measures being able to keep up with development, especially now as advancement of the medium will no doubt open up fresh opportunities to advertisers. It may be the time for policy makers to consider whether there is a need to set up a body to regulate "standards" in the advertising industry.

Notes

1. These government bodies are administrative organs of the government in enforcing of its policy or regulation. They are not created to regulate or uphold "standards" of the trade. They do not undertake the role of the Federal Trade Commission (FTC) in the United States or the Advertising Standards Authority (ASA) in the United Kingdom.
2. The Advertising Law of the People's Republic of China was promulgated on October 27, 1994.
3. For example, see A. Kolah (2002): *Essential Law for Marketers*, Butterworth-Heinemann; E. E. Clark and J. Livermore (1994): *Australian Marketing Law* The Law Book Company Limited, B. Clarke and B. Sweeney (2000): *Marketing and the Law*, 2nd edition, Butterworths and Spilsbury S (1998): *Guide to Advertising and Sales Promotional Law*, Cavendish Publishing Limited.
4. For example, *Tolley v J S Fry and Sons Limited* [1931] AC 333 a defamation case which arose from the implication of an advertisement affecting the status of an amateur golfer.
5. *Lau Tak Wah Andy v. Hang Seng Bank Limited* (Unreported) CACV 612 of 2001. At the time of preparing the revision of this chapter the authors were aware that Mr. Lau had just taken out legal action in the Mainland to enforce his image rights.
6. *Theft Ordinance* (Cap. 210 Laws of Hong Kong section 25).
7. These classes involve Disciplinary Hearing appeals or Obscene Articles Tribunal appeals. Readers are encouraged to look up the relevant cases contained in the Hong Kong Judiciary website at http://judiciary.gov.hk/tc/index/index.htm.
8. Readers may find the document or updated information at the website of the HKISPA at http://www.hkispa.org.hk/mission.htm.
9. For a full description of the Broadcasting Authority, readers are encouraged to consult the official website of the Broadcasting Authority. The authors have referred to the text of the organization in preparing the background of the Broadcasting Authority in this article.
10. See the Guideline to the Application of the Competition Provisions of the Broadcasting Ordinance. Broadcasting Authority, February 16, 2001.

11. Competition Investigation Procedures, Broadcasting Authority and Complaints Archive. Broadcasting Authority, February 16, 2001.

12. The Commerce, Industry and Technology Bureau is responsible for the enforcement of its policy. A very important aspect is the maintaining of the Obscene Articles Tribunal, see below.

13. The Office of the Telecommunication Authority of Hong Kong is the executive branch of the Telecommunications Authority for the enforcement and implement of its policy.

14. For the full version see the official site of the Broadcasting Authority at www. hkba.org.hk.

15. The archives cover a collection of complaints and appeal from the period of January 2001 to August 2004 at the time of preparing this article.

16. The reader is also encouraged to consult the official website of the Telecommunications Authority for the background and complaint case files of the Telecommunications Authority. The authors acknowledged reference to the material on the website in the preparation of this part of the article.

17. *Annual Report 2002–2003*. Consumer Council.

18. A recent report in the *Apple Daily* dated March 2, 2005 concerning prosecution of a sex boosting drug under the *Undesirable Medical Advertisements Ordinance* (Cap. 231 Laws of Hong Kong) is an illustration (Case ESS12570/2003). The advertisements to which the product was promoted included, but not necessarily the advertisement being prosecuted, a fictitious account of the effect of the drug from the experience of prostitutes.

19. For a general but dated survey see Chapter 15 in W. Y. Leung and J. Chan (Eds) (1995): *Media Law and Practice in Hong Kong: A New Discourse*. Commercial Press (HK) Ltd.

References

Calfee, J. E. 1997. *Fear of persuasion: A new perspective on advertising & regulation.* Monnaz, Switzerland: Agora Association.

Hong Kong Broadcasting Authority, Government of the Hong Kong SAR. 2004. *Generic code of practice on television advertising standards.* Hong Kong: Broadcasting Authority.

Gibbbons, T. 1998. *Regulating the media.* 2nd ed. London: Sweet & Maxwell.

Leung, W. Y., and J. Chan, eds. 1995. *Media law and practice in Hong Kong: A new discourse.* Hong Kong: Commercial Press (HK) Ltd.

Lo, P. Y. 2002. *Media and communications. Halsbury Laws of Hong Kong.* 2002 Reissue. Vol. 18 (2). Hong Kong: Lexis Nexis Butterworths.

Petty, R. D. 1992. *The impact of advertising law on business and public policy.* Westport, OT; London: Quorum Books.

Richards, J. I. 2000. *Advertising law & ethics.* http://advertising.utexas.edu/research/law/index.html (accessed 10 March 2005).

Sawant, P. B., and P. K. Bandyopadhyay. 2002. *Advertising law & ethics.* Dehli: Universal Law Publishing Co.

Wright, R. G. 1997. *Selling words—Free speech in a commercial culture.* New York: New York University Press.

Chapter 7

The Symbolic Meaning of Advertising

Katherine T. Frith
Jessie Xinyan Ho

Introduction

The conventional way that marketers define advertising is to describe it as messages that "impart information about products which consumers use to make brand choices" (Domzal and Kernan 1992). The limitation of this definition is that it falls short of giving us the whole picture. Advertising does much more than impart product information; it tells us what products signify and mean. It does this by marrying aspects of the product to aspects of culture. In other words, embedded in advertising's messages about goods and services are the cultural roles and cultural values that define who we are, how we live, and how we interact with others.

As an example, let us take a TV commercial that was shown around the world and won international awards (McAllister 1998). In this automobile advertisement, the manufacturer showed the car being driven through various countries. In China, the car passed by a group of Chinese people doing *tai chi* exercises on the Great Wall. In Mexico the car passed a Mexican farmer who was standing near the road wearing a big sombrero. In this way viewers around the world were shown glimpses of how people lived in other parts of the globe.

Yet, as we know, not everyone in China practices *tai chi*, nor does everyone in Mexico wear a sombrero. But by using certain symbols to represent other cultures the advertisers were able, in 30 seconds, to symbolically represent other parts of the world. By exaggerating or magnifying certain aspects of culture advertisers use symbolism and "magnification" to quickly get their message across. From the advertiser's point of view, the bottom line is profit and sales. Advertisers have little time for character development. The average reader of a magazine spends about four or five seconds on each page. Research on television viewing has confirmed that advertisers have only a few seconds to gain our attention, so the advertiser must compress the sales message. To show that a car is accepted by people worldwide, the easiest thing to do this is to use symbols like *tai chi* or sombreros to stereotype people.

In this chapter we look at some of the ways symbols are used in advertising. Advertisements reflect society, in a sometimes slightly distorted way, and by undressing the ad (Frith 1998) or demystifying the way advertising is symbolically constructed we can begin better to understand the meanings of advertising.

Undressing the Ad

It is important to understand that advertisements are not just messages about goods and service but are also social and cultural texts. Solomon (1988) has pointed out:

> As long as you are unable to decode the significance of ordinary things, and as long as you take the signs of your culture at face value, you will continue to be controlled by them. But once you see behind the surface of a sign into its hidden cultural significance, you can free yourself from that sign and perhaps find a new way of looking at the world. You will control the signs of your culture rather than having them control you. (p. 8)

To be able to read advertisements critically we must begin to incorporate "popular culture as a serious object of politics and analysis" (Giroux 1988, 164). While all culture is worthy of investigation, advertisements are often regarded as trivial or at best part of the mundane world of popular culture (McCracken 1982). However, in critically reading even something as seemingly insignificant as an advertisement we can begin to see "the political, social, and cultural forms of subordination that create inequities among different groups as they live out their lives" (Giroux 1988, 165). This type of critical reading enables students to view aspects of popular culture within a broader social, cultural, and political context. In the case of advertising, which has historically been linked to marketing and sales, it allows us to discover the broader social and cultural implications of these seemingly simple messages.

The benefits of critically examining the whole advertising message, not merely the surface or sales message, is that it helps to sharpen one's critical sensibilities. As McCracken (1982) points out, this can "counteract the non-critical response so often conditioned by the mass media" (p. 31). The methodological tools we will be using to deconstruct ads are interdisciplinary, drawing on a variety of theoretical positions including literary theory, feminist critique, postmodernism, and semiotic analysis. In fact demystification of any aspect of mass culture "is most successful when several methodologies are jointly employed" (McCracken 1982, 31).

One way to begin to understand what advertisements mean (Stern 1992) is to learn how to deconstruct them. Deconstruction is a critical theory of European origin (Saussure 1966; Barthes 1972; Levi-Strauss 1970; Foucault 1970; Lacan 1968). Its proponents find the real significance of texts not in their explicit meaning, nor even in their implied meaning, but in their unintentional meanings, or as one author states: "in the slips, evasions, and false analogies that betray the text's ideology" (McConnell 1990, 100). In essence, deconstruction is a way of reading against the text, or as John Fiske (1989) and Stuart Hall (1974) would say, taking an "oppositional" reading. The aim of deconstruction is to expose the social and political power structures in society that combine to produce the text.

We recognize that interpreting symbolic meaning by means of deconstruction, visual text analysis, oppositional reading, and similar qualitative approaches is unavoidably colored by the context of social and political values and beliefs brought to the task by the analyst. Bearing this in mind, the authors—one an American who has been living and teaching in Asia for more than a decade, the other a Singaporean who has spent considerable time in Hong Kong—shared the task and came to consensus on the findings.

Analyzing the cultural content of an advertisement involves interpreting both the verbal and visual aspects of the advertising text to determine not only the primary sales message but also additional secondary social or cultural messages. Advertisements reflect society, in a sometimes slightly distorted way (Pollay 1986), and by undressing or demystifying ads we can begin to see the role advertising plays in the creation of culture.

One of the most useful techniques for critically deconstructing both the surface and the deeper social and cultural meaning of advertisements is a form of visual textual analysis (Dyer 1982). As we begin to analyze the symbolic meaning of ads, you may find yourself disagreeing with some of our interpretations. This is because *not everyone holds the same beliefs*. Visual messages are polysemous, that is they can be interpreted in several different ways. In learning how others deconstruct advertising messages we begin to realize that advertising only "makes sense" when it resonates within certain belief systems.

To deconstruct an ad we must take it apart layer by layer, like peeling an onion. As we move from the surface message to deeper social messages you will begin see how this system of meaning works.

Analyzing Social Relationships

In his book, *Culture and the Ad: Exploring Otherness in the World of Advertising*, William O'Barr (1994) explains that all advertisements contain ideology. He defines ideology as "ideas that buttress and support a particular distribution of power in society" (p. 2) and notes that ideology is, by nature, always political. Wernick (1991) says that ideology is elided or hidden. In order to undress the ideological messages in advertising we must ask questions about the roles people play both in the ads and in society. Who is in charge? Who holds the power? Who is weak? Who is dominant and who is subordinate (O'Barr 1994)? These types of questions allow us to begin to see the deeper social structures that are circulated and recirculated in advertising.

Feminist scholars, for example, are able to expose hidden masculinist assumptions in advertising by using a method of sex-role reversal (Stern 1992). This can be done by asking yourself: can you exchange the man for the woman in the ad? Would the story still make sense, or would it seem ridiculous? Erving Goffman (1978) was the sociologist who first identified how certain advertising poses symbolized power relationships and how the positioning of women in submissive poses in ads reflected their inferior position in society. Thirty years ago he identified symbolic behaviors in advertising presentation and it is interesting to note that many of these poses are still used today in global advertisements (Frith and Mueller 2004).

In order to analyze the social relationships or symbolic power relationships in an ad you can begin by describing *the story* that is being depicted on the surface of the ad. First, describe the characters in the ad, the props, and the surface elements like the color scheme (Dyer 1982). Explain what the props or symbols signify and how they might support certain hierarchical relationships. Explain what the positioning of the models in the ads symbolizes. The ways in which models are posed symbolizes power structures. Who appears to have the power or control in the story? How is power expressed? Does one person have *power over* another? We can ascertain the power positions by determining who appears to be stronger, or bigger, or more in control of the situation (Goffman 1978).

Sometimes, by exchanging the characters in the ad, we can begin to see how certain types of roles are normalized by advertising. Take automobile advertising for example. Who is traditionally shown driving the car and who is in the passenger seat? Sometimes by exchanging the roles people play in ads we can determine what roles are considered "normal" in a society. Would it seem abnormal to see a woman driving the family car, for example? By exchanging the roles characters play in ads we can often reveal the deeper social structures that go unnoticed in everyday life. As Barbara Stern (1992) explains:

> The method's rationale is that exposure of cultural mores depends on a researcher's ability to engage in self-conscious introspection, for only by viewing what appears "normal" from an outsider's perspective—that of the "other"— can common assumptions about natural behavior be exposed as merely partial worldviews. (p. 12)

O'Barr (1994) points out that asking these types of questions enables us to discover important facts about social relationships that may be normally hidden from view. He points out that while equality is not precluded as a possible message in the discourse of advertising, advertisements are "seldom egalitarian" (p. 4). The most frequently depicted qualities of social relationships in advertising are: hierarchy, dominance, and subordination (O'Barr 1994).

Now let us look at an ad that appeared in the men's magazine, *FHM*, in Singapore in 2004. This ad also appeared in the men's magazine in Hong Kong since it was a regional ad. Singapore and Hong Kong have certain similarities in culture and language, so often global advertisers will run the same ad in both places as the advertisers consider Greater China to be one large market. While certain cultural values are similar there are obviously differences between Hong Kong and Singapore; nonetheless we can look at these ads from Singapore and examine how power is symbolically expressed. In this ad we will examine how cultural values are symbolically expressed.

Case Study: *Sennheiser* headphones (Figure 7.1)

The Surface Meaning of the Ad

In this ad we see a young man standing on the street with crowds walking by. He is casually dressed with the trendy look of messy hair and unshaven face. He has a pair of headphone on and his eyes are closed. The product is pictured at the bottom of the ad. The slogan above reads, "A Sanctuary of sound." The tagline below states, "Turn on, tune in and block out." The smaller text reads, "A hectic sidewalk. The rush-hour traffic. Wherever. With music you can escape the crowded urban jungle. Simply slip on a pair of Sennheiser headphones. And let the music take you someplace special. Full-sized sound. Compact design. Choose the PX series from Sennheiser for street ready performance." The sales message is that Sennheiser can give you quality music which will block out all other noises. The ad is aimed at young Asian men. The advertiser is trying to tap into the psyche of men who are trying to get away from the hectic lifestyle in Asia by saying that Sennheiser can offer refuge with quality sound.

Figure 7.1: An advertisement for Sennheiser headphones

Advertisement courtesy of Sennheiser Electronic Asia Pte Ltd.

The Symbolic Meaning of the Ad

In this ad, note that the background is blurred and out of focus and that the only thing in focus is the young man. Symbolically this ad advocates an alternative lifestyle of music and escapism. One might read it as saying that the only thing that this young man focuses on is his own individual wants and needs while society, represented by the blurred background, is less important. In fact this youth is in his own world; in his world, his music offers a symbolic "sanctuary of sound."

The cultural value of *individualism* is not a particularly strong cultural value in most Asian societies, which historically have tended to be more collectivist in structure. In Singapore all of the three major Asian races—the Chinese, the Malay, and the Indians—have certain shared values. In 1989, using "shared values" that reflect cross-cultural commonalities, the then Deputy Prime Minister Goh Chok Tong put forward a five-point set of shared values that has been used as a blueprint to forge a single national identity that all Singaporeans can abide by.

- Nation before community and society before self
- Family as the basic unit of society
- Community support and respect for the individual
- Consensus, not conflict
- Racial and religious harmony

It is interesting to note that the first value stresses "society before self." Yet the advertiser in this ad, Sennheiser, admonishes youth to "turn on, tune in and block out." Like most developing countries in Asia, Singaporean youth are getting messages from advertisers to adopt a more individualistic value system, to think of themselves as the basic unit of society, and to block out the more traditional values that surround them.

Conclusion

Advertising manipulates symbols to create meaning. The values expressed in advertising mirror the value systems of the advertisers. Advertisers are part of a commercial world, and their aim is to sell products and services. In this chapter we have traced a few of the methods that can be used to examine the symbolic world created in advertising and have deconstructed two ads that appeared in one of the men's magazines that is sold in Singapore.

The argument here is not so much that advertising is intrinsically problematic but rather that advertising creates symbolic meanings and then circulates and recirculates these values and myths, thus shaping our attitudes and beliefs. The importance of studying the symbolic messages in advertisements is that it allows us to move away from the role of spectator to become more conscious of the ways in which symbols are used to create meaning in advertising.

References

Barthes, R. 1972. *Mythologie.* New York: Hill and Wang.

Domzal, T. J., and J. B. Kernan. 1992. Reading advertising: The what and how of product meaning. *Journal of Consumer Marketing* 9(3):48–64.

Dyer, G. 1982. *Advertising as communication.* London: Methuen.

Fiske, J. 1989. *Reading the popular.* Boston: Unwin Hyman. a–b

Foucault, M. 1970. *The order of things.* London: Tavistock.

Frith, K. T. 1998. *Undressing the ad: Reading culture in advertising.* New York: Peter Lang.

———, and B. Mueller. 2004 *Advertising and societies: Global issues.* New York: Peter Lang.

Giroux, H. 1988. Border pedagogy in the age of postmodernism. *Journal of Education* 170(3):162–81.

Goffman, E. 1978. *Gender advertisements.* Cambridge, MA: Harvard University Press.

Hall, S. 1974. Encoding and decoding. *Education and culture.* Birmingham, UK: Centre for Cultural Studies.

Lacan, J. 1968. *The language of self.* New York: Basic Books.

Levi-Strauss, C. 1970. *The raw and the cooked.* London: Jonathan Cape.

McAllister, M. 1998. Sponsorship, globalization and the summer olympics. In K. T. Frith, ed. *Undressing the ad: Reading culture in advertising.* NY: Peter Lang.

McConnell, F. D. 1990. Will deconstruction be the death of literature? *The Wilson Quarterly* 4.

McCracken, E. 1982. Demystifying *Cosmopolitan:* Five critical methods. *Journal of Popular Culture* 16(2):30–42.

O'Barr, W. 1994. *Culture and the ad: Exploring otherness in the world of advertising.* Boulder, CO: Westview.

Pollay, R. 1986. The distorted mirror: Reflections on the unintended consequences of advertising. *Journal of Marketing* 50(2):18–36.

Saussure, F. 1966. *Course in general linguistics* (Trans. Wade Baskin). New York: McGraw Hill.

Solomon, J. 1988. *The signs of our times.* Los Angeles: Jeremy Tarcher.

Stern, B. 1992. Feminist literary theory and advertising research: A new "reading" of the text and the consumer. *Journal of Current Issues and Research in Advertising* 14(1):9–21.

Wernick, A. 1991. *Promotional culture: Advertising, ideology and symbolic expression.* Newbury Park, CA: Sage.

Chapter 8

Advertising and Consumer Culture

Susanna Wai-yee Kwok

Introduction

*T*he omnipresence of advertising and its success in attracting attention and promoting ideas have managed to permeate our daily lives and beliefs. Today, advertising jingles, slogans, and selling phrases are perhaps more popular and influential than any other doctrines, beliefs, or ideologies. Reports have also shown that the institutions of family, religion, and education have become noticeably weaker over the past few decades (Barnouw 1978; Berman 1981; Real 1977; Skolimowski 1977) whereas the potential for advertisements to penetrate our consciousness and channel our very modes of thinking are seen as plausible—if not for individual advertisements then at least for advertisements in aggregate.

Advertising is not merely an economic tool aimed at selling; it is an ideological mirror of consumer society and a cultural expression of the changing norms and collective values of its contemporaries (Marchand 1985; Skov and Moeran 1995; Cheung and Ma 1999). In this chapter the "reflection hypothesis" is proposed in order to review the history and development of Hong Kong newspaper advertisements and the cultural values manifested in them over the past 50 years, from 1949 to

1998.[1] The textual part of the study will be cross-analyzed within the political, social, economic, and cultural environment of Hong Kong to provide a holistic view in understanding the cultural characteristics and values that are being conveyed in the advertisements. The findings will serve as a base from which to discern the role of advertising as a carrier of cultural values in Hong Kong. They will also help to examine the importance of advertising as a medium for the construction of reality in a society.

Advertising as a Carrier of Cultural Values

Advertising is an economic as well as a representational practice. Its aim is to persuade people to buy a product, to increase sales and thus maximize profits. But it is also a cultural practice because, in order to sell it must first appeal, and in order to appeal it must engage with the values and meanings the product has accumulated within a culture and try to construct an identification between the consumers and those cultural values (Gay et al. 1997). Williamson (1978) in her book also explicitly stated that advertisements were one of the most important cultural factors moulding and reflecting current lifestyle. They were a ubiquitous and inevitable part of everyone's lives, and exerted a tremendous influence on cultural development.

On the cultural effects of advertisements, Pollay (1986) and Holbrook (1987) addressed the issue of to what extent advertisements mirror or shape our society. Pollay stated that advertisements were a "distorted mirror" with troubling images, whereas Holbrook contended that the nature of advertisements was pluralistic, and the ability of advertisements to distort was mild and gentle. However, both views lead to the crucial concern that advertisements do exert a cultural effect on society and further research to investigate this issue is recommended.

Previous Cultural Studies on Hong Kong Advertising

A study by Kwok and Wong (1995) concluded that Hong Kong culture is moving towards "a Western style urban consuming society." The interpretation of text and image with respect to the advertised product still remained at the "image-thing" and "functional appropriation" level.

Chan (1999) examined newspaper advertisements over the past 50 years and concluded that the set of dominant values was a combination of utilitarian and symbolic values that laid emphasis on product features as well as human feelings.

Wong (1999a) conducted a longitudinal study of Hong Kong advertising and concluded that "the development process of the production of meanings in advertising and the transformation of Hong Kong culture and society was in fact the advancement of a progressive hierarchy of needs." Wong (1999b) gave an historical account of Hong Kong newspaper advertisements and suggested that advertisements collected from past newspapers not only witnessed the growth in professionalism of the advertising industry in Hong Kong, it also depicted the role of a particular product at a specific period of time and its changes with the advent of a materialistic culture within the Hong Kong context.

A review of past studies of the cultural history of advertising show that scholars agree that there is a correlation between advertising and cultural values. However, there is a divergence on whether these reconstructed values manifested in advertisements merely mirror society, or have been designed to shape it. In historical longitudinal studies the agreed common ground is that the values manifested in advertising reflect the changes in social trends.

Construction of Reality

Back in the twenties, Lippmann in his book *Public Opinion* (1965) noted that people could not possibly experience most events on a firsthand basis.

> For the environment is altogether too big, too complex, and too fleeting for direct acquaintance ..., we have to reconstruct it on a simpler model before we can manage with it (p. 11).

The concept of the "social construction of reality" was first developed by Berger and Luckmann (1966) and later elaborated on and discussed by various communication scholars. Adoni and Mane (1984) used the concept to explain interactions among individuals, society, and culture, while Tuchman (1978) and others also applied the concept in analyzing news in the media. They suggested that the world of everyday life is a world originating in people's thoughts and actions, and is maintained as real by the continuous indoctrination of particular values through different social vehicles such as the mass media.

Under the sociology of knowledge, human reality is defined as socially constructed reality. It perceives society as part of a human world, made by people, inhabited by people, and in turn making people into an ongoing historical process. Human beings depend on the knowledge they obtain from different social vehicles (newspaper advertisements in this study) to construct their picture of the world. On the other hand, advertisers in planning their campaigns also need to consider the "social reality," i.e., the constraints of the contextual environment. As a result, some academicians and practitioners have suggested that advertising follows and reflects but never leads society; it "reflects" rather than "moulds" social reality. Thus the "reflection hypothesis" suggested in this study appears pertinent to an understanding of advertising and its relationship to cultural values.

The Reflection Hypothesis

The phrase "reflection hypothesis" is borrowed from Tuchman (1978) and the section on "reflection theory" in the book edited by O'Sullivan and others (1994).

The "reflection hypothesis" suggests that the mass media reflects the dominant social values in a society, which means that the advertisers have their own agenda for the target market. The hypothesis supports the argument that in order to play safe and attract audience, the media will have to reflect social values that appeal to a heterogeneous group whose interests are diverse and whose orientations are more inclined towards being conservative. It is also suggested that as the mass media, in this case advertisements, has to attract audience who are generally interested in familiar images, the content cannot move too far ahead of public opinion. Hence the gatekeepers or advertisers need to feel safe and to be contemporary (Wilson 1981).

With regard to the "reflection hypothesis" (Figure 8.1) the media have to reflect social reality or values, especially the dominant values in

Figure 8.1: The Reflection Hypothesis

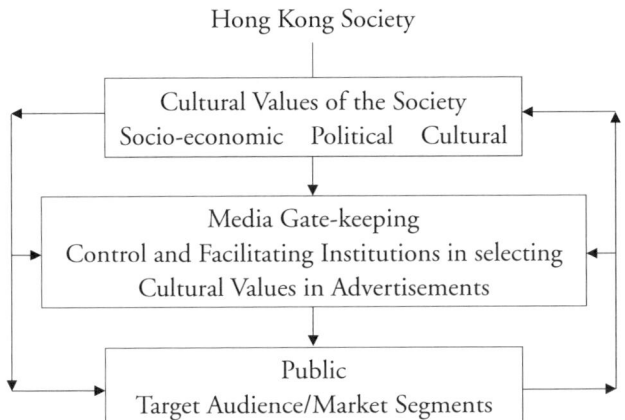

Hong Kong Society

Cultural Values of the Society
Socio-economic   Political   Cultural

Media Gate-keeping
Control and Facilitating Institutions in selecting
Cultural Values in Advertisements

Public
Target Audience/Market Segments

society, in order to attract an audience. It is important to note that this is not a model with unidirectional flow. All the variables assert a certain degree of influence forwards and backwards in the model. As Shooter (1984) has indicated, communication determines how reality is experienced and the experience of reality affects communication. In addition, whatever the circumstances, media gatekeepers (advertisers) have to direct their advertising messages towards the public that they wish to persuade and influence. In this way the target public indirectly exerts an influence on the manner in which advertisers make their decisions. What they reflect in their advertisements is an already-existing and self-evident reality that exists independently of its representation in the media. The doctrine (the advertising discourse) should have its form, substance, or actions explained in terms of a form, substance, or agency outside it (Hong Kong society).

The concepts and theories reviewed above form the basis of the research question in this study:

How were different social realities (cultural values) portrayed in the media, (symbolic social reality—newspaper advertisements) by different advertisers to different social classes (target audience/market segments) within Hong Kong society during the period from 1949 to 1998?

A Content Analysis Study of Newspaper Advertisements (1949–1998)

With regard to the latitudinal aspect of the study, "foodstuff" and "clothing" display advertisements in Hong Kong were analyzed across four different newspapers which catered for different market segments. As for the longitudinal aspect of the study, the two above-mentioned categories of advertisement in Hong Kong were analyzed within the local context against its different stages of development.

Time Spans

After considering the socio-economic, political, and cultural developments in Hong Kong, Chan's demarcation dividing the study period into three different stages (Chan 1992) was adopted.

1st Time Span	The Refugee Society in a Borrowed Place (1949–1967)
2nd Time Span	Rise of Local Identity and Economic Takeoff (1968–1984)
3rd Time Span	Political Transition and Gradual Democratisation (1984–1998)

As indicated in Table 8.1, the first time span commenced with the influx of more than 2 million refugees in 1949. They treated Hong Kong as a temporary home, but they helped Hong Kong to build up its industry. This stage ended with the extended riots in 1967, which also marked the birth of the television era in Hong Kong. The second time span coincided with the period when a Hong Kong identity was being established and an affluent middle class was emerging. Industrial growth was rapid and the Hong Kong economy started to take off. It ended with the completion of the Sino-British Joint Declaration in 1984, which marked the beginning of the long transitional period leading to the transfer of sovereignty in 1997. This span also witnessed the increasing penetration of mass media, especially television, within the territory. Lastly, the third time span witnessed endless Sino-British negotiations and arguments, the birth of party politics, and gradual democratization.

Hong Kong suffered from spasmodic setbacks in economic growth due to the political impact of these processes and, culturally, from being at a crossroads between resinicization and globalization. In communications development a growing diversification of the media with the introduction of satellite television and cable television was observed during this time.

Table 8.1: Hong Kong 1949–1998

1st Time Span 1949–1967	2nd Time Span 1968–1984	3rd Time Span 1985–1998
Political	Political	Political
• British colony: centralized powers, Governor had absolute power	• There was not much reform of the political system	• Radical political reform introduced in 1992 by Governor Patten, this encouraged greater democracy and freedom of expression
• Westerners were superior	• Student Movements in 1970s especially in universities	• Sino-British negotiations, severe discrepancy and tension
• Political refugees, transitory	• Sino-British negotiations in the early 1980s	• Growth of political and pressure groups
• 1967 Riot	• Sino-British Joint Declaration signed in 1984	• Basic Law issued in 1990
		• Transfer of sovereignty in 1997
Social	Social	Social
• Influx of more than 2 millions Chinese refugees	• Number of people born locally increased, roots in Hong Kong	• Political transition caused a serious brain drain, need to coagulate the society
• Overcrowding, poor living conditions	• Hong Kong identity began to be established	• Return to motherland, some advocated patriotism
• Hope for a stable livelihood	• Recreation of social strata	• Expansion of tertiary education, better educated
• Elite education, lack of opportunities for the general public	• Emergence of affluent middle class	• More outspoken
• Lack of medical care	• Free primary education	• Better quality of life
• Emotionally, strong ties with the mainland	• Institutionalized social welfare	• Greater consumer satisfaction
	• Rising consumption	• Environmental concern
	• Growth of nuclear family	

Table 8.1 (Cont'd)

1st Time Span 1949–1967	2nd Time Span 1968–1984	3rd Time Span 1985–1998
Economic • Growth of manufacturing industry • Invariably long working hours • Surplus labor • In the 1950s, wages for unskilled workmen was about $3–5/day	Economic • International trade center • Successful business • Better infrastructure and cultural venue • In the 1960s, wages for unskilled workmen were about $6–15.80/day; $14–31.50 in mid-1970s	Economic • Spasmodic setbacks in economic growth • Developed country • Affluent society • Gateway to China • Growth of service industry • High spending power, "company added values" • In 1997, per capita GDP at constant (1990) market prices was over four times that of 1967 • Average wages were $11,384/month
Cultural • Mainland refugees vs. local Hong Kong population • Survival over modern city life • Adhere to traditional rural values	Cultural • People born locally move away from traditional values • From "rags-to-riches" • Materialistic consumption • Rapid influx and strong influence of western ideas • Localization, domestically-produced TV programs	Cultural • Materialistic society • Fashion conscious, indulge in brand names and labels • Constant influx of ideas from abroad • 1997 issue, identity crisis in early 1990s • Resinicization, cultural internationalization • Patriotic and affectionate to Chinese culture • Hong Kong culture, based on own experiences and developments
Media • Newspapers and radio only • Wired TV in 1957, limited subscribers • Wireless TV by end of 1967	Media • Increasing penetration of mass media: TV, newspapers and radio • Local Cantonese pops became popular	Media • Diversification of the media: Satellite TV and Cable TV • Cut-throat price wars in the newspaper industry • Sensational reporting of *Oriental Daily* and *Apple Daily*

Types of Advertisements Studied

A popular Chinese proverb says: "clothing" (*yi*), "food" (*shi*), "residence" (*zhu*), and "transport" (*xing*) are the four basic necessities for human beings. It would thus be of great significance to analyze these four categories of advertisements throughout the study period in order to identify fundamental values. However in the fifties and early sixties the Hong Kong population was still suffering from the effects of poverty and was still fighting for survival. Cars and real estate were beyond people's means, and advertisements for them were rare. This research, therefore, concentrates on the first two items, "foodstuff" and "clothing," in order to obtain a productive comparison across the different time periods.

Besides food, the term "foodstuff" in this research was also defined as including beverages such as tea, milk, coffee, fruit juice, and their equivalents, which are essential to families nowadays. Restaurant advertisements, which were oriented towards food consumption, were also studied. Altogether eight subproduct categories were grouped under the heading "foodstuff," namely, family food, beverages and tea, soft drinks, snacks, health food, restaurants, supermarket/food stores and others. The category "clothing" included product subcategories such as men's wear, women's wear, children's wear, underwear/hosiery and accessories such as footwear. Retail advertisements for clothing such as boutiques/department stores that emphasise clothing, tailoring and others were also included.

Selection of Newspapers

This research studied four different newspapers that catered for different market segments,[2] namely, *Sing Tao Daily* (Sing Tao), *South China Morning Post* (SCMP), *Sing Pao Daily News* (Sing Pao), and *Ming Pao Daily* (Ming Pao), which covered 38% of the total newspaper readership in the mid-eighties although this dropped to only 15% by the end of 1998 after the newspapers price war. By the end of 1998, Ming Pao with 5% of the newspaper readership was ranked as the third best selling newspaper in Hong Kong, followed by Sing Pao and SCMP (both at 4%), and lastly Sing Tao with 2% of the newspaper readership (ACNeilsen 1990; 1999).

Comparing the readership profiles of the four newspapers with government statistics from the by-census conducted in 1996, we can better understand the demographic differences between the newspapers' readers. The official statistics showed that at the age of 15 and over, only 21.3% of the Hong Kong population (Census and Statistics Department 1996) had attained a post secondary/university level education. Sixty-one percent of the SCMP readership however reported having had post-secondary/university education, and 39% and 34% of the Ming Pao and Sing Tao readership respectively. Sing Pao, at 12% was the only newspaper that has a readership profile showing lower levels of educational achievement than is average in Hong Kong. As for monthly household income, nearly 24.9% of Hong Kong households earned HK$30,000 or above. However, SCMP reported 45% and Ming Pao 22% of their readership as earning HK$35,000 or above per month. Sing Tao and Sing Pao reported 13% and 17% of their readers earning HK$35,000 or above. In conclusion, the readers of SCMP are definitely the wealthiest segment of society. Ming Pao caters for the middle or middle-upper class, while Sing Tao and Sing Pao are for the middle-lower class.

Sampling of Advertisements

The four different newspapers were examined within the time frame of January 1, 1949 to December 31, 1998. As Ming Pao was first published in 1959, it was therefore examined from this time until December 1998.

All "foodstuff" and "clothing" display advertisements in the four newspapers were included in this study. Identical advertisements were also included as their high frequency would definitely have a significant impact on their target audience. Systematic random sampling was used and every newspaper published on the sixteenth of every alternate month was studied.

Framework of Cultural Values

Content analysis was used to study and analyze the cultural values found in Hong Kong newspaper advertisements in a systematic, objective, and quantitative manner. The headlines, captions, body copy, and illustrations of the sampled advertisements were thoroughly examined in order to decide what the manifested cultural values were. The present study employed a different method compared to that used in past studies of cultural values. Instead of a single dominant value based on the overall impression of the advertisement, every cue that was related to all of the items suggested in the operational definitions of cultural values was coded, as an advertisement would convey more than one cultural value.

The Cheng and Schweitzer cultural values framework, a modification of Pollay's (1983) framework, was adopted in this study. After a pilot test, four values that applied in the unique Hong Kong situation were added including "variety," "professional," "from/of abroad," plus an "unclassified" category (Table 8.2).

Table 8.2: Framework of cultural values

Values	Operational definitions
Adventure	This value suggests boldness, daring, bravery, courage, or thrill. Skydiving is a typical example.
Beauty	This value suggests that the use of a product will enhance the loveliness, attractiveness, elegance, or handsomeness of an individual.
Collectivism	The emphasis here is on the individual in relation to others typically in the reference group. Individuals are depicted as integral parts of the group.
Competition	The emphasis here is on distinguishing a product from its counterparts by aggressive comparisons. While explicit comparisons may not mention the competitor's name, implicit comparisons may use such words as "number one" or "leader."
Convenience	A product is suggested to be handy and easy to use.
Courtesy	Politeness and friendship toward the consumer are shown through the use of polished and affable language in the commercial.
Economy	The inexpensive, affordable, and cost-saving nature of a product is emphasized in the commercial.
Effectiveness	A product is suggested to be powerful and capable of achieving certain ends.
Enjoyment	This value suggests that a product will make its user wild with joy. Typical examples include the capital fun that beer or soda drinkers demonstrate in some commercials.

Table 8.2 (Cont'd)

Family	The emphasis here is on family life and family members. The commercials stress family scenes: getting married, companionship of siblings, kinship, being at home, and suggest that a certain product is good for the whole family.
Health	This value recommends that the use of a product will enhance or improve the vitality, soundness, strength, and robustness of the body.
Individualism	The emphasis here is on the self-sufficiency and self-reliance of an individual, or on the individual as being distinct and unlike others.
Leisure	This value suggests that the use of a product will bring one comfort or relaxation.
Magic	The emphasis here is on the miraculous effect and nature of a product, e.g., "Bewitch your man," "Heals like magic."
Modernity	The notion of being new, contemporary, up-to-date, and ahead of the times is emphasized in a commercial.
Natural	This value suggests spiritual harmony between man and nature by making references to the elements, animals, vegetables, or minerals.
Neatness	The notion of being clean and tidy is stressed in a commercial.
Nurturance	This value stresses giving charity, help, protection, support, or sympathy to the weak, disabled, young, or elderly.
Patriotism	The love of and the loyalty to one's own nation inherent in the nature or in the use of a product are suggested.
Popularity	The focus here is on the universal recognition and acceptance of a certain product by consumers, e.g., "Best seller," "Well-known nationwide or worldwide".
Quality	The emphasis here is on the excellence and durability of a product, which is usually claimed to be a winner of medals or certificates awarded by a government department for its high grade or is demonstrated by the product's excellent performance.
Respect for the Elderly	The commercials display a respect for older people by using a model of old age or asking for the opinions, recommendations, and advice of the elders.
Safety	The reliable and secure nature of a product is emphasized.
Sex	The commercial uses glamorous and sensual models or has a background of lovers holding hands, embracing, or kissing to promote a product.

Table 8.2 (Cont'd)

Social Status	The use of a product is claimed to be able to elevate the position or rank of the user in the eyes of others. The feeling of prestige, trend-setting, and pride in the use of a product is conveyed. The promotion of a company manager's status or frame by quoting his words or showing his picture in the commercial is also included.
Technology	Here the advanced and sophisticated technical skills to engineer and manufacture a particular product are emphasized.
Tradition	The experience of the past, customs, and conventions are respected. The qualities of being historical, time-honored and legendary are venerated, e.g., "With eighty years of manufacturing experience," "It's adapted from ancient Chinese prescriptions."
Uniqueness	The unrivaled, incomparable, and unparalleled nature of a product is emphasized, e.g., "We're the only one that offers you the product."
Wealth	This value conveys the idea that being affluent, prosperous, and rich should be encouraged and suggests that a certain product or service will make the user well-off.
Wisdom	This value shows respect for knowledge, education, intelligence, expertise, or experience.
Work	This value shows respect for diligence and dedication of one's labor and skills. A typical example is that a medication has given back to a desperate patient his or her ability to work.
Youth	The worship of the younger generation is shown through the depiction of younger models. The rejuvenating benefits of the product are stressed, e.g., "Feel young again!"
From/Of Abroad	This value indicates that there is an appreciation for goods from abroad or originates from abroad, e.g., "Chocolate from Swiss."
Authority	This value shows respect for professionals or endorsement from experts.
Variety	To indicates that diversity and choices are being offered, and people have freedom of choice.
Unclassified	Advertisements that are information based only. No cultural values listed above are manifested.

Source: Modified from Cheng and Schweitzer (1996)

Cultural Values in Advertisements

Altogether a total of 4,080 advertisements were studied. The SCMP had the largest number of advertisements: in total 2,071 advertisements were studied (50.8%). Ming Pao had the second largest number—712 advertisements (17.5%) were studied. This was followed by Sing Pao (693 ads at 17%) and Sing Tao (604 ads at 14.8%). There was a drastic drop in the number of "foodstuff" and "clothing" advertisements found in Sing Tao during the third time span (68 ads only); this was due to the fact that it had repositioned itself in the late eighties as an authoritative real estate newspaper. On the whole there was a steady decline in the aggregate total of sampled advertisements in the newspapers over the three time spans, especially with the growing popularity of television in the third time span.

Aggregate Cultural Values by Time Spans

As for the aggregate cultural values of the four newspapers measured over time, the F-value indicates that 24 out of the 35 value categories proved to show considerable change across the study period ("unclassified" excluded). This clearly indicates that the cultural values manifested in advertisements did evolve with the societal changes occurring in Hong Kong. Table 8.3 highlights the top 10 most frequently used cultural values included in the four newspapers within the three different time spans. The percentage beside the value, for example, "quality" for the first time span (1949–1967), shows that more than 29% of the total number of sampled advertisements from this time span were found to convey the value of "quality." It was also the most frequently conveyed value in that period. Among the top ten most frequently used cultural values, seven of them showed a significant change in use over time (i.e., "economy," "quality," "variety," "from/of abroad," "enjoyment," "modernity," "competition," and "collectivism") (Table 8.3). This clearly indicates that the cultural values manifested in advertisements did vary with time.

Table 8.3 shows that "economy" (34.4%) was the most frequently used value, except during the first time span (1949–1967). Other frequently used values across the whole study period were "quality"

Table 8.3: Top 10 most frequently used cultural values by time spans
(Aggregate Total)

	1949–1967 (N=1669/19 years)		1968–1984 (N=1384/17 years)		1985–1998 (N=1027/14 years)		Aggregate Total (N=4080/50 years)		F-value
		%		%		%		%	
1	Quality	29.1	Economy	37.0	Economy	41.5	Economy	34.4	29.4***
2	Economy	27.9	From/Of Abroad	25.9	Variety	28.1	Quality	26.4	6.9***
3	Variety	23.9	Quality	25.9	From/Of Abroad	25.2	Variety	24.8	4.1*
4	From/Of Abroad	19.6	Variety	23.5	Quality	22.7	From/Of Abroad	22.6	8.7***
5	Enjoyment	18.0	Modernity	16.8	Enjoyment	18.2	Enjoyment	16.7	5.2**
6	Health	14.6	Enjoyment	14.1	Collectivism	14.6	Modernity	14.3	6.3**
7	Competition	14.3	Competition	14.0	Courtesy	13.6	Competition	13.4	3.4*
8	Modernity	13.7	Beauty	12.9	Popularity	12.8	Popularity	12.9	0.2
9	Popularity	13.3	Popularity	12.5	Modernity	11.9	Collectivism	12.2	4.0*
10	Leisure	11.6	Collectivism	11.8	Beauty	11.1	Beauty	11.9	1.0

*   p < 0.05
**   p < 0.01
*** p < 0.001

(26.4%), "variety" (24.8%), "from/of abroad" (22.6%) and "enjoyment" (16.7%), and all remained in the top five most frequently used values throughout the study period.

"Economy" exhibited a significant growth in the second and third time spans. This seemed to contradict the societal and economic advances in Hong Kong that commenced in the late sixties. Nevertheless by identifying the products and reading between the lines it was found that clothing advertisers were actually launching all kinds of "sales," such as Christmas and New Year sales, to persuade consumers to buy more for themselves or as gifts for friends whereas these were relatively rare in the fifties. The crucial characteristics of the fashion industry are to be fashionable and up-to-date. Hence it is a practice of the fashion industry to clear their stock before the next season commences, thus realizing the stock into funds for further production. In the eighties and nineties a large proportion of the clothing category advertisements were for international brand names that practised such a marketing cycle, which involved a number of sales within a given year.

Two similar studies on "foodstuff"[3] advertisements conducted by the author earlier reported that the use of "economy" showed a comparatively greater discrepancy across different newspapers than that seen in the present study. In comparing the SCMP with Sing Tao and Sing Pao, it was found that only around 11% of the advertisements examined in the SCMP conveyed the value of "economy," whereas of those examined in the latter two papers a total of nearly 29% and 40% respectively were found to convey this value (Kwok 2000a; 2000b). These results imply that the unique marketing cycle of the clothing industry has a significant impact on the kind of cultural values manifested in the advertisements.

Cultural Values by Newspapers

Analyzing the correlation of cultural values across the four different newspapers to see whether a cultural spectrum existed in Hong Kong was essential in this research. Nevertheless, it should be noted that the samples from the four newspapers were out of proportion.[4] In order to understand the differences or similarities between the Chinese and English media, the author recoded the newspapers into two groups:

Chinese newspapers included Sing Tao, Sing Pao, and Ming Pao with a total of sampled advertisements at 2,009 whilst the SCMP represented English newspapers with 2,071 advertisements. *T*-tests were conducted to analyze the change of cultural values in newspapers of different languages. The recoding was also meaningful in view of the demographic differences of the four different newspapers.

Advertisements in SCMP, which were targeted at the wealthier level of society with higher education and better incomes, witnessed a demand for more entertainment in life. Among the top 10 most frequently used values, seven of them showed a significant change over time in terms of the percentage measured (i.e., "variety," "quality," "from/of abroad," "economy," "enjoyment," "modernity," and "uniqueness.") (Table 8.4).

To this target group of people, foodstuff and clothing were much more than basic necessities and to them the emphasis was on the "quality" of the product, diversity, and choice, and even the product originality. As Table 8.4 shows, "variety" (25.8%) scored the highest frequency followed by "quality" (24.7%) and "from/of abroad" (24.4%) respectively. It was also observed throughout this research that there was a marketing cycle in the clothing industry with seasonal sales that emphasized cost-saving. The marketing cycles of the fashion industry mentioned previously could explain why "economy" was among the top 5 most frequently used values in SCMP, which caters for the middle and upper classes.

If we compare the top 10 most frequently used aggregate cultural values by newspapers, Chinese combined against SCMP, Table 8.4 indicates that 8 of them show a significant difference between the two different kinds of newspapers.

In analyzing the values from utilitarian and symbolic dimension[5] Chinese newspapers had a higher score for the utilitarian dimension; values such as "economy" and "quality." On the other hand, English newspapers, namely SCMP, scored higher for the symbolic dimension; values such as "from/of abroad," "enjoyment," and "beauty" (Table 8.5). The results to a large extent are found to conform to the readership profiles of and differences between the two kinds of newspapers. Readers of the Chinese newspapers tended to be in the lower income brackets. The advertisers, therefore, emphasized quality products at affordable or

Table 8.4: Top 10 most frequently used cultural values by time span (SCMP)

	1949–1967 (N=1046/19 years)	%	1968–1984 (N=670/17 years)	%	1985–1998 (N=355/14 years)	%	Aggregate Total (N=2071/50 years)	%	F-value
1	Quality	29.4	From/Of Abroad	29.7	From/Of Abroad	29.0	Variety	25.8	4.9**
2	Variety	28.0	Economy	27.3	Variety	27.6	Quality	24.7	20.7***
3	Enjoyment	21.4	Quality	23.7	Economy	25.6	From/Of Abroad	24.4	14.1***
4	Economy	20.0	Variety	21.5	Enjoyment	15.8	Economy	23.3	6.8***
5	From/Of Abroad	19.5	Competition Modernity	16.7	Quality	12.7	Enjoyment	17.9	9.6***
6	Competition	16.6	–		Tradition	12.4	Competition	15.8	2.9
7	Beauty	14.6	Beauty	13.6	Beauty	11.8	Modernity	14.2	3.4*
8	Leisure	13.8	Enjoyment	13.4	Competition	11.5	Beauty	13.8	0.9
9	Modernity	13.7	Uniqueness	11.9	Modernity	11.0	Leisure	12.1	2.7
10	Convenience	11.8	Leisure	10.3	Leisure	10.7	Uniqueness	9.6	3.3*

*   p < 0.05
**   p < 0.01
*** p < 0.001

Table 8.5: Top 10 most frequently used cultural values by newspapers (Chinese combined against SCMP)

		Chinese Newspapers Combined N=2,009 %	SCMP N=2,071 %	*t*-value
1	Economy	45.8	23.3	4.0***
2	Quality	28.1	24.7	2.4*
3	Variety	23.8	25.8	1.5
4	From/Of Abroad	20.8	24.4	2.8**
5	Enjoyment	15.5	17.9	1.9*
6	Modernity	14.4	14.2	0.2
7	Competition	10.9	15.8	4.5***
8	Popularity	17.4	8.5	8.4***
9	Collectivism	16.1	8.4	7.5***
10	Beauty	9.9	13.8	3.9***

*   p < 0.05
**   p < 0.01
*** p < 0.001

cost-saving prices, and they adopted a more practical, down-to-earth, and realistic approach. Also the readers, who were mostly Chinese, valued "family" and "collectivism" and hence most of the restaurant advertisements stressed that dining out was a good chance for family gatherings, and that buying clothes as gifts for family was essential especially at festivals.

On the other hand, aiming at SCMP readers with higher income levels, advertisers placed emphasis on value-added features rather than the basic values. They stressed that their products were "from/of abroad," that eating out was for "enjoyment" of the food and the environment, and lastly, their products would enhance the attractiveness ("beauty") of their target audience. Thus, advertisements in SCMP emphasized hedonism, the pursuit of high living and self-gratification.

Cultural Values by Products

In the process of the analysis an additional factor not considered at the beginning of the study emerged and deserves mentioning. That is that different products would to a great extent exert influence on the kind of cultural values conveyed in the advertisements, for instance, as seen in the marketing cycle of the clothing retail industry.

Performing the *t*-test for cultural values by product showed that 26 out of the 35 cultural values exhibited significant differences at the 0.05 confidence level. For the top 10 most frequently used cultural values by products, Table 8.6 shows that although 6 of them were the same (i.e., "economy," "variety," "from/of abroad," "quality," "popularity," and "competition"), their percentages of frequency of use varied widely. The most used value by clothing advertisers was "economy" at more than 44% but the frequency of use for this value was only 25.7% for foodstuff advertisements. This high frequency could also illustrate the impact of the marketing cycle found in the clothing industry mentioned earlier. Furthermore, the diversity and variety of the product (32.5%), and whether the product originated from abroad (28.6%), were major selling points for the clothing advertisers in attracting their target audience.

On the other hand, "quality" (31.4%) ranked first for foodstuff advertisements and this only held fifth place in clothing advertisements with around 21% usage. The freshness and quality of the food were the main selling points for foodstuff advertisers. Restaurant owners were also keen to portray dining out at their restaurants as enjoyable

Table 8.6: Top 10 most frequently used cultural values by products

	Clothing N=1,905	(%)	Foodstuff N=2,175	(%)
1	Economy	44.3	Quality	31.4
2	Variety	32.5	Enjoyment	29.3
3	From/Of Abroad	28.6	Economy	25.7
4	Modernity	23.5	Health	18.8
5	Beauty	21.5	Variety	18.1
6	Quality	20.7	Competition	17.9
7	Leisure	12.5	Collectivism	17.5
8	Popularity	8.5	From/Of Abroad	17.4
9	Competition	8.2	Popularity	16.8
10	Professional	7.8	Convenience	13.1

events ("enjoyment" at 29.3%). Furthermore, this pleasant experience could be achieved at a reasonable or affordable price ("economy" at 25.7%).

Among the 26 values which showed significant difference, it was found that 17 of them were closely correlated with foodstuff advertisements and the other 9 values were more often conveyed in clothing advertisements. In addition it was found that foodstuff advertisements tended to be more utilitarian and clothing advertisements to adopt more symbolic values. Besides "economy," "convenience," "effectiveness," "health," and "quality" were more likely to be manifested in foodstuff advertisements; the family or health food popular in the first time span placed strong emphasis on health consciousness and the effectiveness of products. Values like "adventure," "beauty," "individualism," "leisure," "modernity," "sex," "variety," and "from/of abroad" were however more likely to be conveyed in clothing advertisements. Ideas like beauty and sexiness or suggestions that wearing a particular dress would make one distinctive and attractive were prominent in clothing advertisements. Further, the up-to-date style, variety of choice, and design originating from abroad were the main emphasis of and prominent in clothing advertisements.

Moreover, values like "family" and "collectivism" were found in restaurant advertisements as the Chinese newspapers stressed that dining out was a good opportunity for a family gathering and advertisements in English newspapers emphasised that it could provide a relaxing occasion for a social gathering.

Conclusion

A total of 4,080 advertisements were analyzed and the "reflection hypothesis" was supported by the results. Findings indicate that there was a significant change in product nature[6] and values conveyed in newspaper advertisements over different time spans. There was also a significant difference between values highlighted in different newspapers, which were aimed at different target audiences. Hence the "reconstructed reality" in newspaper advertisements has reflected the evolution of cultural values over time and across the different socioeconomic sectors of Hong

Kong society over the past 50 years. It was also found that product nature had a significant influence on the values conveyed in advertisements. The results showed that there was a strong association among the list of cultural values used by the advertisers, their contemporary contextual environment, and also their target customers.

Analysis of the results indicated that as Hong Kong society became more affluent there was a shift from basic physiological needs to esteem needs. The use of utilitarian values constantly declined; on the other hand the use of symbolic values steadily increased over time. This indicates a close correlation with socioeconomic developments in Hong Kong as shown in Table 8.1.

The conclusions drawn are further illustrated in the summary shown in Table 8.7, in which all of the analyses yielded positive results and supported the research question. Cultural values proved to vary over time, among different target segments or social classes, and also varied according to the product nature. The results were also found to confirm the "reflection hypothesis" proposed in this research. However, it is necessary to stress that the "reflection hypothesis" is useful in studying the advertising industry as a whole rather than individual cases. It is understandable that an indisputable unanimous result would be very unlikely. It would, therefore, be acceptable if the majority held a similar stance and worked accordingly.

The results of this study confirmed that the power of advertisers to mould is limited but the research design and the findings are unable to answer the question "why"—Why the advertisers made such decisions within their contemporary social system? In order to achieve a more

Table 8.7: **Summary of cross tabulations on the aggregate totals**

	Significance Score ("unclassified" excluded)
Cultural values by time	24 out of 35 values (68.6%)
Cultural values by newspapers languages (English & Chinese)	18 out of 35 values (51.4%)
Cultural values by products	26 out of 35 values (74.3%)

comprehensive view of the topic, field study in advertising agencies or direct participation in the work of advertisers can help us to diagnose "why" and "how" such decisions are made—How these big advertisers via gatekeeping possess the power to choose the kind of values to be manifested in advertisements?

Notes

1. The chosen 50 years witnessed the most crucial developments in Hong Kong contemporary history, from the influx of more than 2 million refugees back in 1949 to the transfer of sovereignty in 1997.

2. Hong Kong is a pluralistic society evidencing a wide range of attitudes, lifestyles, and behaviors. Because of this distinctiveness, both scholars and professionals in the advertising industry have classified the population into meaningful market segments. The view that different newspapers with different editorial profiles cater for specific social groups was adopted in this study.

3. The two studies on "foodstuff" advertisements included comparisons between *South China Morning Post* and *Sing Tao Daily*, and between *South China Morning Post* and *Sing Pao Daily News*. As with the present research, the study period was from 1949 to 1998, and the modified operationalizations of the Cheng and Schweitzer cultural values framework were adopted.

4. SCMP with 2,071 advertisements contained more advertisements than the sum of those in the three Chinese newspapers (Sing Tao with 604 ads, Sing Pao with 693 ads, and Ming Pao with 712 ads).

5. In order to achieve a more meaningful interpretation of the results two different cultural dimensions, namely "utilitarian" and "symbolic" were introduced. The "utilitarian" dimension emphasizes the pragmatic and useful features of a product rather than its luxurious or decorative traits and includes values such as "economy" and "quality" that put emphasis on value for money; other values include "convenience," "effectiveness," and "health". On the other hand, some advertisements might place special attention on the "symbolic" dimension, which emphasizes image, luxury, and value-added qualities; values such as "enjoyment," "from/of abroad," and "variety" to name a few.

6. The changes in product nature are of two different aspects: i) the subcategories, i.e., the most popular advertiser in the 1950s was "beverage & tea" and this was replaced by "restaurant" in the late 1960s; ii) the advertisers under the same sub-category, i.e., "restaurant" in the 1950s and 1960s referred to teahouses with affordable prices and in the 1980s and 1990s the category referred to cafés or restaurants in prestigious hotels.

References

ACNielsen. 1984–1999. *Hong Kong advertising expenditure.* Hong Kong: ACNielsen.

Adoni, H., and S. Mane. 1984. Media and the social construction of reality: Toward an integration of theory and research. *Communication Research* 11(3):323–40.

Barouw, E. 1978. *The sponsor: Notes on a modern potentate.* New York: Oxford University Press

Berger, P. L., and T. Luckmann. 1966.) *The socialconstruction of reality.* Middlesex: Penguin Books Ltd.

Berman, R. 1981. *Advertising and social change.* London: Sage Publications.

Census and Statistics Department, HKSAR Governemnt. 1996. *1996 Population bycensus main report.* Hong Kong: Census and Statistics Department.

Chan, J. M. 1992. Mass media and socio-political formation in Hong Kong, 1949–1992. *Asian Journal of Communication* 2(3):106–29.

Chan, K. W. 1999. Cultural values in Hong Kong's print advertising, 1946–1996. *International Journal of Advertising* 18(4):537–54.

Cheng, H., and J. Schweitzer. 1996. Cultural values reflected in Chinese and U.S. television commercials. *Journal of Advertising Research* 36(3):27–45.

Cheung, C. H., and K. W. Ma. 1999. *Advertising modernity: "Home", space and privacy.* Hong Kong: Hong Kong Institute of Asia-Pacific Studies, The Chinese University of Hong Kong.

du Gay, P., S. J. Hall, M. H. Linda, and K. Negusk. 1997. *Doing cultural studies: The story of the Sony walkman.* London: Sage Publications.

Holbrook, M. B. 1987. Mirror, mirror, on the wall, what's unfair in the reflections of advertising? *Journal of Marketing* 51:95–103.

Kwok, W. Y. 2000a. *The eating culture in Hong Kong (1949–1998).* Paper presented at the meeting of The 3rd International Postgraduate Symposium on Hong Kong Culture and Society, March, Hong Kong.

———. 2000b. *The eating culture in Hong Kong: A heterogeneous analysis (1949–1998).* Paper presented at the meeting of International Association for Media and Communication Research, August, Singapore.

Kwok, Y. C., and S. Y. Wong. 1995. Hong Kong sixties advertising image. In M. Turner and I. Ngan, eds. *Hong Kong sixties designing identity*, 439–533. Hong Kong: Hong Kong Arts Centre.

Lippmann, W. 1965. *Public opinion.* Ontario: First Press Paperback, The Macmillan Company.

Marchand, L. 1985. *Advertising the American dream: Making Way for modernity, 1920–1940.* Los Angeles: University of California Press.

O'Sullivan, T., J. Hartley, D. Saunders, M. Montgomery, and J. Fiske. 1994. *Key concepts in communication and cultural studies.* 2nd ed.. London: Routledge.

Pollay, R. W. 1983. Measuring the cultural values manifest in advertising. In J. H. Leigh and C. R. Martin Jr., ed. *Current Issues and Research in Advertising*, 71–92. Ann Arbor, MI: University of Michigan Graduate School of Business Division of Research.

———. 1986. The distorted mirror: Reflections on the unintended consequences of advertising. *Journal of Marketing* 50(2):18–38.

Real, M. R. 1977. *Mass-mediated culture.* New Jersey: Prentice Hall.

Shooter, J. 1984. *Social accountability and selfhood.* New York: Basil Blackwell.

Skolimowski, H. 1977. The semantic environment in the age of advertising. In T. H. Ohlbren and L. M. Berk, eds. *The New Languages: A Rhetorical Approach to the Mass Media and Popular Culture*, 91–101. New Jersey: Prentice-Hall.

Skov, K, and B. Moeran, ed. 1995. *Women, media and consumption in Japan.* Surrey: Curzon Press.

Tuchman, G. 1978. *Making news: A study in the construction of reality.* New York: The Free Press.

Williamson, J. 1978. *Decoding advertisements: Ideology and meaning in advertising.* London: Marion Boyars Publishers Ltd.

Wilson, S. J. 1981. The image of women in Canadian magazines. In E. Katz and T. Szecsko, eds. *Mass Media and Social Change*, 231–45. California: Sage Publications.

Wong, S. Y. 1999a. *Advertising and the transformation of Hong Kong culture and society since 1945.* Unpublished doctoral dissertation. Hong Kong Polytechnic University.

———. 1999b. *Advertising, culture & everyday life I: Hong Kong newspaper advertisements, 1945–1970.* Hong Kong; Luck-Win Book Store.

Chapter 9

Gender and Advertising: The Promotional Culture of Whitening and Slimming

Anthony Fung

*T*he cultural nexus between women and advertising has been a capitalist phenomenon. In Hong Kong, gender portrayal and women's images in advertising started receiving attention from women's groups and academics in the early late 1980s (e.g., Chai 1988). The central issues concerned at that time were gender inequality and bias in advertising. In 1992 a systematic study by the Association for the Advancement of Feminism (1992) revealed that a significant number of ads still used the female form to attract an audience, reinforcing the gender role and stereotypes carried by these ads. Fewer than 5% of the ads promoted the value of gender equality. A decade later, a similar gender-role effect was found in television commercials in Hong Kong with 90% of the content categories showing no difference in presentation, credibility, and role (Furham et al. 2000). Comparing Indonesian television commercials, the same study also suggested that gender stereotypes in ads is a pan-Asian phenomenon, a trend which seems more apparent in Asia and in particular in Hong Kong (Furham et al. 2000, 2631–32). In the study of Hong Kong and Singapore commercials, women were more often seen in dependent roles (Siu 1996). Young and Chan (2002) also arrived at the conclusion that there is a tendency toward a homogeneous Asian culture in terms of gender values.

The intriguing question here is what is unique in Hong Kong that makes its ads stand in contrast to the West as more biased and stereotypic (c.f., Leung 2004). The problematic seems not just simply an equality and fairness issue related to women, but more related to a cultural and gender phenomenon as a consequence of the politico-economic context of Hong Kong.

In this chapter I would suggest that specific gender relations in advertising are highly connected to the mature, capitalistic environment of Hong Kong which sets the economic agenda largely independent of moral and cultural considerations. In an historical analysis of the media's gender role since the 1960s, Sze and Lo (1990) suggested that women's status is tied closely to economic development—a proposition that even a cursory look at a Hong Kong's women's magazines will readily confirm. Analyzing the relationship between identity and consumption (women models variously featured in different classes of advertisement to cater to different class consumption), Fung (2002) found that women's magazines provide the vital advertising information necessary for women to embody beauty so as to maintain their communities.

In the following analysis, rather than focusing on discussing gender inequality or bias, I would like to examine the cultural connection between advertising and the construct of beauty in Hong Kong. From a sociological perspective I would like to discuss specifically two concepts, skin whitening and body slimming, and how their symbolic meanings shape, construe, and interrogate the gender culture in Hong Kong.

Skin Whitening and Beauty

Among all the commodities available in the highly capitalistic society of Hong Kong, cosmetics and skin and body care products are definitely the favorites for female consumers. According to ads for the Japanese whitening product Fancl (which features Gigi Leung, one of the most impressive and professional spokespersons for skin whitening) "whitening" facial products are regarded as the "savior" of Chinese yellow-skinned women. Along with Fancl's slogan of "super white" there are mottos from SKII ads which feature "egg white" and the "double white" of Pond's and the "Pink White" of Bioré.

This promotional culture has helped fuel a booming business in whitening creams throughout Asia. According to ACNielsen in 2002 the sale of facial-whitening products in Hong Kong grew by 35% in both value and volume, outpacing the overall facial-moisturizing category which grew by 18% in volume and 15% in value respectively (Prystay 2002).

The fundamental support for skin-whitening in the Chinese Hong Kong culture may be linked to intrinsic nature as well as cultural interpretation of color. Normally, dark color stands for secrecy, mystery, and deepness. Nevertheless when it comes to skin complexion, people seem to conceive that whiteness is more mystical and whimsical. Traditional Chinese women believe the Chinese axiom: "one portion of whiteness can hide three portions of ugliness." Their adoration of whiteness is based mainly on the fact that culturally they value a white skin color higher than other criteria of beauty. For professional women whitening is not just a matter of cultural satisfactoriness; it affects their status as career women. They believe that a white skin is connected to civilization, progressiveness and the renaissance of Anglo-Saxon traditions. These professionals who succumb to white-skin discourse are infused with a western sense of modernity that gives them an extra modicum of assurance and confidence in their work and in their interactions with bosses and clients. In general, females of a darker skin color—not only the yellowish Chinese but also black people—find that light skin is more attractive than their own skin complexion (Bond and Cash 1992). This promotional culture seems to have penetrated markets in a number of different developed countries.

Myth and Fairytales in Advertisement

The success of the skin-whitening culture lies in attaching the signification of modernity to white skin. The agent of choice to carry and manifest this Western modernity of whiteness is the Hong Kong celebrity; first by linking celebrities with traditional folklores and customs, and second by making use of symbolic meanings in selling the whitening culture. Hong Kong, the meeting point between East and West, is strategically rich in both Chinese and Western legends, folklores, customs, and stories. The advertisers are able to make use of the audience's familiarity with these cultures, in particular some easily understood and popular fairytales, to connect consumption and advertising culture. Complicated symbolic social and cultural values are embedded in fairytales, ranging from realistic and socially acceptable values to various fantasy aspirations. All these significations in ads constitute what Barthes (1973) called myth available and produced in consumption. The audience believes that the advertisements are both mythical and miraculous and hence represent optimism. While immersing themselves in the existing capitalist culture—ruthless, aggressive, and competitive in nature—consumers are also much attracted to this out-of-this-world image in the hope, in some sense, of becoming the celebrity by consuming the product. In the case of Hong Kong the Western fairytale of *Cinderella* has been used to draw consumers into identifying themselves with the white-skinned princess and with white-skin products.

The best example of this ad is the Fancl commercials with Gigi Leung personified as Cinderella. She possesses the natural beauty of whitened skin, the same quality with which Cinderella the princess is born. On the other hand her life parallels that of Cinderella in the fairytale. She started her acting career as a pure, introverted, and quiet girl—the girl next door in the film *Full Throttle* (1995). After her self-transformation and repackaging from her record company EEI of Warner Music Hong Kong, she became a stylish and elegant lady credible enough to serve as a marketing spokesperson. This change reassembles the dramatic life of Cinderella who with the blessing of a fairy was able to attend the ball and meet her prince. In fact Gigi presented the same story in the love lullaby *Cinderella* in her album *Sparking Fire* (2000). When Gigi Leung promoted Fancl in 1999, what made the audience believe was not just the selling messages that the ads conveyed, but the entire Cinderella image that Gigi personified. Her princess-like image matched squarely with the perfect lady model who has been de-colored.

Slimming, Love, and Beauty

If we see the consumption of beauty products for the transformation from a yellowish girl to a white-skinned lady—which Western girls are naturally—as a kind of Western cultural imagination, we can also conceive of body slimming as a type of cultural formation and identification. It is true that in developing societies, including the old China, there are peoples who still gauge female beauty by sheer bulk and accordingly force brides to go through excessive fattening before marriage as a sign of possessing reproductive vigour. But in contrast, nowadays, in many developed countries including Hong Kong brides prefer to go through an exhausting slimming regime to create a sylph-like figure which is then forever recorded for veneration in wedding photographs and video film (Thomas 2004). Slimming practices such as corsetting and body contouring have long histories in the West. In the Hong Kong society, in general, the root of body shaping is thought to be more connected to Chinese culture in that the Hong Kong Chinese are more familiar with traditional body-shaping techniques such as foot binding. Additionally, and perhaps more importantly, physically the Chinese are seen as being smaller and thinner than Westerners.

Studies in 2003 by Caritas Hong Kong found that slimming ads in the media played a vital role in creating the fashion of slimming. In this study 61.8% of the women said that they had attempted to engage in some sort of weight-reduction activity. This is not to say that all women in Hong Kong are passive acceptants of this mediated slimming culture. In fact, the same study suggested that the respondents interviewed in general disagreed that women should be evaluated merely on the basis of appearance. At the same time 43% felt that the culture of emaciation was a public pressure on them (*Sing Pao Daily News*, June 16, 2003).

In Hong Kong it is estimated that around 30% of the pages of entertainment magazines are slimming advertisements directed at women (Hong Kong Association for Democracy and People's Livelihood, March 7, 2004). Ads from slimming salons use famous female artists to carry the message. The ads of Marie France Bodyline wholesales the weight loss achieved by Christy Chung and Cass Phang—as well as their sexy bodies—after their pregnancies. The ads mainly target family women and housewives, and also directly appeal to middle-class women by featuring Flora Chan who is known to role-play forensic doctors, lawyers, and other professionals on television. With these three married (or once married) ladies selling slimming ads with the motto "you can get married," they reassure married women of keeping their beauty and offer the suggestion that they too can be part of the beauty community. There were also the highlights of Royal Body Perfect with Carina Lau and Michele Yeh, and Lisa Wong wearing swimming suits, as evidence of the effectiveness of the slimming process. Celebrities' personal witness with their own bodies not only promoted the fashion of body contouring; it also embedded these celebrities as powerful symbols of professionalism capable of generating more signs, discourse, and symbols for slimming.

Really Show, Ads, and Surrealism

The ads selling body slimming go beyond product promotion, which purely features slimming medication, herbal tea, diet meals, or slimming programs. Inserted ubiquitously in print and the broadcast media, on billboards on cross-harbor tunnels, on skyscrapers and inside and outside public transport, are examples of slimming success and the news and facts about innovative products, healthy tips, and advice for nutrition. The narratives of those who have experienced the vicissitudes of fatness and revitalization after slimming are also featured. In these "ads," fat tummy and strong arms are framed and assumed to be the enemies of women, while a perfect slim body is the model of beauty. With just a short headline mentioning the sponsors' brands, many of these ads deliberately avoid promoting specific products and services.

This is what I call an "info-ad," an ad in which it is hard to distinguish facts from advertisement, real from unreal, and the products from news. This ad trend was adopted by the local Hong Kong media which boosts their popularity by launching programs and dramas about the slimming culture. This further blurs the boundaries between promotion, information, and programming. Among all these info-ads one common form is the "reality show" on television and in the print media. This metamorphoses promotional culture into the everyday life of the people. A typical ad of this sort usually compares the body size, health conditions, and psychological well-being of the women before and after the slimming trial. Many of these ads also specifically target would-be brides who are expected to be close to the ideal of beauty prior to marriage.

Various ad campaigns for different services and products create a slimming culture atmosphere with slimness as the signifier and beauty as the signified. Emaciation and body recontouring is now a symbol of achievement in the culture of Hong Kong. Such an achievement is more than beauty since today—a healthy body and a balanced life are always used as the official pretext for selling body recontouring. As stated above, whereas commercials about skin-whitening products sell Western pallor as a culture of superiority and modernity, ads about slimming products and services highlight the real physical and psychological benefits of "returning to the basics"—of a healthy body.

As a consequence of these "reality shows" or info-ads what is mediated in the everyday life of audiences are imaginaries—non-real, flamboyant, and symbolic—which are ironically more real, vivid, and appealing than the objects that the images represent. Even though it is written explicitly on the print ad or shown with subtitles on television that these are promotional messages after being bombarded by all these messages, the audiences do not have the ability to, or perhaps do not bother to, distinguish images from objects because what is real and unreal, fact and promotion, signifier and signified, can no longer be separated. Culturally, images of beauty have become more real or super-real than reality and the signified has overwhelmed the signifier—a condition of surrealism that happens in a highly capitalist society.

The Intertextualities of Advertising Texts

This surreal culture of beauty is now sustained by the totality of the celebrity icon and intertextual links between different signifiers and the signified. Nowadays Gigi's Cinderella-like image is not only a signification which corresponds to the original signifier—the Fancl product itself—but it also operates in such a way that the signified continuously, consistently, and repeatedly generates other significations and symbols across different media or in different texts in the same medium. For example, the Cinderella image of Gigi started in the movie *Full Throttle* (1995) and extended in the love comedy *100% Once More* (1996), and then finally to the epic story of *Turn Left Turn Right* (2003). Although Gigi did not explicitly sell skin products and slimming services in these movies, audiences unconsciously link the symbols and signs of the fictional characters with the conception of beauty that Gigi was imbued with.

The slimming ads also worked in tandem with other media in a more planned and strategic manner in Hong Kong. The classic example is the fusion of film text and advertising texts in promoting slimming. Sammi Cheng, a leading artist and singer in Hong Kong and spokesperson for Modern Beauty Salon with a reported salary of HK$10 million, was the actress chosen for *Love on a Diet* (2001), which made HK$38 million in ticket sales. The movie featured stars Sammi Cheng (Mini Mo) who falls in love with the fat knife salesman Andy Lau (Fatty Lau). When Mini loses her love relationship with the Japanese pianist Kurokawa, she spirals into eating binges to become a "300 lb. fatty." Fatty Lau believes that the solution to her problem is to lose weight in order to regain her relationship. In the end, unsurprisingly, Fatty builds affection for Mini and becomes her lover. Using the subtitle "What people will do for love!" the movie equates love with slimming and betterment with the perfect body shape. At the apex of the film's promotion the entire media, including the news media, was full of the slimming message; whether from the movie or from the beauty salon no longer seems to be important.

The Asian Female Complex and Promotional Culture

With the multiplication of the signified in the above intertextual borrowing and appropriation, ads in Hong Kong conjure a slim body silhouette which represents confidence, affluence, and female dignity as opposed to "other non-qualified women." This very pale and inconspicuous silhouette for that perfect body should also be strikingly white. In sum, while Hong Kong Chinese yellow-skinned professional women believe that whitening is a pilgrimage to a higher social status, which is connected to Western modernity, they simultaneously yearn to keep a body of oriental petiteness. The consequences of promotional consumption construct an Oriental women complex, the paradox that Hong Kong women themselves want to maintain their own Chinese body images of slenderness but at the same time debase their own non-white skin color. Such detest of the Oriental yellow is much stronger than in the old days which may only be because many regard their darker skin as not as superior as white skin, which can camouflage other "faults." At present wanting to have the whitish skin of the West seems to be the only psychological and cultural solution to becoming an Oriental diva, one combining the best female qualities of both East and West. Perhaps this phenomenon, as mentioned at the beginning of this chapter, is unique to Asian professional women who, becoming more financially independent and resourceful—and situated in a booming and emerging culture and economy—still bear the legacy of social learning which originated in the modern West.

To disentangle this Oriental complex one has to first deconstruct the intertextual fantasy, significations, and images of the slimming and skin product ads. Subjective power and critical ability are not enough to resist the inherent ideologies. The failure of deconstruction is not because women consumers are not educated or non-responsive but because body decoloring and emaciation are culturally—and perhaps universally—packaged for those social classes who need to demonstrate their status, prestige and power. The women who have the economic power to consume this promotional culture and to turn their bodies into commodities are reluctant to give up their superiority over other women who do not.

Thus, as expected, any feminist movements in contesting the conception of beauty as a "slim body and white skin" have to rely on a minority of educated women who have the channels and intellectual power to deconstruct public information and advertisements (e.g., Choi 1992). Fortunately we are starting to see collective efforts to generate alternative voices deconstructing the myth of skin whitening. Social and feminist groups have also proposed legal measures to curb exaggerations in ads and to oppose the cultural stigmatisation of those women who choose to remain outside this advertising influence. Some women's groups such as the Hong Kong Federation of Women have organized a series of workshops and seminars to promote this oppositional discourse, e.g., "blind slimming is not beauty; highlighting healthy is the beauty."

Finally, as a person who lives in a highly mature capitalist city, I would not sanctimoniously judge those fairytales and surreal stories promoting commodities. It is not the consumption *per se* but our lack of pluralistic values and lifestyles and an appreciation beyond simple tolerance of the women who are less willing to be treated as commodities.

Reference

Association for the Advancement of Feminism, The. 1992. *The gender consciousness on television commercials: A preliminary report.* Hong Kong: The Association for the Advancement of Feminism (In Chinese).

Barthes, R. 1973. *Mythologies.* London: Jonathan Cape.

Bond, S., and T. Cash. 1992. Black beauty: Skin color and body images among African–American college women. *Journal of Applied Social Psychology* 22(11): 874–88.

Chai, Y. M. 1988. Women's image under advertising culture. *Cultures in Transition* 2 (March 1):13–14 (in Chinese).

Choi, P. K. 1992. Waiting for new women magazine. *Gender Studies Information* 1(5):31 (in Chinese).

Fung, A. 2002. Women's magazines: Construction of identities and cultural consumption in Hong Kong. *Consumption, Markets and Culture* 5(4):321–36.

Furnham, A., T. Mak, and L. Tanidjojo. 2000. An Asian perspective on the portrayal of men and women in television advertisements: Studies from Hong Kong and Indonesian television. *Journal of Applied Social Psychology* 30(11):2341–64.

Hong Kong Association for Democracy and People's Livelihood. 2004. http://www.adpl.org.hk/content03/b/20040307.htm (accessed June 16, 2003).

Leung, L. 2004. Fashioning (Western) sexuality for sale: The case of sex and fashion articles in cosmopolitan Hong Kong. In C. H. Ng and C. W. Cheung, eds. *Reading Hong Kong Culture*, 420–41. Hong Kong: Oxford University Press.

Prystay, C. 2002. Critics say ads for skin whiteners capitalize on Malaysian prejudice. *Online Wall Street Journal*, April 30, 2002. http://www.calbaptist.edu/dskubik/white_skin.htm (accessed June 16, 2003).

Sing Pao Daily News. 2003. June 16. http://news.sina.com.cn/o/2004-03-07/18531987593s.shtml (accessed June 16, 2003).

Siu, W. S. 1996. Gender portrayal in Hong Kong and Singapore television advertisements. *Journal of Asian Business* 12(3):47–63.

Sze, M. H., and Y. Y. Lo. 1990. Public forum: Women's images were distorted? Mass Media Awareness Seminar. In *Mass Media and Women in the 90s'*, 63–71. Hong Kong: Hong Kong Christian Service Communications Centre.

Thomas, P. 2004. Beauty is shape. http://www.fashion-era.com/beauty_is_shape.htm (accessed February 23, 2004).

Young, S. M., and K. Chan. 2002. Gender portrayal in Hong Kong and Korean children's TV commercials: A cross-cultural comparison. *Asian Journal of Communication* 12(2):100–19.

Acknowledgements

This paper was fully supported by a grant from the Research Grant Council of Hong Kong Special Administrative Region (Project no. CUHK4274/03H).

Chapter 10

Advertising and Children

Kara Chan

Introduction

*T*oday advertising penetrates into the life of every person, including children. The children's market is important to advertisers because they are seen as a current market for a variety of goods and services, a future market as tomorrow's customers, and an influential market for family purchases (McNeal 1987). A survey of 2,400 children aged 7–12 years in six countries, including China, Japan, France, Germany, United Kingdom, and the United States, indicated that their estimated annual spending power ranged from US$1.7 billion in Germany to US$11.3 billion in the U.S. Children actively participated in family purchase decisions in a number of product categories (Carey et al. 1997). The newly emerging middle class, high populations, and one-child policies in some Asian countries mean that these "little emperors" have more and more influence over how the family money is spent. Research has suggested that children in China have been quick to make demands and exercise "pester power." They are often the first to learn of new products from the mass media, retail outlets, and parents. Chinese children considered television to be the most important information source on new products (McNeal and Ji 1999).

Advertisers target children because of their high disposable income, their early establishment of loyalty to certain brands, and a conventional wisdom that young adults buy products on impulse (Fox 1996). Many parents and critics fear that children are susceptible to commercial appeals because young viewers lack the necessary cognitive skills to process the highly persuasive messages and make appropriate judgments about them (Choate 1975). Educators and researchers have attempted to design programs that will teach children about the intent of advertisements and help children construct defenses against commercial messages (Pecora 1995). Twenty-five years of consumer socialization research have yielded impressive findings on the developmental sequence characterizing the growth of consumer knowledge, skills, and values as children mature throughout childhood and adolescence. There is much evidence to show that as children grow in cognitive and social terms there is growth in knowledge of products, brands, advertising, parental influence strategies, and consumption motives and values (John 1999).

Children in Hong Kong are exposed to a large amount of advertising, particularly through television advertising. According to a weekly ACNielsen television rating report the average rating report, the average rating of TVB-Jade, the dominant Chinese channel, from 7:00 a.m. to 12:45 a.m. at midnight on a school day in February 2001 for children of 4–14 years was 11 rating points (equivalent to an audience size of 100,000). Children watched a lot more television during school holidays. The average rating of TVB-Jade on an Easter holiday was 16 rating points (45% more audience than on a typical school day). A child spending three hours per day watching television may be exposed to 20,000 commercials every year. A survey of Hong Kong adults indicated that a majority accused television advertising of having adverse effects on children. They perceived that television advertising leads children to pester their parents (Chan and Ruidl 1996). A McDonald's television commercial featuring a boy who told lies to get approval to visit the restaurant was under serious attack by parents. The advertisers decided to pull the commercial before the Hong Kong Broadcast Authority started an investigation (Chan 1997). There are stringent regulations in Hong Kong governing television advertising targeting children. For each hour of television broadcast there should not be more than 10 minutes of advertisements for both adult as well as children's viewing hours. The basic principle is that television commercials should not take advantage of the natural credulity and sense of loyalty of children. The presentation of commercial information must not result in physical, mental, or moral harm to children. Commercials that are frightening, anxiety-provoking, or which contain violent, dangerous or antisocial behavior cannot be directed toward children. Children in commercials also need to display good manners and good behavior. If there is a reference to a competition in an advertisement aimed at children, the value of the prizes and the chances of a child winning one must not be exaggerated. The true size of the product advertised and any free gift for children should be depicted in a way that makes this easy to judge (Hong Kong Broadcast Authority 1993).

This chapter aims to answer the following questions:

a) Do children understanding the nature and the purpose of television advertising?
b) What kind of television commercials do they like and do they not like?
c) Do they understand the key messages in television commercials?
d) Do children perceive television advertising to be truthful? How do they judge whether commercials are true or not?
e) Do children watch television commercials and what are their attitudes toward television advertising?
f) Does children's attention to and attitudes towards television advertising relate to perceived truthfulness?
g) What is children's perception of parental influence on their exposure to TV advertising?
h) How are the above related to the stage of cognitive development a child has reached?

The current study adopts John's (1999) theory of consumer socialization. The theory identifies distinct stages of cognitive and social development and postulates that children would manifest differences in the ways they select, evaluate, and use information. Children's response to television advertising will therefore be analyzed by age group.

Most of the research literature on advertising and children is based on research conducted in Western societies. There are very few comparable studies from Asian countries. When referring to Chinese perspectives towards child development, Confucianism is one Chinese ideology that has been widely investigated by Chinese and Western researchers. Some important characteristics include an emphasis on children's moral orientation (Ekblad 1986); filial piety (Hsu 1981; Kelly and Tseng 1992), self-fulfillment (Kelly and Tseng 1992; Suzuki 1980), good manners and the importance of education (Chiu 1987; Ekblad 1986; Ho 1989). The implications of all these studies suggest that Chinese parents tend to be more concerned about moral behavior in commercials and they will exert more control over their children's behavior.

Cognitive Development and Children's Understanding of Television Advertising

In Western studies of child development, Piaget's (1970) theory of cognitive development has provided substantial guidance to research related to the communication process of advertising to children. The theory proposes that a child's ability to think and reason progresses through a series of distinct stages that are closely related to age. Integrating Piaget's (1970) stage theory of cognitive development and Selman's (1980) stage theory of social development, John (1999) proposes a model of consumer socialization that is shown to be particularly useful in characterizing children's responses to advertising. In the model (Table 10.1), learning to be a consumer is a developmental process from the perceptual stage (3–7 years) to the analytical stage (7–11 years) to the reflective stage (11–16 years). In the perceptual stage, children can grasp concrete knowledge only. Their consumer knowledge is characterized by perceptual features and distinctions based on a single and simple dimension. They are egocentric and unable to take others' perspectives into account. Children in the analytical stage are able to grasp abstract knowledge. Concepts are thought of in terms of functional or underlying dimensions. They are able to analyze marketplace information in two or more dimensions and can acknowledge contingencies. They have developed new perspectives that go beyond their own feelings and motives and can take a dual perspective—their own and that of others. Children

Table 10.1: Cognitive developmental models

Piaget's model of cognitive development (1970)	Sensorimotor (0–2 years) knowledge of the world depends on current sensory experience and activity; do not have the concept of object permanence	Preoperational (2–7 years) highly egocentric; believe what they perceive is real, do not have the concept of conservation	Concrete operational (7–11 years) can plan strategies and consider consequences, cannot think of actions in the abstract; fail to use the same principles in new situations	Formal operational (11–18 years) understand abstract principles, able to think of ideas apart from objects, still apply concrete strategy for problems not so experienced
Selman's model of social-cognitive development of perspective taking (1980)	Stage 0 (3–6 years) Undifferentiated and egocentric; unaware of others' perspectives	Stage 1 (6–8 years) Differentiated: aware of different perspectives in others	Stage 2 (8–10 years) self-reflective role taking: beginning to think from another's perspective	Stage 3 (10–12 years) third-person: simultaneously consider own and another's perspective
John's model of consumer socialization (1999)	Perceptual stage (3–7 years) grasp concrete knowledge only, focus on perceptual features, unidimensional, egocentric, unable to take others' perspective, can distinguish commercials from programs based on perceptual features	Analytical stage (7–11 years) understand abstract knowledge, think in terms of functional or underlying dimensions, analyze information in two or more dimensions, understand contingencies, can distinguish commercials from programs based on persuasive intent	Reflective stage (11–16 years) more sophisticated understanding of marketing concepts, think and reason in more reflective ways, focus more on the social meanings of the marketplace, able to understand persuasive intent as well as the specific advertising tactics/appeals used in commercials	

Stage 4 (12–15+ years) Societal: compare perspectives with social system in the reflective stage possess a multidimensional understanding of marketing concepts such as branding and pricing. They shift into more reflective ways of thinking and reasoning and focus more on the social meanings and underpinnings of the consumer marketplace. In terms of advertising knowledge children in the perceptual stage can distinguish commercials from programs, based on perceptual features such as length. Children in the analytical stage can distinguish commercials from programs based on persuasive intent. Children in the reflective stage are able to understand persuasive intent as well as the specific advertising tactics and appeals used in the commercials (John 1999). John's theoretical framework, by combining that of Piaget and Selman, points in the direction of a positive effect of age on understanding of a social concept such as television advertising.

Most of the studies of children's communication processing of television advertising have supported these two theories. Studies have generally indicated that children's ability to distinguish programs from commercials increases with age (Meringoff and Lesser 1980), as does their comprehension of television advertising and its persuasive intent (Blosser and Roberts 1985; Rubin 1974; Ward 1972). Some understanding of advertising intent usually emerges by the time most American children turn 7 to 8 (Bever et al. 1975; Rubin 1974). Furnham (2000) reported that research among German children found that nearly two out of three 6-year-olds can make the distinction between programs and commercials and can grasp the intent behind commercial messages. An experiment with 108 children in United Kingdom found that none of the 6-year-olds, a quarter of the 8-year-olds and a third of the 10-year-olds were able to understand the persuasive intent of television advertising (Oates, Blades, and Gunter 2002).

A Study that Measures Hong Kong Children's Understanding of Television Advertising

Six undergraduate students were recruited and, through personal sources, interviewed 448 Chinese children of 5–12 years in Hong Kong. The children were from a quota sample of equal numbers of boys and girls for each school year from kindergarten and grades 1–6. Personal

Table 10.2: **Structure of the questionnaire**

Variable measured	Question	Type
Understanding of television advertising	When we are watching television, sometimes the program stops and there are other messages coming up. These messages are called the TV commercials. Can you tell me, What are TV commercials? What do TV commercials want you to do? Why do TV stations broadcast TV commercials?	Open-ended
Recall favorite and most disliked commercials	What is your favorite commercial? Why do you like it the most? What is your most disliked commercial? Why do you dislike it the most?	Open-ended
Recall brand name	Please tell me which brand uses the slogan XXX.	Open-ended
Comprehension of television advertising	(show storyboards) Please tell me what this commercial says.	Open-ended
Perceived truthfulness	Do you think commercials are mostly true/mostly not true/partly true?	Close-ended
	How do you know if they are true or not true?	Open-ended
Attention	Do you watch TV commercials?	Close-ended
Parental influence	What do your parents teach you about TV commercials?	Open-ended

interviews were conducted at public libraries, churches, restaurants, and parks near school areas in May 1998. Each interview took approximately 20 minutes. Table 10.2 summarizes the structure of the questionnaire. A coding menu was developed for open-ended questions after reviewing all the responses.

Children were prompted about their awareness and knowledge of television advertising. The interviewer mentioned that "when we are watching television, sometimes the program stops and there are other messages coming up. These messages are called commercials." The children were asked what commercials are, what their purposes are, and why television stations broadcast commercials. Table 10.3 summarizes their responses. In response to the question "What are TV commercials?" 46% of the children reported without aid that televisions commercials are messages to introduce products. In response to the question "What do commercials want you to do?" a much higher number of children (60%) reported that TV commercials want them to buy things. In response to the question "Why do television stations broadcast commercials?" 19% of the children reported that they want people to buy things and 22% reported that TV stations want money to make programs. The results consistently show a sharp increase in understanding of "What are TV commercials," "What do TV commercials want you to do," and "Why do TV stations broadcast commercials" from age 8 onwards. Younger children aged below 8 had difficulty verbalizing what constituted a commercial. Younger children viewed television advertising as part of the entertainment offered by the television station. Some thought that television stations broadcast commercials in order to test whether the commercials were funny and to attract audiences. While understanding of the purpose of advertising generally increased with age, children aged 12 responded no differently than children aged 8–11 on all three questions.

The results on children's cognitive responses to television advertising obtained in this study are similar to previous studies in Western societies. Age-related changes in understanding are consistently found. A remarkable increase in understanding of what advertising is and the purpose of television advertising at children aged 8 years is consistent with John's (1999) model. The children entering this stage of consumer socialization are able to think conceptually and organize the selling idea in a more coherent manner. However, the apparent growth in understanding of television advertising has to be weighted against the relative abilities of younger and older children to express themselves verbally, as well as their ability to articulate the difference between programs and commercials. Answers to the three questions "What are television commercials," "What do TV commercials want you to do," and "Why do television stations broadcast commercials" reveal a range of responses at different levels of understanding of television advertising. Many younger children, who found difficulty in expressing what

Table 10.3:   Children's understanding of television advertising

	Age group and cognitive stage (%)					
	5–7 (N=165) perceptual	8–9 (N=114) early analytical	10–11 (N=117) late analytical	12 (N=52) reflective	Total N=448	Chi-square statistics
What are TV commercials?						113.2***
Low	77	35	19	38	47	
Medium	16	59	73	58	46	
High	7	6	8	4	7	
What do TV commercials want you to do?						63.4***
Low	53	18	17	42	34	
Medium	8	5	8	2	6	
High	39	77	75	56	60	
Why do TV stations broadcast commercials?						67.4***
Low	77	56	32	38	56	
Medium	4	4	3	2	3	
High	19	40	65	60	41	

Low: no concept of advertising, including "Don't know" cases.
Medium: understand that TV advertising shows things, introduces products, introduces new products
High: understand that TV advertising promotes products, sponsors TV programs, or that TV stations carry ads for money.

commercials are, could still identify that the commercials wanted them to buy things. A higher proportion of children aged 9–10 years could recognise the institutional function of television advertising. The findings have public policy implications: that younger children need greater protection against persuasive marketing communication in the mass media. Children over 8 years have probably developed a cognitive defense and understand the selling intent of television advertising.

Liked and Disliked Commercials

Children were asked to recall their favorite television commercials and the commercial they disliked the most. Altogether 222 and 115 commercials were mentioned as the favorite and the most disliked commercials respectively.

Commercials for food and drink, toys, and mobile phones were most frequently cited as commercials children liked. These three product categories accounted for nearly 80% of the total number of recalls. Older children (aged 10–12) lost interest in toy commercials and developed a marked appreciation for mobile phone and sports goods commercials. The children liked these commercials because the commercials were interesting and funny, they liked the products, or they liked the characters/celebrities used. Older children liked commercials using celebrities. This accounted for their high appreciation of mobile phone commercials that used film stars and pop singers as endorsers. Many children cited McDonald's, Kinder chocolate, and Yakult drink commercials as their favorite commercials because the story lines were cute and entertaining. The children liked commercials with cartoon figures, a funny story or their favorite film/television stars.

Commercials that children disliked the most consisted of a high proportion of mobile phones commercials, food and drink commercials, public service announcements, and supermarket commercials. These four categories accounted for 55% of the total number of recalls. The children disliked these commercials because they did not understand them, they found them boring or horrifying, or they disliked the products (particularly for liquor and female personal products). The respondents found some Public Service Announcement advertisements terrifying. For example, respondents mentioned an antidrug commercial that featured distorted images of a young man after taking drugs, and a commercial about a fire accident in the household.

Some children disliked commercials that were exaggerated and false. Some children did not like certain commercials because of "incorrect" behavior. For example, a 9-year-old girl said she did not like any beer commercials because they contained pornography. An 11-year-old girl did not like a Yakult drink commercial featuring a young boy showing passion for a little girl because "love affairs is no good at that age." Children learned about proper behavior from public service announce-ments. For example, they learned that shoplifting and driving under the influence of alcohol were not acceptable behavior. Older children criticised certain commercials for the use of celebrities that they did not like. An interesting observation was that celebrities polarized reactions from fans and non-fans. For example many children who liked the mobile phone commercial featuring pop singer Leon Lai disliked another mobile phone commercial featuring singer Aaron Kwok. Advertisers need to recognize the trade-offs of using a celebrity. What appeals to one group is likely to drive away another group.

The findings that children liked food and beverage commercials were similar to those obtained by Ward (1972) and Yavas and Abdul-Gader (1993). This is probably because children are more familiar and experienced with the product category. Fun and enjoyment is the main reason for liking a commercial in both Hong Kong and in the research literature. However, there are differences in the reasons for disliking commercials. Hong Kong children frequently mentioned "product" and "incorrect behavior" as reasons. This indicates that the Chinese children place more emphasis on the moralistic orientation of commercials than Western children. They hold stronger beliefs about good and bad product categories as well as social behavior. Compared with findings of Ward (1972) and Yavas and Abdul-Gader (1993), Hong Kong children more frequently mentioned "celebrity/personality" as a reason for both liking and disliking. This suggests that the use of "personal" or "social" influence appeals more to Chinese children than Western children. This may also be due to the heavy use of celebrity commercials in Hong Kong.

For the favorite commercials, a majority of respondents (85%) recalled the brand names. For the most disliked commercials, nearly 60% mentioned the brand names. This indicates that brand recognition is stronger for liked brands than disliked brands.

Recall of Brand Names from Slogans

Very often slogans are used in the commercials to enhance recall. In the study we investigate whether children can associate the brand names with the slogans used in the commercials. Three slogans of three commercials (two chocolate brands and a milk powder brand) are tested. The children were asked "please tell me which brand uses the slogan xxx." It was found that the overall broad recall from the slogan was low (18% to 32%), confirming previous findings that brand names were difficult to remember. Slogans help little in brand recognition for children. Advertisers should consider other strategies to enhance brand recognition, such as incorporating brand names in slogans and package recognition.

Comprehension of Television Advertising

The children were presented with six-screen storyboards of four selected commercials and were asked to explain what the commercials said. The four commercials were selected to represent products that could be easily understood by children (chocolate and tea), products that were difficult to understand (taxis using gas fuel), and the government's prosocial messages (a public service announcement about equal rights between females and males). The results in Table 10.4 indicate that there is a significant difference in the respondents' comprehension of television advertising. The overall proportion of children who could give the key messages ranged from 27% to 63%. All Chi-square values were significant, indicating that comprehension was consistently related to age. Children aged 5–7 had difficulty in identifying key messages. They seemed to be preoccupied with what a commercial should say or what they were interested in knowing. In the case of both the chocolate and tea commercials, a lot of children mentioned that the commercial was about the good taste (coded as "partial understanding"). They failed to recognize that there were a variety of selling points for food. The children's comprehension was clearly limited by personal experience. The commercial about taxis using gas fuel caused the most confusion because driving was unfamiliar to them. Many children mixed up public service announcements advocating similar issues, including the use of unleaded fuel or turning off the engine when the car stopped. Surprisingly prosocial messages communicated well even to younger children when they were presented in a "children-friendly" way. The public service advertisement on "equal rights" gave some specificity to the idea in an animated form featuring animated boy and girl characters. After a voice-over that everyone had the right to choose his or her occupation, the girl said that she wanted to be a doctor. The boy rejected her idea and the voice-over asserted equal rights.

Table 10.4: **Children's comprehension of four selected commercials**

	Age group and cognitive stage (%)				Total	Chi-square statistics
	5–7 perceptual	8–9 early analytical	10–11 late analytical	12 reflective		
Kinder Chocolate						35.5***
Full understanding	53	68	73	64	63	
Partial understanding	31	27	26	37	29	
Don't know	16	5	1	0	8	
Lipton 3 in 1 tea						68.8***
Full understanding	19	41	61	60	40	
Partial understanding	48	40	26	36	39	
Don't know	33	19	13	4	21	
Taxi using gas fuel						57.1***
Full understanding	11	25	45	42	27	
Partial understanding	33	34	32	33	33	
Don't know	56	40	23	25	40	
Equal rights						115.1***
Full understanding	33	75	86	87	63	
Partial understanding	25	4	3	2	12	
Don't know	42	21	11	12	25	

Responses were coded as "full understanding" if they contained the key messages (Kinder Chocolate: a cat wants to get the chocolate; Lipton Tea: refreshing or relief from pressure; Taxi using gas fuel: gas fuel produces less smoke; Equal rights: girls can do the jobs they want to do.)

The findings reveal that comprehension of advertising content varies greatly depending on children's cognitive development and the style of presentation. Using simple dialog, concrete examples, and animated figures, the children demonstrated a fairly good understanding of prosocial messages. This finding should be encouraging for government officials and educators. The government should produce more campaigns in a children-friendly way in order to cultivate prosocial behavior and to protect children's interests. For example, younger children can learn how to respond to sexual harassment through a government publicity campaign.

Perceived Truthfulness of Television Advertising

While understanding of the purpose of advertising improves with age, belief in the truthfulness of advertising tends to decline over age. With comprehension of persuasive intent comes cynicism and distrust about the advertised product (Rossiter 1980). Distrust begins to emerge by the second grade (age 8) and is evident for most sixth graders (age 14) (Gaines and Esserman 1981; Rossiter 1980). Skepticism about advertising becomes stronger as children move into adolescence. For example, the percentage of U.S. kindergarteners, third graders, and sixth graders believing that advertising never or only sometimes tells the truth increases from 50% to 88% to 97% respectively (Ward, Wackman, and Wartella 1977). In a national survey of over 500 British children aged 4–13, only 6% thought that commercials "always" tell the truth, while 15% thought that they "quite often" are truthful. Most (60%) reported that commercials "sometimes" tell the truth, the remaining 20% perceived commercials as "rarely or never" telling the truth (Greenberg, Fazal, and Wober 1986). Perceived truthfulness of advertising did not depend on gender or social class of the children, but depended mainly on age. The youngest children were most likely to believe that commercials tell the truth while older children were more skeptical (Greenberg, Fazal, and Wober 1986).

Children also develop a better understanding of why commercials are sometimes untruthful. For example, kindergarteners cannot state the reason why commercials lie while older children connect lying to persuasive intent (Ward, Wackman, and Wartella 1977). Van Evra (1995) argued that children become less likely to be persuaded with age because they use other sources for the information they need and depend less on television advertising. The commercials therefore become less personally relevant to the child.

Decreased attention during commercials and selective viewing of commercials with age has been found in many studies (Sheikh, Prasad, and Rao 1974; Ward 1972; Ward, Levinson, and Wackman 1972; Zuckerman, Ziegler, and Stevenson 1978). Girls were found to pay greater attention to commercials than boys (Greenberg, Fazal, and Wober 1986). Attention to television commercials depended on personal factors and stimulus factors. Personal factors include parental and peer influence, level of motivation, and attitudes towards commercials. Stimulus factors include the nature of the television program, the content of the commercial, and the product advertised (McNeal 1987).

A study was conducted that measure Hong Kong children's perceived truthfulness of television advertising. Table 10.5 summarizes Hong Kong children's perception about the truthfulness of television advertising. Nearly equal proportions of children perceived that commercials were mostly true (42%) and mostly not true (40%). Fourteen percent of respondents perceived that commercials were partly true. The result for children aged 5–7 was bimodal. They either perceived commercials to be "mostly true" or "mostly not true" and very few of them considered commercials "partly true." Perceived truthfulness of television advertising generally declined with age for both boys and girls. Boys and girls differed mainly in the percentages of those perceiving commercials to be "partly

Table 10.5: Children's perceived truthfulness of television advertising

	Age group (%)					Chi-square statistics
	5–7	8–9	10–11	12	Total	
Television advertising is	(N=165)	(N=114)	(N=117)	(N=52)	(N=448)	32.3***
Mostly true	55	33	37	33	42	
Partly true	7	16	16	23	14	
Mostly not true	31	47	46	40	40	
Don't know	7	4	1	4	4	
For boys	(N=82)	(N=57)	(N=60)	(N=25)	(N=224)	20.5*
Mostly true	56	35	38	24	43	
Partly true	9	9	17	20	12	
Mostly not true	30	54	45	56	43	
Don't know	5	2	0	0	2	
For girls	(N=53)	(N=57)	(N=57)	(N=27)	(N=224)	20.4*
Mostly true	53	32	35	41	42	
Partly true	6	23	16	26	37	
Mostly not true	31	40	47	26	15	
Don't know	10	5	2	7	6	

$*$ <0.05 $***$<0.001

true" and "mostly not true." A higher percentage of girls perceived that commercials are partly true while a higher percentage of boys perceived that commercials are mostly not true.

Table 10.6 summarizes how children know whether TV advertising is true or not. The majority of the children's judgments were based on perception of advertising content as well as intrusive feelings. Fifty-six percent of children said they perceived commercials mostly not true because the content seemed so or they felt so. Other frequently mentioned reasons for perceiving commercials true were through encountering the product (having seen the product: 26%; having tried the product: 17%) and from word of mouth (16%). Other frequently mentioned reasons for perceiving commercials not true were having tried the product (22%) and from word of mouth (18%). Chi-square test results indicated that the reasons given by those perceiving commercials mostly true were

Table 10.6: How children know whether television advertising is true or not true

Reason*		Age group (%)				
	Mostly ad is true (T)	5–7	8–9	10–11	12	Total
	Mostly not true/	N=75	37	44	18	174
	partly true (NT)	N=57	68	60	32	226
Content seems so/	T	34	38	41	56	38
I feel that it is	NT	49	63	49	69	56
Other people say so	T	24	19	7	0	16
	NT	37	10	16	3	18
Have (not) seen the	T	25	22	32	22	26
product	NT	2	3	1	6	3
Have tried the product	T	16	16	16	22	17
	NT	12	19	33	22	22
Other@	T	1	5	4	0	3
	NT	0	4	0	0	1

* coded from open-ended responses
@ excluded for compilation of Chi-square statistics because of its small number
Chi-square value for those considered advertising is mostly true =11.4 (n.s.)
Chi-square value for those considered advertising is mostly not true or partly true = 28.9 (p < 0.001)

similar for children of different age groups. However, the reasons given for suspicion were different according to age groups. Skepticism about advertising for the youngest children came mainly from others' opinions, while that for the older children came mainly from their personal experience. Bases for judgments did not differ by gender.

Hong Kong children were not totally susceptible to advertising appeals. Even children aged 5–7 cast doubts on the truthfulness of commercials. It was interesting to find that children's bases for skepticism about advertising vary by age. Younger children relied mainly on the advertising content or had been told to doubt advertising. This study is limited in that most of the interviewers did not follow up on children's sources of information about the truthfulness of commercials. Young children probably learn about truthfulness of commercials from parents, siblings, teachers, or other adults. Older children have more consumer experience and are more likely to draw upon themselves to cast doubt on the commercials. In the case of over one fifth of those who perceived commercials are mostly not true or partly true it was because they had tried the product. According to findings in Western societies, belief in the truthfulness of television advertising declines with age. The current finding is consistent with John's (1999) theory of consumer socialization. As children enter the analytical stage they are better able to differentiate between imaginary portrayals in the commercials and real-life experiences. Children, as consumers, are better able to compare user experience with advertising promises. As most of the children in Hong Kong relied on the commercial content to make judgments about its trustworthiness, existing regulations on message presentation should be maintained.

Attention to and Attitudes toward Television Advertising

Table 10.7 summarizes Hong Kong children's self-reporting of their attention to TV advertising and their attitudes toward television advertising. Attention generally declined with age. When compared with results from a survey on Hong Kong adults, Hong Kong children paid more attention to TV advertising than adults. Results indicated that Hong Kong children liked TV advertising. Children aged 5–7 were

Table 10.7: **Children's attention to and attitudes toward TV advertising**

| | Age group (%) | | | | | Chi-statistics | HK |
	5–7	8–9	10–11	12	Total	square	adults@
Don't watch at all	2	5	2	0	3	21.0 *	2
Watch sometimes	46	59	54	52	52		76
Watch often	29	23	36	31	29		20
Watch every time	23	13	8	17	16		2
Dislike very much	4	2	2	0	2	40.0 ***	1
Dislike	18	18	10	8	15		7
Neutral	12	30	39	40	27		34
Like	59	48	46	44	51		49
Like very much	7	2	3	8	5		10

@ source: Chan (1995)

bimodal. They either "like" or "dislike" the commercials—very few of them reported a neutral answer. Attitudes differed by age group for boys as well as girls. Younger children liked TV advertising while older children took a neutral position. Older girls reported a greater drop in liking of commercials than older boys did.

Attention to commercials was positively related to the perceived truthfulness of TV advertising ($r=0.14$, $p<0.01$). Those who perceived commercials to be mostly true paid more attention to them than those who perceived commercials to be mostly not true. Attitude toward commercials was positively related to the perceived truthfulness of TV advertising ($r=0.21$, $p<0.001$). Those who perceived commercials to be true were more likely to say they liked them. Attitude toward commercials was positively related to attention ($r=0.28$, $p<0.001$). Those who liked commercials were more likely to watch them.

Parental Influence

Table 10.8 summarizes the children's perception of parental influence on what to learn and what not to learn from commercials. The actual parental influence was not measured in the current study as parents were not questioned directly. Children reported more don'ts than do's. Children perceived that their parents were concerned about the consumption of "bad" products including drugs, cigarettes, and liquor. Hong Kong children also reported that their parents asked them not to imitate violent and dangerous actions. Some children reported that their parents were concerned about illegal behavior (e.g., stealing) and incorrect behavior (e.g., telling lies). Children reported that parents use commercials to teach them to study hard and be good children. They also reported that parents used commercials to teach them about maintaining good health and a tidy environment. Parental guidance put emphasis on topics related to health, safety, and proper behaviors in children. Children seldom reported that their parents use commercials to teach them about consumer rights and purchasing decision making. Although Hong Kong parents perceived that television advertising took advantage of children (Chan 1995), children did not perceive that

Table 10.8: Children's perception of parental influence on what to learn
from television advertising

	No.
<u>Don'ts</u>	124 (73%)
don't take illegal drugs	38
don't copy violent behaviour	33
don't copy incorrect behavior (tell lies, watch bad movies, read bad books, etc.)	13
don't steal/corrupt	11
don't smoke	9
don't copy dangerous actions	9
don't imitate a specific cartoon figure	8
don't drink alcohol	3
<u>Do's</u>	45 (27%)
study hard	13
maintain good health	8
be good to parents	3
be a good child	9
keep Hong Kong clean/conserve the environment	7
others	3
Total mentions	169 (100%)

their parents helped them to become competent consumers. Surprisingly, children's rights as consumers are not fully respected. Fostering a consumer culture empowering consumers to be conscious of their rights and obligations is one of the main areas of work of the Hong Kong Consumer Council (Hong Kong Consumer Council 1998). Over the past decades the Consumer Council has launched several campaigns to encourage dissatisfied consumers to lodge complaints with it. However, none of these campaigns are targeted at children. Publicity campaigns about children's consumer rights and ways to collect consumer complaints from children should be developed. Perhaps consumer education should start with the parents, teachers, community leaders, and administrators. Parents and teachers should discuss with children their consumer rights and support them if they wish to express dissatisfaction.

Conclusion

To conclude, the majority of Hong Kong children aged 8 and above knew what advertising was and had developed an appreciation of television commercials. Older children were aware of the selling intention as well as the institutional function of television advertising. Understanding of television advertising, recall of brands from slogans, and comprehension of advertising content were clearly related to the stage of consumer socialization of children. Advertisers targeting children should make the commercials funny and interesting so that children will like them and remember their brands. Hong Kong children did cast doubt about television advertising. Perceived truthfulness of commercials decreased with age. Hong Kong children also enjoyed television advertising and paid a lot of attention to it. Perceived truthfulness of television advertising had a positive association with children's liking of and attention to these messages. Children reported that their parents were more concerned about the influence of commercials on their health and moral standards. Commercials were perceived as teaching aids for becoming good citizens and avoiding hazardous product categories. As a result of the study, continuing consumer education, and media literacy programs for children and adults should be encouraged.

References

Bever, T. G., L. S. Martin, B. Barbara, and G. J. Thomas. 1975. Young viewers' troubling response to TV ads. *Harvard Business Review* 53 (November–December): 109–20.

Blosser, B. J., and D. F. Roberts. 1985. Age differences in children's perceptions of message intent. *Communication Research* 12 (4):455–84.

Carey, G., X. Zhao, J. Chiaramonte, and D. Eden. 1997. Is there one global village for our future generation? Talking to 7–12 year olds around the world. *Marketing and Research Today* (February):12–16.

Chan, K. 1995. *Hong Kong television advertising: The good, the bad and the ugly.* Hong Kong: Department of Communication Studies, Hong Kong Baptist University.

———. 1997. Television advertising regulation and public opinions in China and Hong Kong [Zhong-gang dianshi guanggao guanli yu shimin yijian]. In T. M. Chan, L. Chu, and C. D. Poon, eds. *Mass Communication and Market Economy* [Dazhong chuanbo yu shichang jingji]. Hong Kong: Lu Feng Society. (In Chinese)

———, and R. Ruidl. 1996. Predicting attitudes toward television advertising: The view from Hong Kong. Paper presented at the 20th IAMCR Scientific Conference and General Assembly, August 18–22, Sydney, Australia.

Chiu, L. H. 1987. Child-rearing attitudes of Chinese, Chinese-American, and Anglo-American mothers. *International Journal of Psychology* 22:409–19.

Choate, R. B. 1975. *Petition of the council on children, media and merchandising to issue a trade regulation rule governing the private regulation of children's television advertising.* Filed before the Federation Trade Commission. Washington, DC.

Ekblad, S. 1986. Relationships between child-rearing practices and primary school children's functional adjustment in the People's Republic of China. *Scandinavian Journal of Psychology* 21:697–715.

Fox, R. F. 1996. *Harvesting minds: How TV commercials control kids.* Connecticut: Praeger Publishers.

Furnham, A. 2000. *Children and advertising: The allegations and the evidence.* London: The Social Affairs Unit.

Gaines, L., and J. F. Esserman. 1981. A quantitative study of young children's comprehension of television programmes and commercials. In J. F. Esserman, ed. J *Television Advertising and Children*, 95–105. New York: Child Research Service.

Greenberg, B. S., S. Fazal, and M. Wober. 1986. *Children's views on advertising.* London: Independent Broadcasting Authority.

Ho, D. 1989. Continuity and variation in Chinese patterns of socialization. *Journal of Marriage and the Family* 51:149–63.

Hong Kong Broadcast Authority. 1993. *Television code of practice on advertising standards.* Hong Kong: Government Printer.

Hong Kong Consumer Council. 1998. *Annual Report 1997–98.* Hong Kong: Consumer Council.

Hsu, F.L.L. 1981. *American and Chinese: Passage to differences.* 3rd ed. Honolulu: University Press of Hawaii.

John, D. R. 1999. Consumer socialization of children: A retrospective look at twenty-five years of research. *Journal of Consumer Research* 26 (December): 183–213.

Kelly, J. L., and H. M. Tseng. 1992. Cultural differences in child rearing: A comparison of immigrant Chinese and Caucasian American mothers. *Journal of Cross-cultural Psychology* 23 (4):444–55.

McNeal, J. U. 1987. *Children as consumers: Insights and implications.* Massachusetts: Lexington Books.

———, and M. F. Ji. 1999. Chinese children as consumers: An analysis of their new product information sources. *Journal of Consumer Marketing* 16 (4):345–64.

Meringoff, L. K., and G. S. Lesser. 1980. Children's ability to cistinguish television commercials from program material. In R. P. Adler, G. S. Lesser, L. K. Meringoff, T. S. Robertson, J. R. Rossiter, and S. Ward, eds. *The effects of television advertising on children*, 29–42. Lexington, MA: Lexington Books.

Oates, C., M. Blades, and B. Gunter. 2002. Children and television advertising: When do they understand persuasive intent? *Journal of Consumer Behaviour* 1 (3):238–45.

Pecora, N. 1995. Children and television advertising from a social science perspective. *Critical Studies in Mass Communication* 12:354–64.

Piaget, J. 1970. The stages of the intellectual development of the Child. In P. H. Mussen, J. J. Conger and J. Kagan, eds. *Readings in Child Development and Personality*, 291–98. New York: Harper and Row.

Rossiter, J. R. 1980. The effects of volume and repetition of television commercials. In R. P. Adler, G. S. Leser, L. K. Meringoff, T. S. Roberson, J. R. Rossiter and S. Ward, eds. *The effects of television advertising on children: Review and recommendations*, 153–84. Lexington, MA: Lexington Books.

Rubin, R. S. 1974. The effects of cognitive development on children's response to television advertising. *Journal of Business Research* 2(October):409–19.

Selman, R. L. 1980. *The growth of interpersonal understanding.* New York: Academic Press.

Sheikh, A. A., V. K. Prasad, and T. R. Rao. 1974. Children's TV commercials: A review of research. *Journal of Communication* 24(4):126–36.

Suzuki, B. H. 1980. The Asian–American family. In M. D. Fantinin and R. Cardenas, eds. *Parenting in a multicultural society.* New York: Longman.

Van Evra, J. P. 1995. Advertising's impact on children as a function of viewing purpose. *Psychology and Marketing* 12(5):423–32.

Ward, S. 1972. Children's reactions to commercials. *Journal of Advertising Research*, 12(April):37–45.

———, D. Levinson, and D. B. Wackman. 1972. Children's attention to television advertising. Vol. 4 of *Television and Social Behaviour*, 491–516. Washington, DC: Government Printer Office.

———, D. B. Wackman, and E. Wartella. 1977. *How children learn to buy: The development of consumer information processing skills.* Beverly Hills, CA: Sage Publications.

Yavas, U., and A. Abdul-Gader. 1993. Impact of TV commercials on Saudi children's purchase behaviour. *Marketing Intelligence and Planning* 11(2): 37–43.

Zuckerman, P., M. Ziegler, and H. W. Stevenson. 1978. Children's viewing of television and recognition memory of commercials. *Child Development* 49: 96–104.

Acknowledgements

The work described in this chapter was fully supported by a Faculty Research Grant from the Hong Kong Baptist University (Project No. FRG/97–98/II-24). Part of this chapter has been published in the *Journal of Marketing Communications*, vol. 6, no. 1 (2000), 37–52 (www.tandf.co.hk/journals) and in the *Advances in Consumer Research*, vol. 28 (2001).

Chapter 11

Advertising and Adolescents

Kara Chan

*I*n this chapter, we will examine three major issues relating to advertising and adolescents. Adolescents are a major target for fashion and beauty products. We are going to study how adolescents consume advertising icons and form attitudes about beauty and body images. The second part of the chapter investigates the potential effect of advertising on adolescents' value orientation, especially on values about the acquisition of possessions. The third part of the chapter examines how Hong Kong adolescents view smoking and cigarette advertising. All three issues are related to concern about consumption of advertising messages and its consequences on the health and well being of the young audience.

Developmental Changes of Adolescents

When children become adolescents their physical, cognitive, and social development continues to change. The manifest physical change in teenagers is that they reach puberty. During the physical development of adolescents not only do their bodies grow rapidly, their reproductive system and secondary sex characteristics are also drastically altered. For the secondary sex characteristics, girls' breasts will develop and boys will grow facial hair.

Due to the combination of rapid body growth and the sexual changes of puberty during adolescence, the early identity formed by children in childhood is no longer appropriate and teenagers enter a period of identity crisis (Erikson 1980). As adolescence is a transitional stage between childhood and adulthood, this period prepares teenagers to become adults. They have to formulate a new identity for their occupational, sexual, and religious roles, and to establish autonomy from their parents so that they can learn to be more independent in decision making. An increase in conflicts between adolescents and parents is predictable because they have divergent views on everyday issues such as chores and personal rights such as dating. Thus adolescents seek personal relationships that value their perspectives and understand their need for emotional support. Peer groups become an inevitable source of these relationships. As a result, peer influence may override parental influence in becoming the most powerful influence on young people during adolescence. This is because peer groups can provide emotional support and protect them from the emotional turmoil caused by the shared identity crisis. Peers share much of their inner feelings and secrets and are more knowledgeable about each other's feelings. As a result, adolescents prefer to identify with peer groups by merging their individual identities with that of the group.

The process by which young people acquire skills, knowledge, and attitudes relevant to their functioning as consumers in the marketplace is defined as consumer socialization (Ward 1974). According to John's (1999) consumer socialization model outlined in Chapter 10, adolescents belong to reflective stage (11–16 years). In this stage they are capable of understanding marketing concepts—for example, branding and pricing— in a multidimensional way. Their ways of thinking and reasoning become more reflective. They emphasize the social meanings that underpin the consumer marketplace. Regarding advertising knowledge, adolescents are competent in understanding both persuasive intent and the specific advertising tactics and appeals used in advertisements.

Adolescents and Body Image

In the following paragraphs the relations between advertising exposure, adolescents' ideal role model, and body image will be discussed.

During childhood, parents are inevitably the role models for children. When children enter adolescence, they realize the limitations of their parents. As they attempt to establish autonomy from their parents, adolescents need to seek role models outside the family environment. Advertising provides a host of potential role models who are attractive, powerful, and glamorous, and from whom adolescents acquire attitudes, values, and behavior. Adolescents may take both real and fictional people shown in the advertisements as their role models because of their exposure to advertisements, and they imitate the values and behavior of those role models (Anderson et al. 2001).

When adolescents choose media figures as their role models, who represent ideals of appearance, behavior, or lifestyle, they may not only identify with them but also compare themselves to them. Adolescents may become involved in contradictory scenarios in the social comparison processes. One is spending more effort to be more like a media role model. Another one is being more aware of the disparity between self and the media models. They may be dissatisfied or even discouraged when they feel that they are inferior to the media role models (Anderson et al. 2001).

Adolescents are a prime target for advertisers of products and personal services for body fitness and beauty. A quick analysis of the types of products advertised in popular youth magazines in Hong Kong indicates that advertisements for clothing, cosmetics and personal care, and facial treatment and slimming, constituted 38–84% of total advertising space (Table 11.1).

One of the characteristics of the role models provided by advertisers is the body images and physical attractiveness of the persons who appear in the advertisements. When adolescents identify with those role models they will become intensely concerned with their own bodily characteristics and physical attractiveness. They will suffer from body dissatisfaction when they feel inferior to the role models, who demonstrate a cultural ideal of beauty that is hard for most ordinary adolescents to meet. Attractiveness in a role model is often defined by Hong Kong advertisers as having a slim and perfect body figure. As a result adolescents will spend both money and time on slimming in order to have a perfect body figure. This is because young people will accept

Table 11.1: **Analysis of types of products advertised in youth magazines**

Title	No. of pages in one issue	No. of pages of ads	% of ad in mag	a) Clothing	b) Cosmetics and personal care	c) Facial treatment and slimming	d) Electronics	e) Movies	f) Food and beverages	g) Services and others	(a) to (c) total
Fashion and Beauty	130	43.5	34%	12%*	43%	14%	0%	2%	9%	15%	69%
Monday	168	92.25	55%	5%	12%	25%	11%	2%	14%	26%	42%
Monday's Bee	98	12	12%	38%	0%	0%	42%	0%	0%	21%	38%
Monday's Honey	98	25.25	26%	20%	56%	8%	4%	0%	0%	12%	84%
Cosmo Girl	154	50.5	33%	23%	56%	0%	10%	0%	0%	12%	79%

* percentage of clothing ads among all mag ads

the ideals portrayed in the advertisements as indicators of the values of society through observational learning and media cultivation.

The choices of role models for adolescents increase beyond parents to popular stars when they enter adolescence. This is because adolescents have not accumulated a great deal of experience in the real world. Advertisements serve as an "early window" for adolescents to acquire knowledge and experience about the world.

In Hong Kong several organizations have carried out surveys investigating Hong Kong adolescents' attitudes toward slimming. Retailing company 7-Eleven conducted a survey and interviewed 329 students, aged 10–24, in 2001. Over one third of the respondents said that their major wish was to have a prefect body figure. This was followed by having a happy life, good academic achievement, meeting more friends, and good communications with parents (Central News Agency 2001).

In order to examine the reasons for adolescents' slimming, the Hong Kong Christian Service conducted another study in 2003 (*Hong Kong Economic Times* 2003). Respondents were 429 Sham Shui Po residents, aged 13–19. Forty-two percent of respondents reported that they had tried slimming measures because of the influence of their peers and the mass media. Forty-five percent of adolescents reported that they learnt the standard of perfect body image from newspapers and magazines, while another 43% reported that they learnt it from television programs and advertisements. Three quarters of respondents agreed that slimming advertisements encourage people to judge a person by his/her appearance. This implies that the influence of mass media on adolescents' development of ideal body image is enormous.

The widespread slimming trend in Hong Kong is also demonstrated by a survey conducted by the Hong Kong Playground Association in 2004. Altogether 991 respondents, aged 11 to 27, participated in the survey (*Va Kio Daily* 2004). Results showed that nearly 80% of the respondents who planned to take measures to reduce weight were either of normal weight or even under-weight. Over half of them thought that there is insufficient information about correct ways of slimming. Over half of them wanted to receive reliable information about slimming from newspapers and magazines. Survey results indicated that there was a gender difference in adolescents and young adults' level of satisfaction with their body. Altogether 71% of female respondents reported that they were not satisfied with their weight and perceived that they were overweight. The percentage for male respondents was 48%. In other words, female respondents were more likely to be dissatisfied with their body images than male respondents.

To conclude, the mass media has vigorously promoted the idea that being slim is important in order to be physically attractive and adolescents and their friends were affected by this. No matter what their weight was, they wanted to be slimmer in order to achieve a perfect body figure. Adolescents must build up a strong value system to resist the influence of advertising on body image.

Consumption and Materialism

Many critics argue that the pervasive consumer messages in the media have led to the adoption of a materialistic orientation by the audience (Cheung and Chan 1996). Pollay (1986) summarizes the themes of materialism to include the belief that consumption is the route to happiness and meaning, and the solution to most personal problems; consumption displaces feelings from people to objects (Leiss 1976); it replaces spiritual development with secular hedonism (Skolimowski 1977); it distorts gross economic goals versus justice and peace; and it encourages ecological wastefulness. Four socializing agents, namely family communication patterns, peer communication, marketplace knowledge, and exposure to materialistic models and values, affect the development of materialistic values. These four agents will be discussed in the following paragraphs.

Parents play an important role in children's consumer socialization through parent–child communication, training, and modeling (Ward, Wackman, and Wartella 1977). Parental concern about children's use of media reflects both personal and cultural differences in the perceived desirability of controlling outside influences on their children such as the mass media (Rose, Bush, and Kahle 1998). Family communication patterns provide a way of assessing the interaction between parents and children, and their media and consumption environment. Previous research has related family communication patterns to parental styles (Carlson, Grossbart, and Stuenkel 1992) and advertising practices (Carlson, Grossbart, and Walsh 1990).

Family communication has been conceptualized as being two dimensional (see Moschis 1987 for a review). The first dimension, socio-orientation, measures vertical, or relationship-oriented patterns of communication. The emphasis is on parental control and children's deference to authority. The second dimension, concept-orientation, measures issue-oriented communication. The emphasis is on the establishment of an independent evaluation of an issue by children. Past studies have identified that family environment has an impact on endorsement of materialistic values. Adolescents in families with a socio-oriented communication structure exhibit higher levels of materialism (Moschis and Moore 1979). Adolescents in families with a concept-oriented communication structure demonstrate lower levels of materialism (Moore and Moschis 1981). Parental styles and practices that did not fully meet children's needs are associated with materialism (Kasser et al. 1995; Williams et al. 2000). Adolescents who communicate less frequently with parents about consumption are more materialistic (Moore and Moschis 1981).

Apart from the qualitative differences in family communications patterns, empirical study also indicates that there are cultural differences in family communication patterns. For example, American mothers, as a group, emphasize independence and individualism more than Japanese mothers, who emphasize social harmony and respect for authority (Itoh and Taylor 1981; Power, Kobayashi-Winata, and Kelley 1992). Rose and others (1998) found that American mothers more often engaged in concept-oriented communication about consumption than Japanese mothers, and Japanese mothers more frequently employed socio-oriented communication patterns.

When referring to Chinese perspectives towards parental styles, Confucianism is one Chinese ideology that has been widely investigated by Chinese and Western researchers. Some major concepts of Confucianism include: the supreme moral person (Lei 1993; Metzger 1992); filial piety (Hsu 1981; Kelly and Tseng 1992); social harmony (Domino 1992); collective decision making (Stander and Jensen 1993);

good manners, and the importance of education (Ekblad 1986; Ho 1989). The implications of all these studies suggest that Chinese parents tend to be more concerned about the moral behavior of their children and that they will exert much more control over their children's behavior. Chan's (2001) study of Chinese children in Hong Kong reported that parents use television commercials to teach children about restrictive consumption behavior (what products they should not buy) and desirable moral behavior (such as protecting the environment). Because of the traditional Chinese values of collective decision, filial piety, and social harmony we expect that Chinese parents are more likely to adopt a socio-oriented communication pattern when communicating with adolescents about consumption.

Communication outside the family also contributes to the difference in level of materialism among children. Adolescents' attitudes toward advertising are positively correlated to the frequency of communication with peers (Moschis 1978). Boush, Friestad, and Rose (1994) predicted that skepticism toward advertising is negatively correlated to adolescents' susceptibility to peer influence. Susceptibility to peer influence is interpreted as "the need to identify or enhance one's image with significant others through the acquisition and use of products and brands, the willingness to conform to the expectations of others regarding purchase decisions, and/or the tendency to learn about products and brands by observing others, and/or seeking information from others" (Bearden, Netemeyer, and Teel 1989, 474). Susceptibility to influence can be subdivided into two dimensions: a normative dimension, which reflects a willingness to comply with wishes of others or to conform with others to enhance one's self-esteem; and an informational dimension, which reflects one's willingness to accept and internalize information from another.

Boush, Friestad, and Rose (1994) predicted that advertising would function as a type of normative influence and hence adolescents who are more susceptible to influence would be less skeptical toward advertising. Empirical findings support this prediction (Bearden, Netemyer, and Teel 1989; 1990). Mangleburg and Bristol (1998) found that adolescents' susceptibility to normative influence is inversely related to their skepticism toward advertising, while adolescents' susceptibility to informational influence is positively related to their skepticism toward advertising. Studies showed that materialism is higher in adolescents who communicate with peers more frequently (Churchill and Moschis 1979; Moschis and Churchill 1978) and are more susceptible to their influence (Achenreiner 1997).

When the level of marketplace knowledge of teenagers increases, they will become more skeptical toward advertising. This is because they are more able to differentiate between truthful and misleading commercials when they are more familiar with a wide variety of brands and stores. In general, greater marketplace experience means better marketplace knowledge. Experienced adolescents will be more able to understand the biased point of view of the marketer's position provided by the advertisements and therefore may in turn have a more skeptical attitude toward such persuasion attempts. Age was found to be positively related to skepticism toward advertising (Boush, Friestad, and Rose 1994). This may be because older adolescents have acquired more experience in the marketplace and are more likely to have had negative experiences than have younger adolescents, and hence they have increased marketplace knowledge and skepticism toward advertising. Research has demonstrated that adolescents' marketplace knowledge is proportionally related to their skepticism toward advertising (Mangleburg and Bristol 1998).

According to Kasser, Ryan, Couchman, and Sheldon's model (2004), materialistic values are frequently found in popular culture, the media and advertisements. People exposed to materialistic models will be more likely to take on the materialistic values through modeling (Bandura 1971) and internalization of these values (Ryan and Connell 1989). Empirical data indicates that television exposure has a positive correlation with materialism for children and adolescents in Western societies (Buijzen and Valkenburg 2003; Churchill and Moschis 1979; Kapferer 1986; Moschis and Moore 1982) and in Asian societies including China, Hong Kong, and South Korea (Chan 2003; Cheung and Chan 1996; Kwak, Zinkhan, and DeLorme 2002; Yang and Ganahl 2004). Another pervasive source of materialistic models is advertising messages. Advertisements encourage consumption through the images of attractive and/or famous product users, the demonstration of social reward by using the products, and the association of the products with wealthy lifestyles (Kasser et al. 2004). Empirical data supports the theory that advertising exposure has a positive correlation with materialism (Buijzen and Valkenburg 2003). Moschis and Moore (1982) conceptualized advertising exposure according to frequency of watching advertisements as well as the reasons for watching. The motives for advertising viewing appear to have two dimensions: seeking information about the products, and seeking images or talking points. A longitudinal study of adolescents found that television advertising exposure had a long run and a short run on adolescents' adoption of materialistic values (Moschis and Moore 1982).

Students from the Department of Communication Studies of the Hong Kong Baptist University conducted a survey in 1998 to investigate adolescents' attitudes towards television advertising in Hong Kong (Chan 1999). They interviewed 95 secondary school students, ranging from form 3 to 6 (equivalent to grade 8 to 11). Respondents reported that they spent an average of three hours watching television every day and over half had an allowance of HK$101–300 (about US$12–38) every week.

According to the survey, respondents' attitudes towards television advertising were favorable. The percentages of respondents that said they disliked television advertising and thought that television advertising was bad were only 11% and 9% respectively. On the other hand, 44% of respondents reported that they liked television advertising and 49% of them thought that television advertising was good.

Regarding perceived marketplace information, 35% of the respondents reported that they were not familiar with the market price of the products. Thirty-five percent reported that they were not familiar with different types of shops. The percentages of respondents that expressed neutrality on these points were 44% and 55% respectively. This shows that adolescents do not have a full grasp of marketplace information. Over half of the respondents reported that the product information provided by television advertising was inadequate. Forty-four percent of respondents thought that the majority of television advertising was not credible. This suggests that respondents are skeptical toward television commercials. This survey is limited since the sample size is rather small.

In 2004, a survey of 289 secondary school students in form 1 to 7 (equivalent to grade 7 to 13) conducted by the Hong Kong Baptist University found that Hong Kong adolescents perceived a strong influence from peers. Table 11.2 summarizes perceived peer influence. When purchasing unfamiliar products, 67% of respondents would seek advice from their friends. This implies that peers are an important source of product information for adolescents. When asking about adolescents' susceptibility to normative influence it was interesting to find that 59% of the respondents would not only buy the brands and products their friends approved of. However, 44% of them expressed the hope that their friends would like the brands and products they purchased. This suggests that adolescents are quite independent in making buying decisions. However, when purchase decisions are made, they want to obtain acceptance from their peers.

Table 11.3 summarizes the response from adolescents about family communication patterns about consumption. Over half of the respondents said that their parents would let them decide how they spent their money. Sixty-five percent of adolescents reported that their parents

Table 11.2: Perceived peer influence (N=289)

Items	Disagree %	Neutral %	Agree %
Informational influence			
If I don't have a lot of experience with a product, I often ask my friends about it.	11	22	67
I usually ask my friends to help me choose the best product.	24	40	36
I look at what my friends are buying and using before I buy.	38	30	32
Normative influence			
It is important that my friends like the products and brands I buy.	22	34	44
I like to know what products and brands make a good impression on my friends.	41	34	25
I only buy those products and brands that my friends will approve of.	59	28	13

Table 11.3: Family communication about consumption reported by adolescents

Items	Never/ seldom %	Some- times %	Often/ nearly every time %
Concept-oriented communication			
My parents let me decide how I should spend my money.	21	28	51
My parents think that I can decide which things I should or shouldn't buy.	24	32	44
My parents say that buying things I like is important even if others do not like them.	31	36	33
My parents ask me for advice when buying things for the family.	39	30	31
My parents ask me what I think about the things I buy for myself.	65	24	11
Socio-oriented communication			
My parents want to know what I do with my money.	37	30	33
My parents tell me I can't buy certain things.	40	34	26
My parents tell me not to buy certain things.	38	41	21
My parents complain when they don't like the things I have bought for myself.	55	32	13
My parents tell me what products and brands I should buy.	73	20	7

never or seldom asked them what they thought about the things they bought for themselves. Over 70% of adolescents reported that their parents never or seldom told them about what brands and products they should buy. Fifty-five percent of respondents reported that their parents never or seldom complained when they did not like the things they bought for themselves. The mean scores for concept-oriented versus socio-oriented communication patterns reported by Hong Kong adolescents were 3.0 and 2.6 on a five-point scale. Results of *t*-tests indicated that concept-oriented communication pattern was more often adopted in the family ($t=7.1$, $df=288$, $p<0.001$). In other words, adolescents in Hong Kong enjoyed a high level of concept-oriented communication about consumption in the family. Socio-oriented communication in the family about consumption was rather limited.

To conclude, Hong Kong adolescents liked television advertising but they were skeptical about it. Although they would seek product information from peers, they would not only select the brands and products that their friends approved of when making buying decisions. The perceived marketplace information of adolescents was not sufficient and they were not satisfied with the information provided by television advertising. They enjoyed significant autonomy and had not been seriously influenced by their parents on purchasing. And family communication about consumption was more concept-oriented than socio-oriented.

Adolescents and Smoking

Television advertising for tobacco was banned in Hong Kong in 1990 so as to prevent adolescents from becoming smokers. In 1999 the Hong Kong Council on Smoking and Health surveyed 21,044 form 1 to 3 secondary students (i.e., grade 7 to 9) about youth smoking and health (Lam, Ho, and Kui 1999). It was found that about one third of the adolescents (34%) first began smoking at the age of 11. Twenty-eight percent of the respondents began smoking at the age of 13 and 14. Sixteen percent of the adolescents started smoking at the age of 9 to 10 and 18% began smoking at the age of 8 or below. Only a small percentage, which is 4% of adolescents, started smoking at the age of 15 or above.

The same survey found that 35% of the respondents had watched or participated in cigarette sponsored activities, such as tennis matches and concerts. Six percent of the students had used empty cigarette packs to exchange for admission tickets for films, sports, competitions, or other entertainment. Another 8% of the students had used empty cigarette packs in exchange for free gifts or goods at a reduced price. Eleven percent of the respondents had been given free publicity cigarettes. Those who had ever smoked (ever-smokers) were more likely to participate in promotional activities that use empty cigarette packs for premiums or tickets than those who had never smoked (never-smokers) (Table 11.4).

A majority of respondents reported that they had seen tobacco advertisements in magazines, newspapers, television, large outdoor billboards, posters, MTR stations, and buses (Table 11.5).

Adolescents reported that they had seen goods with cigarette advertisements. The mostly frequently seen items were lighters (29%), ash trays (23%), watches (12%), hats (11%), and T-shirts (10%). Ever smokers were much more likely to perceive cigarette advertisements to be attractive than never-smokers (Table 11.6).

Table 11.4: Smoking status and participation in cigarette promotion activities

	Ever-Smokers %	Never-Smokers %
Use empty cigarette packs to exchange for admission tickets	12	3
Use empty cigarette packs to exchange for free gifts and reduced price goods	14	5
Watch or participate in cigarette sponsored activities	43	32

Table 11.5: Media on which tobacco advertisements were seen recently

Media	%
Newspapers	66
Magazines	62
MTR stations	48
Television	44
Large outdoor billboards	42
Posters	40
Buses	40
Railway station	24
Hand bills	24
Movies	18
Taxis	17
Mini buses	16
Radio	15
Trams	14
LRT stations	12
Internet	10
Ferries	9
Others	11

Table 11.6: Smoking status and perceiving cigarette advertisements as attractive

	Ever-Smokers %	Never-Smokers %
Marlboro	41	7
Salem	41	7
Kent	16	3
Camel	11	2
Mild Seven	8	1

To sum up, about one third of adolescents had watched or participated in cigarette sponsored activities and less than one tenth had used empty packs to exchange for tickets, gifts or goods. Most adolescents were exposed to tobacco advertisements. Few respondents perceived cigarette advertisements as attractive, but such perception was strongly associated with smoking experience. As age at first smoking was mainly 11 to 12, antismoking publicity should begin as early as ages 9 to 10. An antismoking campaign aimed at adolescents should be perceived by them as attractive and persuasive and use multiple channels, including media and interpersonal resources.

References

Achenreiner, G. B. 1997. Materialism values and susceptibility to influence in children. In M. Brucks and D. J. MacInnis, eds. *Advances in consumer research*, vol. 24, 82–88. Provo, UT: Association for Consumer Research.

Anderson, D. R., A. C. Huston, K. L. Schmitt, D. L. Linebarger, and J. C. Wright. 2001. Self-image: Role model preference and body image. In *Early childhood television viewing and adolescent behavior*, 108–18. Boston: Blackwell.

Bandura, A. 1971. *Social learning theory*. Morristown, NJ: General Learning Press.

Bearden, W. O., R. G. Netemeyer, and J. E. Teel. 1989. Measurement of consumer susceptibility to interpersonal influence. *Journal of Consumer Research* 15 (March):472–80.

———. 1990. Further validation of the consumer susceptibility to interpersonal influence scale. In M. E. Goldberg, ed. *Advances in Consumer Research*, vol. 17, 770–76. Provo, UT: Association for Consumer Research.

Boush, D. M., M. Friestad, and G. M. Rose. 1994. Adolescent skepticism toward TV advertising and knowledge of advertiser tactics. *Journal of Consumer Research* 21 (June):165–75.

Buijzen, M., and P. M. Valkenburg. 2003. The unintended effects of television advertising: A parent-child survey. *Communication Research* 30 (5): 483–503.

Carlson, L., S. Grossbart, and K. J. Stuenke. 1992. The role of parental socialization types on differential family communication patterns regarding consumption. *Journal of Consumer Psychology* 1 (1):31–52.

———, S. Grossbart, and A. Walsh. 1990. Mothers' communication orientation and consumer-socialization tendencies. *Journal of Advertising* 19 (3):27–38.

Chan, K. 1999. Television Advertising and Hong Kong Adolescents. *Media Digest* (June):14–15

———. 2001. Children's perceived truthfulness of television advertising and parental influence: A Hong Kong Study. In M. C. Gilly and J. Meyers-Levy, eds. *Advances in Consumer Research*, vol. 28, 207–12. Provo, UT: Association for Consumer Research.

———. 2003. Materialism among Chinese children in Hong Kong. *International Journal of Advertising and Marketing to Children* 4 (4):47–61.

Central News Agency. 2001. Majority of Hong Kong adolescents wish to have a perfect body figure. July 30.

Cheung, C. K., and C. F. Chan. 1996. Television viewing and mean world value in Hong Kong's adolescents. *Social Behavior and Personality* 24(4):351–64.

Churchill, G. A., and G. P. Moschis. 1979. Television and interpersonal influences on adolescent consumer learning. *Journal of Consumer Research* 6 (June):23–35.

Domino, G. 1992. Cooperation and competition in Chinese and American children. *Journal of Cross-Cultural Psychology* 23 (4):456–67.

Ekblad, S. 1986. Relationships between child-rearing practices and primary school children's functional adjustment in the People's Republic of China. *Scandinavian Journal of Psychology* 21:697–715.

Erikson, E. H. 1980. *Identity and the life cycle.* New York: Norton.

Ho, D. 1989. Continuity and variation in Chinese patterns of socialization. *Journal of Marriage and the Family* 51:149–63.

Hong Kong Economic Times. 2003. The trend of slimming has strongly influenced adolescents. November 20.

Hsu, F.L.L. 1981. *American and Chinese: Passage to differences,* 3rd ed. Honolulu: University Press of Hawaii.

Itoh, F., and C. M. Taylor. 1981. A comparison of childrearing expectations of parents in Japan and the United States. *Journal of Comparative Family Studies* 12 (4):449–60.

John, D. R. 1999. Consumer socialization of Children: A Retrospective Look at Twenty-Five Years of Research. *Journal of Consumer Research* 26 (December): 183–213.

Kapferer, J. N. 1986. A comparison of TV advertising and mothers' influence on children's attitudes and Values. In S. Ward, T. Robertson and R. Brown, eds. *Commercial television and European children*. Hants, England: Gower Publishing Company Limited.

Kasser, T., R. M. Ryan, C. E. Couchman, and K. M. Sheldon. 2004. Materialistic values: Their causes and consequences. In T. Kasser and A. D. Kanner, eds. *Psychology and consumer culture*, 11–28. Washington, DC: American Psychology Association.

———, R. M. Ryan, M. Zax, and A. J. Sameroff. 1995. The relations of maternal and social environments to late adolescents' materialistic and prosocial values. *Developmental Psychology* 31:907–14.

Kelly, J. L., and H. M. Tseng. 1992. Cultural differences in child rearing: A comparison of immigrant Chinese and Caucasian American mothers. *Journal of Cross-cultural Psychology* 23 (4):444–55.

Kwak, H., G. M. Zinkhan, and D. E. DeLorme. 2002. Effects of compulsive buying tendencies on attitudes toward advertising: The moderating role of exposure to TV commercials and TV shows. *Journal of Current Issues & Research in Advertising* 24 (2):17–32.

Lam, T. H., S. Y. Ho, and C. Y. Kui. 1999. The youth smoking and health survey. http://www.info.gov.hk/hkcosh/download/report/en_report07.pdf. (accessed December 12, 2004).

Lei, T. 1993. Metzger's model for the modern moral man. Paper presented at the International Conference on Moral and Civic Education, November, Hong Kong.

Leiss, W. 1976. *The limits of satisfaction*. Toronto: University of Toronto Press.

Mangleburg, T. F., and T. Bristol. 1998. Socialization and adolescents' skepticism toward advertising. *Journal of Advertising* 27 (3):11–21.

Metzger, T. 1992. The thoughts of Tang Chun-I (1909–1978): A preliminary response. Proceedings of the International Conference on Tang's Thoughts, Hong Kong, 165–98.

Moore, R. L., and G. P. Moschis. 1981. The role of family communication in consumer learning, *Journal of Communication* 31(Autumn):42–51.

Moschis, G. P. 1978. Teenagers' responses to retailing stimuli. *Journal of Retailing* 54 (4):80–93.

———. 1987. *Consumer socialization: A life-cycle perspective*. Lexington, MA: Lexington Books.

Moschis, G. P., and G. A. Churchill Jr. 1978. Consumer socialization: A theoretical and empirical analysis. *Journal of Marketing Research* 15 (November):599–609.

———, and R. L. Moore. 1979. Family communication patterns and consumer socialization. In *Advances in consumer research*, vol. 6, W. L. Wilkie and A. Arbor, eds. 359–63. Michigan: Association for Consumer Research.

Moschis, G. P., and R. L. Moore. 1982. A longitudinal study of television advertising effects. *Journal of Consumer Research* 9 (December):279–86.

Pollay, R. W. 1986. The distorted mirror: Reflections on the unintended consequences of advertising. *Journal of Marketing* 50 (April):18–36.

Power, T. G., H. Kobayashi-Winata, and M. L. Kelley. 1992. Childrearing patterns in Japan and the United States: A cluster analytic study. *International Journal of Behavioral Development* 11 (2):185–205.

Rose, G. M., V. D. Bush, and L. Kahle. 1998. The influence of family communication patterns on parental reactions toward advertising: A cross-national examination. *Journal of Advertising* 27 (4):71–85.

Ryan, R. M., and J. P. Connell. 1989. Perceived locus of causality and internalization: Examining reasons for acting in two domains. *Journal of Personality and Social Psychology* 57: 749–61.

Skolimowski, H. 1977. The semantic environment in the age of advertising. In T. H. Ohlbren and L. M. Berk, eds. *The new languages: A rhetorical approach to the mass media and popular culture*, 91–101. Englewood Cliffs, NJ: Prentice-Hall.

Stander, V., and L. Jensen. 1993. The relationship of value orientation to moral cognition: Gender and cultural differences in the United States and China explored. *Journal of Cross-cultural Psychology* 24 (1):42–52.

Va Kio Daily. 2004. Eighty percent of the people having taken measures to slim in Hong Kong still want to slim when being normal weight. March 20.

Ward, S. 1974. Consumer socialization. *Journal of Consumer Research* 1 (September): 1–14.

———, D. B. Wackman, and E. Wartella. 1977. *How children learn to buy.* Beverly Hills, CA: Sage.

Williams, G. C., E. M. Cox, V. A. Hedberg, and E. L. Deci. 2000. Extrinsic life goals and health risk behaviors in adolescents. *Journal of Applied Social Psychology* 30:1756–71.

Yang, H., and D. J. Ganahl. 2004. A cross-cultural study between American and Chinese college students regarding television viewing, materialism, beliefs and attitude toward advertising. Paper presented at the Association for Educators in Journalism and Mass Communication 2004 Convention, Advertising Division, August 4–7, Toronto, Canada.

Notes on Contributors

Fanny Fong-yee CHAN is an M.Phil. graduate in School of Communication, Hong Kong Baptist University. She graduated from the University of Hong Kong, with her major in Psychology and double-minor in Statistics and Media Studies. Her research interests include advertising, persuasion, humor, psychology of handwriting and calligraphy.

Joseph Man CHAN is Professor and former Director at the School of Journalism and Communication, The Chinese University of Hong Kong. His publications concern international communication, political communication, and communications development in Greater China. Among the books he co-authored or co-edited are: *Mass Media and Political Transition: The Hong Kong Press in China's Orbit* (New York: Guilford, 1991), *Global Media Spectacle* (Buffalo: SUNY Press, 2002), *In Search of Boundaries: Communication, Nation-States and Cultural Identities* (Westport: Ablex, 2002). He has served as a President of the Chinese Communication Association. He has been a visiting scholar at Harvard University and Oxford University.

Kara CHAN is Professor at the Department of Communication Studies, Hong Kong Baptist University. She teaches advertising and communication research methods. She has worked in the advertising and public relations profession. She was a statistician for the Hong Kong Government before joining the University. Her research areas include Hong Kong and China's mass communication, advertising, and consumer behaviors. She was a Fulbright Scholar at Bradley University, Illinois from 1999 to 2000. She is the co-author (with James McNeal) of *Advertising to Children in China* (Hong Kong: The Chinese University Press, 2004).

Katherine T. FRITH is Associate Professor at the School of Communication and Information, Nanyang Technological University of Singapore. Prior to working in Singapore, Dr. Frith was Associate Professor and Chair of the Advertising and Public Relations Program in the College of Communications at the Pennsylvania State University in the United States. Dr. Frith has published three books, including *Advertising and Societies: Global Issues* (New York: P. Lang, 2003) and *Advertising in Asia: Communication* (Ames: Iowa State University Press, 1996), *Culture and Consumption* (Ames: Iowa University Press, 1996). She has also written 12 book chapters and over 30 scholarly articles in communications journals.

Anthony FUNG is Associate Professor at the School of Journalism and Communication, The Chinese University of Hong Kong. His recent research focuses on gender and youth identity, popular culture and cultural studies, and new media technologies. He has published in major communication and cultural studies journals, such as *Journal of Communication Inquiry, Gazette: A Journal for International Communication, Sex Roles, World Communication, Cultural Studies,* and *Mass Communication & Society.* He is the co-author of *Television Formats and the East Asian Cultural Imagination* (in press).

Benny HO is a project manager in a media and advertising company focusing on the China market, and owned jointly by the United States, European and Chinese sectors. His research interest is marketing communication.

Jessie Xinyan HO is currently pursuing a career in advertising. She graduated with honors from the School of Communication and Information, Nanyang Technological University of Singapore. Her major was Public and Promotional Communication. Her research interests include advertising, persuasion, gender studies, semiology, and social culture.

Susanna Wai-yee KWOK is Instructor at the Department of Marketing, The Chinese University of Hong Kong. She has worked in the advertising and marketing profession before joining the University. Her research interests include integrated marketing communication, generational marketing, cultural studies and advertising, and corporate communication.

Ernest F. MARTIN, Jr is Associate Professor of the School of Mass Communications, Virginia Commonwealth University. He was previously Assistant Dean at the College of Communication and Media Sciences, Zayed University (United Arab Emirates), as well as Chairman of the Department of Communication Studies, Hong Kong Baptist University. He has worked professionally for more than 10 years with Cox Enterprises, Koplar Communications and Frank Magid Associates. He is co-author of *Free Expression and Five Democratic Publics: Support for Individual and Media Rights* (Cresskill, NJ: Hampton Press, 2004).

Gerard PRENDERGAST is Associate Professor of Marketing at Hong Kong Baptist University. His research is in the area of marketing communications and his publication have appeared in journals such as *Journal of Advertising, Journal of Advertising Research, Public Relations Review, International Journal of Advertising,* and *Journal of Marketing Communications.* He is also a member of several editorial boards.

Chris Fei SHEN is an M.Phil. graduate in School of Communication, Hong Kong Baptist University. He received his bachelor's degree from Tongji University, Shanghai, China, majoring in advertising. His main research focus includes social impacts of mass media and political communication. He is now a doctoral student at Ohio State University.

Chao-wai WONG is a Barrister-at-Law. He read Law in the United Kingdom where he attained his LLB and LLM. He also obtained a MA from the University of Hong Kong. He taught law at the University of Hong Kong and the City Polytechnic of Hong Kong, which is now renamed as the City University of Hong Kong. He is currently an adjudicator with the Obscene Articles Tribunal.

Wendy Siuyi WONG is teaching at the Department of Design, York University, Canada. She has published extensively on Chinese and Hong Kong visual culture and history including graphic design, comics and advertising images. Her books on Chinese visual culture and comics history include *Advertising, Value, and Consumer Culture: Hong Kong Television Commercial, 1970–1989* (2003), *An Illustrated History of Hong Kong Comics* (1999), and *Advertising, Culture & Everyday Life I: Hong Kong Newspaper Advertisements, 1945–1970* (1999). Wong was a visiting scholar at Harvard University in 1999–2000. She was the 2000 Lubalin Curatorial Fellow at the Cooper Union School of Art.

Subject Index